Sweet Mysteries

Dwain L. Kitchel, Sr.

Sweet Mysteries

Dwain Kitchel Sr.

TENNESSEE VALLEY
Publishing®

Knoxville, Tennessee
2002

Published by:
     Tennessee Valley Publishing
     PO Box 52527
     Knoxville, Tennessee 37950-2527
     email: info@tvp1.com

Printed and bound in the United States of America.

Library of Congress Cataloging-in-Publication Data

Kitchel, Dwain L. (Dwain Lorne), 1933-
     Sweet Mysteries / Dwain L. Kitchel, Sr.
          p.   cm.
     ISBN 1-882194-83-7
     1. Life.   I. Title
     BD431.K55 2002
     128- -dc21

2002010521

Dedication

This book is dedicated to my wife, **Margaret,** and my daughter, **Elizabeth**, who encouraged and helped me through every phase of the project. My love and respect for these two ladies know no bounds.

Acknowledgments

The author is indebted to Dee Clem for her editing skills that strengthened this work. Also, he is indebted to Andy Wright—a *contentious*, independent soul who thinks for himself, is long on opinions and is unintimidated by anyone else's age, rank, education, wealth, knowledge or experience. Andy's certainty about that quicksilver commodity called truth, juxtaposed with the author's uncertainty, helped find *a reasoned path* in this world of mysteries.

About Endnotes

Notes are employed extensively in *Sweet Mysteries* for reference, credit and clarification purposes and the reader is encouraged to make use of them. These notes are presented at the end of each chapter.

Contents

Contents (Continued)

Introduction

There is a restlessness in my soul, as there is in yours. From where this genetic imprint originates, we cannot know. It is a mystery. A portion of my restlessness has spilled onto the pages of this book.

Presented here is an assortment of facts, follies and mysteries. The aim is to heighten our appreciation of the contradictions and wonders of life. If the attempt is successful, you will recognize honesty and the pervasive attempt to persuade you (and me) that we should listen to ourselves. This presentation is chiseled from leaden facts, but let not their weight diminish the truth that we exist in a world where it is our mysteries and not what we know that provide us with our greatest spiritual comfort and ultimate refuge from our restlessness.

♭♭ One ♭♭

To Dream the Impossible Dream[1]

(Imagination)

On March 28, 1970, a 7.8 magnitude earthquake wrenched western Turkey and some islands on the eastern coast of Greece. Mostly rural areas were involved and less than 2,000 deaths were reported, so as world events go this was not big. But, huge chunks of landscape were turned inside out.

More than twelve years later, on July 23, 1982, a Greek accountant and amateur rock hound, George Peloponesus, was poking around an area hit by the 1970 earthquake and collecting crystalline rocks. Peloponesus ventured deep inside a cave located on one of Greece's small uninhabited islands, near the eastern coast of Greece in the Aegean Sea. Here, he found some choice rocks, but of more interest he found an unusual parchment. The parchment was tightly sealed in a hollowed out rock casing that had been fastened together with some reddish material and was lying in the midst of a jumble of fragmented rocks which must have broken loose during the last earthquake. While fragile, the parchment held together quite well.

Peloponesus donated the goatskin parchment to the University of Athens in Greece. The University's scholars determined the parchment was ancient Greek (before 1600 B.C.), and by early winter of 1982 they deciphered its writings. It was a story that, in turn, was handed down to the ancient Greeks by the Sumerians who lived about 1500 years earlier in the Tigris-Euphrates river valley, about 1400 miles east-southeast of Greece. How this transfer from the Sumerians to the ancient Greeks came about was a mystery. The story made little sense to either of these ancients. But, in spite of the certain encryption errors, it begins to makes some sense with the information now available in the twenty-first century.

♭♭ Sumerian's Experience ♭♭

A Sumerian narrated his story, as follows:

I left the field in the late afternoon and was fishing for perch when my eyes were drawn to the heavens and, for no reason that I could understand, I fell into a deep rapture. After a short period, I awoke as if from a night's sleep. I know it wasn't long because there was still light. I had this message that had no meaning to me spinning in my aching head. Although I tried to will it away, it refused to leave my consciousness; so I left my cane and hurried to my friend's abode. Soab, my friend, was a scribe and he wrote the message exactly as it poured like poisoned food from my mouth. The words had no utility, only embarrassment for me, but they explained how they were put into me by an adventurer from long ago.

Here there was a break, then the message that Soab scribed continued.

This was an exciting time for our scouting party. We had been traveling for what seemed an eternity and now we were ready to commence the surface examination. There were only six of us and my dual duties were navigation officer and mission historian. *My Lord our spirits were high*, especially mine since I nailed the navigation and parked us dead on target on the valley floor. This was no mean feat for one in their first renewal. The crew members called me "Navigator," and I could detect an admiring and friendlier tone in their voices since we had landed. I won't say I was strutting around, but I was more than a little proud of my navigation achievement. True we had precision astro-instruments, but it took some doing to sling shot us past 10^{13} stars, black masses, dark matter, find the optimum intergalactic entryways, and accelerate at the proper angle through the universe bubble, to land on this insignificant rock. I say insignificant, but it had two outstanding features that were extremely important to us—(1) An intense electromagnetic field, that would allow us to replenish our craft's power system and (2) An abundance of H_2O.

As we moved from our craft, there was no sense of motion. Light was cresting over the eastern range of mountains in a multitude of hues—oranges, purples and shades of silver that mixed with the blackness, then drove it away, poof, like a magician casting off a dark spell. And there we were—bathed in the star's light. Horizon to horizon in every direction the terrain was consumed by magnificent light. The air was heavy with stinking sulfur that caused us to adjust our odor sensors. There were jagged mountains surrounding us on three sides and to the south the valley faded away into distant knolls. There was no cellular life, only stark rocky landscape that had been pushed and shoved and smoothed out in places by several billion years of solar winds, ice movements, meteor bombardments, and core and subsurface upheavals.

We were located 65 degrees latitude and 65 degrees longitude on the 3^{d} distant mass from star 0723's epicenter, which had established its own atmosphere, cooled to accessible temperatures and stabilized in its orbit about star 0723. We tagged it 0723-3.

Our first task was to stretch our miserable bodies, then make repairs on our craft and replenish it for the long journey back home. We had mastered the use of harmonic photon accelerators, bidirectional gravity shields and bidirectional mass convertors which enables us, within limits, to convert mass to energy and energy back to mass. This ability permits us to remove the cloak of illusion from the dimension called time and the parameter called motion and allows us to travel at speeds beyond light speed. The fuel we use for our craft is electromagnetic energy and photons (the most plentiful energy source in the universe). Our bidirectional gravity shields allow us to accelerate and deaccelerate, using the great masses located throughout the universe. Our photon nets and gravity shields are in great need of repair. This will be done by our engineering officer. Our crew consists of the captain, engineering officer, geophysics officer, astrophysics officer, genetics officer and myself. I've listed us in decreasing order of rank, so you see as the lowest ranking member of the crew I can't strut too much. Each of us provides backup for another. The backup teams are: (1) captain and engineering officer, (2) astrophysics and geophysics officer, and (3) the genetics officer and myself.

After our repairs were made, we pricked, prodded, surveyed and analyzed the mass makeup and core temperature patterns; calculated the orbit trajectory with other Cosmos masses; and decided 0723-3 had a good chance of surviving for another ten-to-twenty-billion years. This met our specifications, so our party merged its rationality and decided this was as good a place as we were going to find to sow our cellular seeds. These biological seeds were diverse, including vegetation and mobile forms for land and water, each having traces of our own nucleic acid containing genetic codes that control the manufacture of proteins and direct the path for organism development.

Following preflight instructions, we interconnected the seed bins with the craft dispersal system, then made 360,000 low altitude passes at creep speed. At each pass, we spewed millions of seeds on 0723-3's surface. Our land-water sensor malfunctioned, thus many water seeds fell on land and land seeds on water. But we knew all of the ingredients were present to populate this barren rock—multiple seeds with our superior genetic coding, a changing environment, the right temperature envelope and chemical makeup (hydrogen, oxygen, carbon and helium), and the presence of moisture and light. Over time, evolution and mutation would do the rest. Our work was finished! So we set sail for home and we were glad to be leaving this uninhabited rock on the outer fringe of the Cosmos.

I suppose it's my own mutative spirit, supplemented by historical and genetics training, that caused me to code this short message into the seed you evolved from. We planted our species cells on 0723-3, after it had made three-and-a-half-billion revolutions about its star, and this message is programmed to transmit to your being after it has made another billion revolutions.

While there was a beginning to you and 0723-3, there is no beginning to our universe, only bubble cycles. The bubbles expand, collapse, expand and collapse, repeating these cycles, insofar as we can determine, forever. It follows then there is no end. There is no Alpha nor Omega. Our form approaches pure energy which permits us to move about the universe. There is a universal but varying relationship between the two fundamental components of the universe—mass and energy. In a broad range it is energy=(mass)(mass momentum variable)(speed of light)^2. The equation becomes complicated, because the speed of light is variable and all mass is transient—either increasing or decreasing in size and is in varying states of motion. The optimum mass momentum variable is one, but is less than one under certain conditions of the universe.

We have charted the mass momentum variable for about 40% of our universe, finding it to vary between 0.75 and 1.0. With the right conditions and harmonic photon accelerators one can increase or decrease the speed of light, thus under certain conditions of mass allowing us to control energy. But everything is relative and/or in a varying state of change. Change is essential to us, because as long as there is change there can be life. Your existence is our attempt to create a new civilization based on our heritage but tempered by the random evolution of a different galaxy; a civilization that we hope eventually will develop science, quality of life and number of renewals beyond our present ability. Our culture now has the option of five renewals for each individual. A renewal is approximately equivalent to the time it takes for 100 revolutions of 0723-3's orbit about its star. We mass hop at will, but stars are too hot and our limited understanding makes us slaves to the random will of the universe. Plus, we understand very little about our neighboring and distant universes where our scientists tell us energy may convulse in strange and unknown patterns with masses that can initiate and terminate bubble cycles.

Enough! Enough!! What kind of science-fiction malarkey is being promoted here? The answer is none. Rather, this malarkey has been used to illustrate one of our greatest realities and gifts—*IMAGINATION* or the ability to fantasize, especially about subjects or situations we cannot control and do not and cannot know the answers to or choose to escape from or enter uninvited into. Here, from an unfertile imagination (mine), some scientific knowledge and less than 2,000 words, an explanation of mankind's creation, UFOs, and scientific relationships has been presented. Perhaps a dumb explanation, but surely no dumber than many classical creation myths.

♭♭ Myths ♭♭

Creation myths generally culminate in the creation of humankind, after which the cosmos begins to resemble the world of human experience. In mythic history, the early world usually is closer to perfection while later phases show the degeneration of the world as it grows more distant from the original creation. The earliest humans are often thought to have extraordinary powers and to have been much closer to the gods than present-day humans. Most creation myths presume the eternity of the world, or at least that part of it reserved for the chosen few. Interestingly, most of the known creation-to-the-end myths have an ongoing struggle between supernatural powers (good versus evil) and a way of cleansing earth of its sinners by great floods or fire.

Many mythologies include stories of self-fertilization or strange fertilizations by or through a creator. These stories are necessary because there must be a way to get mankind started. Also there is the matter of the heavens, land, water, air, light and fire that must be explained. In Egyptian mythology, only the ocean existed, then the sun came out of an egg that appeared on the surface of the water, while in Vodun mythology a sky-serpent first created the waters of the earth. The movement of his giant coils formed the valleys and mountains of earth and the heavens. In the Sumerian flood myth, the gods became angry with mankind and destroyed them with a great flood. But a worthy man, Ziusudra, built a great boat and saved his family and the animals. This myth was imagined two-thousand years before Noah and his ark. The civilizations of Greece, India, China, Babylonia, and several Indian tribes of South America, including the Mayan and Aztecs, all have their version of a great-flood myth. In Genesis, God does it all in six days, then disappointed with the sinners He created He floods them out of existence except for worthy Noah, his family, and some birds and animals.

♪♪ Imagination ♪♪

But let us return to *imagination*—the creator of myths, large and small. At an early age, most children understand the value of fantasy. Watch them become animated and their eyes brighten as they happily wiggle and verbalize "a pretend" or know that you are pretending with them. As we pass from childhood to adulthood and become the keepers of our planet and progenitors of our species, most cultures promote suppression of imagination in favor of the importance of the reality (work, careers, family, social obligations, etc.) of our everyday worlds. As one grows older and approaches the end of their life cycle, many become reacquainted with imagination's value. Most grandparents tell better stories to their grandchildren than parents do to their children, not only because they have more experience or time on their hands, but because they give freer rein to their imaginations. Aristotle was one of the greatest realists in history and he spent a long and productive lifetime (sixty-two years) gathering and interpreting facts and opposing mysticism. Yet, in the last year of his life, he wrote to his close friend Aristipater, "The more I am by myself, and alone, the fonder I have become of myths."[2]

Imagination is at the same time a sweet mystery and a wonderful reality. It knows no racial, sexual, cultural, intellectual, physical, or financial limits. Imagination is not bound by age, beauty or social status. It allows us to remove spatial, time, you-name-it boundaries and visit exotic and nonexistent places, perform great feats, enjoy forbidden pleasures and solve unsolvable problems. Imagination, according to the song "The Impossible Dream," permits us to right the unrightable wrong and dream the impossible dream. Imagination leads the way, in fact, for many to right unrightable wrongs and achieve the here-to-fore impossible. Imagination also can create mundane problems in everyday life as this personal story about a frangipani plant illustrates.

The Frangipani

I made a foolish mistake forty years
Ago when I wasted a frangipani plant
While holding off a band of buccaneers
Who stormed our tranquil household habitat.
They sailed in over elm from distant shores,
With flying skull and cross-bone semaphores,
To plunder our hard-earned family stores.

Absorbed in sport of great import I played
Alone on flagstone porch and waved my stick
And dreamed those daydreams that invade
The noblest game when there appeared this slick
Two-masted frigate that darkened the sky,
Then, winged close like some phantom butterfly
And lit so near I heard its rigging sigh.

The clanging sounds of grappling hooks rang loud
As fast the ghastly ship was wed to home
And smell of brine and stinking pirate crowd
Engulfed me like a veil of spoiled sea foam.
Mad shrieks and shouts and flashing blades spanned
The hemp in heed to the captain's command:
"Kill them all lads and load the contraband!"

Inflamed with burning hope to save my folks
And duty clear, I sprang to stop the scum.
With new-born sword carving savage strokes
I slew the first few drunken flunkeydom
And deftly parried so swift and bold
The rest paused. "Make way mates!" the captain crowed
"I'll cut the boy's heart from its bloody hold!"

Silence beset the crew, as sailors stood
Arrear, and framed the captain's rum breath
Which wheezed refrains I clearly understood
As battle cries that signified my death.
I slowed his charge with spins and a quick tack
And stalled him by feinting a high attack,
Next, thrusting low, I slit his scrotal sac!

Swish! .... Perhaps a turbulent sea wind
Flushed my fancy fed feats away for now
I found sap clinging to undisciplined
Cutlass turned stick and—*Oh God No!*—somehow
I'd gelded Granny's favorite plant prize.
Attempts at stalk splints soon made me realize
That my aims were better aimed at alibis.

The dread of detection gave no relief
Until Granny's weekly garden tour
And my call was the first echo of grief
That sounded from a sad fact's disclosure.
Having fully rehearsed my alibi,
I heeded the summon—casual, humble-pie—
Prepared my innocence to sanctify.

Dear Granny's eyes each glistened with a tear
And though she neither scolded nor accused
Those tears stripped away the false veneer
So that one downcast glance introduced
The truth. She knew and knew I knew she knew.
I blubbered and failed the interview,
But Granny just said "Shush...I'll plant anew."

> Lots of lessons have been learned since that date
> And mistakes made by that boy matador
> Would need a handsome book to tabulate.
> But for you now in your heaven,
> And perhaps it helps his score,
> Please hear this truth Dearest Granny:
> He's never killed another frangipani.

Our individual lives are balancing acts. If we move too far into a world of fantasy, our behavior is termed bizarre and we can be classified as psychotic or mentally disturbed. We can hallucinate—see, hear, or feel something that isn't there, or be delusional, or have a false belief that appears obviously untrue to others in our culture. For example, a person might believe they received a message concerning the origin of planet earth's population and need to be the messenger of that information or whack a plant while fantasizing. According to my friend, Andy Wright, whom I will seek assistance from throughout this work, that is bizarre behavior! Andy's given name actually is *Always*, but his high school friends took the sting out of his parent's awkward sense of humor by calling him Andy. A tradition that will be maintained here. Some of Andy's college companions chose to call him "Never," and there are times when he demonstrates they were on the *"wright"* track.

Nigel Thomas warns that notwithstanding imagination being a familiar word in our everyday language, it is a very complex and contested concept.[3] It, like many cognate terms, often appears to have radically different senses and connotations when used in different contexts. Traditionally, imagination means the mental capacity for experiencing, constructing, or manipulating "mental imagery." Imagination is synonymous with fantasy and is responsible for inventiveness and creative, original, and insightful thought in general, and, sometimes, for a much wider range of mental activities dealing with the non-actual, such as supposing, pretending, 'seeing as,' thinking of possibilities, and *even being mistaken*. Imagination particularly is associated with thinking about things that are not actually present to the senses—things that are not really there.

That's one of the problems we face with language. It seems everything, even imagination, is so complicated that it depends on which foot you are standing, where you are standing, when you are standing, who is listening, why they are listening, etc., ad nauseam. Nevertheless, it is believed the reader will recognize the meaning(s) of imagination in this work as Andy and your writer step back and forth between reason, experience, faith, intuition, and imagination or fantasy in our effort to understand some of the issues and problems facing mankind in the twenty-first century. If this work appears didactic, it isn't meant to be for the reader—only for Andy. Andy responds with a warning that the fact-driven dialogue, found here, seems to migrate, with a will of its own, toward preachy, debatable conclusions.[4]

Chapter Notes

1. *To Dream the Impossible Dream* is a phrase from the hit song "The Impossible Dream" ("The Quest"). The song is based on *Don Quixote* by Cervantes and was performed in the Broadway musical *Man of La Mancha*, words and music by Joe Darion and Mitch Leigh.

2. *Aristotle, Volume I, Great Books of the Western World*, (Chicago, London, Montreal: Encyclopaedia Britannica, Inc., 1952).

3. Nigel J.T. Thomas is an expert on the subject of imagination. To learn about ancient and medieval conceptions, history of different philosophical views, and scientific research concerning the mind and imagination, visit his website at http://www.calstatela.edu /faculty/nthomas.

4. Facts presented in this book are drawn from the work of many others. Credits and supporting comments are contained in notes located at the end of each chapter. Of course, any errors or misrepresentation of the facts are the responsibility of this author.

Two

Songs of Our Own

(Mysteries of the Mind)

ometimes we walk alone, sometimes the songs that we hear are just songs of our own. Wake up to find out that you are the eyes of the world, but the mind has its beaches, its homeland and thoughts of its own. Wake now, sometimes the songs that we hear are just songs of our own.[1] The Grateful Dead entertained us with their string rock rhythm, and, thanks primarily to Robert Hunter, many of their lyrics are poetic gems. Certainly, the above lyrics are true to the mark—***sometimes the songs that we hear are just our own fantasies***.

Millions of people claim knowledge of past lives, ghosts, abductions by aliens, encounters with deities, mystic experiences or other special mystic abilities, such as predicting future events. Most of these individuals are conscious of their claims while others have been made aware of their special experiences only through hypnosis or trances that open their subconsciousness. While a percentage of these claims are hoaxes or jokes, there can be no doubt that a substantial number are serious claims made by honest, intelligent individuals. In thousands of cases documented by psychologists, physicians and other professionals there is no evidence of fraud or collusion between the subjects and those documenting their unbelievable experiences. The credibility of these experiences is enhanced by the astonishing level of emotion and detail revealed, some of which is verifiable. Are any of these claims reality or are they voodoo fantasies or illusions of the mind? These questions beg an answer!

Andy Wright quickly points out that the Bible is filled with examples of miracles, conversations between God and mortals, the presence of angels and the power of Satan over the minds of the unholy. Therefore, Andy knows that many of these claims are not only true in the minds of the believers; they are real. He uses the immensity of space as a tool to demonstrate the plausibility of other beings and insists that billions of people at some point in their lives (including his own) have had isolated déjà vu experiences (feeling like you've been there before) or premonitions (believing something is going to happen and it happens). Bookshelves are filled with individual accounts and group studies that claim to verify the validity and reality of mind travels, aliens, prophecies, occult experiences, ghosts, angels, past lives and other mysterious encounters. So, what is one to believe?

Lack of understanding has been a "hallmark" of humans throughout history; and because some fail to understand mysteries or miracles does not disprove their reality. Remember fantasies are reality, while what one fantasizes often is not and will not become a reality. In the year of my birth, 1933, which wasn't that long ago, only mystics could have foretold with a straight face the miracles that man would walk on the moon in the twentieth century and would stir up a mixture of inanimate materials, creating something that could be used to solve a host of mathematical and scientific problems, communicate between the masses, and provide easy access to more than a thousand times the information contained in the Library of Congress. Yet, today most twelve-year-old Americans know that humans walking on the moon are old-hat, and they understand and accept the reality of digital computers and the Internet.

In *The Experts Speak*, Christopher Cerf and Victor Navasky provide numerous examples of experts having to eat their proclamations and predictions.[2] For example, an expert editorial, in an 1865 *Boston Post* article, advised readers "Well-informed people know it is impossible to transmit their voices over wires and that were it possible to do so, the thing would be of no practical value." Lord Kelvin, pioneer genius in thermodynamics and electricity, in 1895 wrote "Heavier-than-air flying machines are impossible," and Lee Deforest, inventor of the Vacuum tube in 1957, declared "man will never reach the moon, regardless of all future scientific advances." Airplanes, computers, the Internet, space travel, radios, telephones and television are miracles of achievement, rather than miracles of experience of the kind associated with reincarnation, encounters with deities, communion with spirits, etc. But the reality of these ideas seemed as far-fetched to the disbelievers of earlier times as the ideas of reincarnation and other unsolved mysteries appear to disbelievers of today. The common denominator of these experience miracles is the human mind. Although the lack-of-understanding factor is ever present, David Hume gave some excellent advice when he said that no testimony of man is sufficient to establish a miracle; such miracles are much more likely to be falsehoods or illusions than reality.[3]

♪♪ Reality or Illusions? ♪♪

Sorting out reality from illusions of the mind requires a rational balance of our lack of understanding with what we do know and understand. And when the subject is the mind, nowhere is there a larger lack of understanding. Steven Pinker, one of the world's articulate cognitive scientists, reminds us that we don't understand how the mind works nearly as well as we understand how the body works.[4] He suggests that our ignorance can be divided into mysteries and problems. When we are faced with a problem, we may not know its solution but we have a measure of understanding and, at least, can attempt solutions; whereas, when we are faced with mysteries, we can only stare in wonder and bewilderment, not knowing what an explanation would look like. Pinker reports that in the late-twentieth century dozens of mysteries of the mind have been upgraded to problems. In fact, advances in brain/mind research in the decade of the 1990s, led the U.S. Congress to pass a resolution that the 1990s was the decade of the brain.

As we make an effort to enter into the realm of the mind, Andy Wright and I, who often disagree, are in full agreement. We are attempting to enter a holy sanctuary (a perfect example of a mystery behind an enigma behind a mystery), and our understanding can best be guided by scientists who have devoted countless hours to the study of the brain, mind and thought processes. The mind is not the brain. Rather, it is what the brain does, excluding physiological functions such as metabolizing fat and giving off heat.

Important insights about the brain are provided by the research of the Harvard neuroscientists Norman Geschwind and Albert Galaburda and the reporting of Terry Armstrong and Nicole Rust. They tell how the uniqueness of our brain-centered behavior has its genesis in fetal development, and that fetal life is critical in determining intellectual and behavioral development.[5,6] Their outline of the brain's development includes:

❑ Formation of the primitive neural elements;
❑ Development and differentiation of the neural plate and neural tube which gives rise to the brain;
❑ Formation of the neural crest on top of the neural tube from which the nervous system, eyes and the bones of the face, and other features emerge;
❑ Formation of germinal zones within the brain;
❑ Cell migration of essential brain cells;
❑ Cell differentiation and maturation during which brain cells find their first locations, grow and establish connections.

Neurons, the major cellular component of the brain, found in the outer layer of the cerebrum known as the cerebral cortex, migrate in fetal life from a tiny 3-mm-long neural tube to their final location.

This occurs in successive stages that result in six cell layers in the cortex. Following the first layer, new layers must make their way past the earlier ones to their final positions in the cortex. Many of these cells migrate to dedicated positions and relegate themselves to tasks such as speech, movement, vision, touch, hearing, smell and taste functions. This entire process requires the constant production of new brain cells during pregnancy, arriving at approximately 100-billion neurons at birth. The brain needs energy. Neural tissue is metabolically greedy, our brains take up 2 percent of our body weight (about 3 pounds), but consume 20 percent of our energy and nutrients. Axons are the output cables of neurons, and most neurons only have a single axon.

Digital computers can operate at more than a thousand million operations per second. By contrast a neuron fires at about one hundred operations per second, therefore a computer is about ten million times faster than a neuron. But, the operations in a computer are mostly serial, one after the other, while neuron axons are wired in parallel. For example, about a million neuron axons are wired from each eye to the brain, all working in parallel or simultaneously. This speeds up the brain process, and because of the redundancy the loss of a few neurons does not have much effect on the brain's responsiveness.

Geschwind and Galaburda developed their understanding of human uniqueness around the concept of brain asymmetry where each side of the brain evidences particular skills. Each hemisphere is superior in certain functions; the left is usually dominant for language and manual skills; the right is more involved in certain spatial, musical, attentional and emotional aspects. They found that increased fetal testosterone levels alter and modify neural development, resulting in brain asymmetry. Their theory seems to explain many aspects of learning disorders and special talents. Increased testosterone in the fetal environment also explains, they contend, why males and females differ on average in patterns of abilities. Males predominate in cases of autism, dyslexia, stuttering and other developmental disorders including reading difficulties. Certain types of special gifts, including music, artistic, mathematical and axial motor skills are also attributed to cerebral asymmetry.

♪♪ Minds Control Personalities ♪♪

Our minds control our personalities which differ in at least six substantial ways, e.g.: whether a person is outgoing or retiring; whether a person worries more than normal or is calm and self-satisfied; whether a person is courteous or rude, trusting or suspicious, careful or careless; and whether a person is daring or conforming. Where do these traits come from? If they are genetic, identical twins should share them (even if separated at birth), and biological siblings should share them more than adoptive siblings. If they are a product of socialization by parents, adoptive siblings should share them, and twins and biological siblings should share them more when they grow up in the same home than when they grow up in different homes. Dozens of studies have tested such predictions on thousands of people in many countries. The studies have examined not only personality traits, but actual outcomes in life—such as alcoholism and divorce. Results of these studies are clear and replicable, and they contain some stunning revelations.[7]

One result has become well known. Much of the variation in personality—about 50 percent—has genetic causes. Identical twins separated at birth are alike; biological siblings raised together are more alike than adopted siblings. That means the other 50 percent must come from the parents and the home. Right? Wrong! Being brought up by a parent accounts, at most, for 5 percent of the differences among individual personalities. Identical twins separated at birth are not only similar; they are virtually as similar as identical twins raised together.[8] Adoptive siblings in the same home are not just different; they are about as different as two children plucked from the population at random. The biggest influence that parents have on their children is at the moment of conception. Psychologist Judith Harris suggests that these studies imply only that children would turn into the same kinds of adults if you left them in their homes and social milieus but switched all the parents around.[9] Khalil Gibran hit the bull's-eye, when he wrote in 1923, long before the proof of these scientific studies, that a parent's relationship to its child is like that of a bow to an arrow.[10] Once the arrow is unleashed, the bow has little influence.

♪♪ Importance of Early Socialization ♪♪

Lise Eliot, research neuroscientist and mother, provides a remarkably apt description of how the brain and mind develop in the first five years of life.[11] The importance of early brain development in our behavior is demonstrated dramatically by children who were isolated from human society. Fortunately there aren't many cases. There are, however, a number of documented cases where children have been locked away and isolated from normal human contact or reared in the wild.

John McCrone, reports there are more than thirty-five reputable cases of wild children; most reared in wolf dens. McCrone contends these records support his thesis that we are born into this world with a mind as naked as our bodies and we have to rely on society to clothe our minds.[12]

The idea of wolves raising children seems far fetched in 2002, but in the nineteenth and early twentieth century, it was common practice in India for rural mothers to leave their babies, unattended, by the side of a field while they worked. Indian wolves were plentiful and so were unattended infants. The Indian wolf is sandy colored and less fearsome than its European or North American counterparts. Occasionally wolves were caught picking up babies and when chased they dropped them with little or no harm. Most infants stolen by wolves were probably eaten, but a few survived and for reasons unknown were kept alive, for a time, by the wolf pack. In the 1850s, an English army officer, Col. William Sleeman, who was stationed in India, wrote of six cases that he felt were reliable.[13]

One of the most famous examples of wild children was two young girls who were found living with wolves in a cave-like den in the jungle of Northern India. They were discovered in 1920 by Reverend Joseph Singh, a Catholic missionary in charge of an orphanage, who kept a detailed diary of his observations of the two girls. When found, the older girl seemed to be about seven years old; the other perhaps a year younger. It seemed apparent that the girls were not sisters, but had been stolen at separate places by the wolves.[14]

When retrieved from the wolves' den, the girls were like animals. They ran or shuffled in a sort of stooped crouch. They were afraid of humans and artificial light and tried to escape the fenced grounds of the orphanage. They preferred to eat with the dogs in the compound. They ate by pushing their face into the food, the way dogs do, and they drank by lapping from a bowl. They both had worms, and within a year, the younger girl died of worms.

The older girl, christened Kamala by Rev. Singh, recovered from worms. Kamala eventually learned to wear clothes and bathe and learned about fifty words of language, before she died from typhoid fever. At death, she was approximately 16 years old.

The girls seemed to have no trace of humanness in the way they acted and thought. They tore off any clothes put on them, would only eat raw meat, slept curled up together in a tight ball and growled and twitched in their sleep. When first brought to civilization, they only came awake after the moon rose; then howled, like wolves, to be let free. There were many unusual incidents, like the time, about one year after being found, that Kamala caught a chicken in the yard, tore it apart with her teeth and hands and ate it raw.

What is most fascinating is what the girls didn't do. When they were captured, they did not display any characteristically human qualities. For example, they did not use tools of any kind, not even a stick. They did not use fire. They did not walk upright. They did not laugh. They did not sing. They used no language, not even grunts.

They used no gestures to communicate. They did not show any affection or attraction or curiosity toward humans. In short, they didn't display human traits that many believe are genetically innate. Kamala did show more signs of personhood after nine years of civilized life. At Kamala's death in 1928, her adoptive mother, Reverend Pakenham-Walsh, commented that "She was still an infant, so to say, of three or four years of age with reference to her growth as a human child."

Another compelling and well-documented case of a wild child is the wild boy of Aveyron.[15] In 1800, a filthy, naked boy about twelve-years old was found grubbing for potatoes in a field near Saint Sernin in Southern France. A villager named Vidal captured the boy who behaved like a frightened beast. There was never proof of the child's family or where he came from or how long he had been living like an animal. But there was no doubt that he survived alone in the wilds for many years, living off nuts, berries, small animals and vegetables he would sneak from farmers' fields. Vidal named him Victor.

When the news spread of Victor's capture, it was learned that he had been captured twice before, about two years earlier in the woods near Lacaune, approximately seventy miles south of Saint Sernin, but escaped both times. Lucien Bonaparte, Napoleon's brother and France's Minister for the Interior, demanded the boy be brought to Paris for close study. Lucien felt that Victor, as a child raised out of civilization, might shed some light on the inherent nature of humans. Victor was about four-and-a-half-feet tall; he was deeply tanned and covered in scars and scratches. He could not speak and did not react when spoken to, but he would twist around at the sound of a walnut cracked across the room. He could make noises such as grunts and murmurs, but he refused to wear clothes, ripping them off. He slept curled up in a ball like an animal and defecated without shame whenever and wherever the urge occurred. He would only eat food such as potatoes, raw meat, walnuts and acorns. His gait was a shuffling run and occasionally he would move on all fours. At first Victor showed an animal blankness and no interest in other humans;

he appeared to have no thoughts except for food and sleep. The only excitement he demonstrated was when he glimpsed the outdoors and tried to escape. He spent hours hunched on the floor, rocking slowly back and forth and staring off into space. In this position, he made dull murmurs and occasionally small convulsions would twitch across his body and face. In spite of intensive efforts to teach him social graces and to speak, he was house-trained but still half-wild, fearful and mute when he died in his forties.

Other reports of wild children or children locked away from normal development reveal similar characteristics, especially regarding language. If a child does not have the benefit of a language-using community during the first three years of life, then the child does not readily acquire language, even with later intensive training. Moreover, the child does not develop into a fully functioning person. This was true in Kamala's case. Most stories about children raised in the wild aren't totally trustworthy,[16] but there have been sufficient quantity and quality of documentation to show they behave more like interesting animals, rather than people. Their lack of language and social training is so far outside the range of what we understand as acceptable that, at best, they are marginal human beings. And, not because of their genetic make-up, but because of how and what they learned or did not learn from their cultural environment. Left outside of a peopled social culture, humans do not develop language and social skills. There can be little doubt that many skills are learned. Certainly the evidence shows that human beings are not innately wise, generous, tool-using, speaking creatures.

A study commenced in 1945, by Rene Spitz followed the social development of babies who were separated from their mothers early in life.[17] Some children were placed with foster families, while others were raised in institutions. The babies raised in institutions had no family-like environment. In some cases, care was provided by nurses who worked eight hour shifts. More than a third of the babies raised in the institution environment died before reaching adulthood.

Twenty-one were still living in institutions after forty years, and most were physically, mentally, and socially retarded.

Humans need physical contact and socialization throughout life. Isolation will bring on hallucinations, apathy, anxiety, and the loss of self confidence. Joel Charon informs us that socialization is synonymous with learning.[18] We are expected to learn the rules, expectations, and truths of our group, whether the group is our family, the army, a social club, a governmental entity, or a kindergarten class. Socialization is the process whereby people acquire personality and learn to thrive in their society. It encompasses the truths, attitudes, gender roles, values, tastes, rules, and goals that people share with one another. The most important time for socialization is during our first decade of life.

We obviously learn throughout our lives and later learning can override and/or build on earlier learning, but the first ten years are extremely important in determining whom we are for the rest of our lives. *All I Ever Really Needed to Know I Learned in Kindergarten*[19] is the title of a best-selling book and is based on this fact. I read the book, knowing the premise, at best, was a gross over-simplification of the truth and at worst a downright error. While the book was witty and entertaining, I came away with my preconceived notion still secure, because we learn throughout our lives. Wisdom is not all in the sandbox and there is a lot more to learn than "cleaning up your own mess." I am reminded of the five-year old girl who told her father that kindergarten was a waste of her time. "Why?" he asked. "Because," she said, "I can't read and I can't write and they won't let me talk." What we've learned by age five or six is very important, but not enough to carry us through a reasonably happy, productive life. But, as the wild children and other cases of isolated children have revealed, children in the first three-to-five years of their lives need a social setting that teaches them language and the basics of human behavior, or they will be socially stunted in a human environment for the remainder of their lives.

♭♭ **Nurture or Nature** ♭♭

Matt Ridley thinks men and women have different minds; the differences being the direct result of evolution.[20] Women's minds evolved to suit the demands of bearing and rearing children and men's minds evolved to suit the demands of rising in a male hierarchy, fighting over women, and providing food to a family. Five mental features that stand out as repeatable and persistent in psychological tests are: (1) females are better at verbal tasks; (2) males are better at mathematical tasks; (3) males are more aggressive; (4) males are better at some visual-spatial tasks such as map reading but females are better at others such as object and location memory tasks, i.e., noticing things and; (5) females are better judges of character and mood.

Nurture reinforces nature; it rarely fights against it. More than 80 percent of the murderers and drunk drivers in America are males, and it's difficult to believe that this fact is due to social conditioning alone. Matt Ridley advises that human nature is a product of culture, but culture is also a product of human nature, and both are the products of evolution. In the 1930s contact was made with New Guinea tribes that were unaware of the outside world's existence. Yet they were found to smile and frown just like Westerners, despite thousands of years without sharing a common ancestor. The smile is the universal sign of man's pleasure and illustrates there are far more similarities of men and their natures than there are differences. Ridley makes an excellent case for the notion that the differences between the natures of men of different races are trivial, compared to the differences between the natures of men and women of the same race. A paradox he points out is that, in spite of the similarities, each individual is unique. Ridley believes this is so because our genes use our bodies and sexual nature to enhance their chance of propagation, because sex is humanity's best strategy for outwitting its constantly mutating predators that are striving for their own genetic survival.

♪♪ Illusions and Delusions ♪♪

Whether the foundation is nurture or nature or some combination, psychologists and magicians, alike, frequently show that our ideas about the workings of the mind can be misleading. They teach us that "seeing and believing" can lead to a lot of erroneous conclusions. Slight of hand, misdirection, motion of objects, distance of objects from the eye, coloring of objects, relationship of lines, textures and shapes, all easily can deceive our visual system, hence our mind which relies on our senses. In some instances our sensory systems aren't fooled, but our mind has been trained so that our brain tells us something is there which isn't. Your brain makes the best interpretation it can, according to its makeup and previous experience and the limited and ambiguous information provided by your eyes and other senses. What we see in the sky are not stars, anymore than seeing Clark Gable, the actor, in *Gone With the Wind* is Clark Gable. What we see is what the stars were light-years ago. Clark Gable has been dead a number of years, likewise, for all we know many of the stars we see are now part of black holes. What our eyes see are often illusions. Certainly this is true when objects are examined on a microscopic scale. For example, a bar of gold appears solid to our eyes, but the nucleus of each of its atoms is so small that enlarged by 10^9 its outer electron shell approximates the size of greater Los Angeles and its nucleus is only about the size of an automobile. Thus, gold is mostly space. It's amazing what the eye can see and the brain can deduce from an object, movie or television screen. If you haven't been fooled thousands of times by reflections, optical illusions, sleight of hand, etc., then you haven't lived long or you are sleepwalking through life.

Past experience shows that people enjoy being fooled, learning about others being fooled, or reading convincing personal accounts that seem to prove miracles are facts rather than illusions or delusions. A recent trip to a large Barnes & Noble bookstore verified that American book buyers in 2002 still enjoy being fooled. One of the best selling book types, now labeled "New Age," are books of this ilk. Books with titles involving the occult, ESP, prophecies, fortune tellers, haunted houses, ghosts, alien encounters, large creatures ("big foot" and other land or water monsters), tarot cards, astrologists, hypnotic spells, magicians, mind travelers, seances, spiritualists, reincarnationists, etc. fill the bookstore shelves.

Charles Mackay wrote about the popular delusions of Europe in his day (1841).[21] Many of these delusions have survived the test of time, such as the prophetic powers of Nostradamus. Mackay writes that Nostradamus lived in a time when astrology was in high favor with superstitious European royalty, especially King Henry II. Nostradamus was born in 1503 and became the personal physician and chief astrologist to King Henry II. Nostradamus didn't receive much fame until his almost unintelligible verses, *Centuries*, were published.[22] His prophecies consist of upwards of a thousand obscure stanzas. They take so great a latitude, both as to time and space, that they are almost sure to be fulfilled in a fashion somewhere in the course of time, especially when the embroidery of true believers is added to the mix. Astrology was Nostradamus's main area of expertise.

♪♪ Prophecies ♪♪

Hundreds of scientific efforts conclude that astrology is a mixture of superstition, quackery and big business; and there is no proof that the influence of the heavenly bodies on individuals can reveal their past, predict their future or determine social events in their lives.[23] It is true that no amount of expert derision is conclusive evidence against the claims of astrologers. But their only proof lies with individuals who are sure astrologers have assessed correctly their personality traits or provided advice that proved to be sound. For every such case, many more can be found where the predictions do not align with the facts.

Close examination of the works of well-publicized prophets, like Nostradamus, Edgar Cayce, and Jean Dixon, reveals that more of their *specific* prophecies were in error than those proven to be accurate. Their misses do not make the pages of those trying to support their belief in mysticism. Jean Dixon, a Capricorn, wrote her syndicated horoscope column weeks before actual publication. Thus, she wrote her horoscope for the day she died—January 25, 1997. This is what she wrote: "Have faith in yourself and a fresh start will prove highly successful. Time is your best ally. Be willing to work hard and put in long hours."[24] This isn't an accurate obituary, but then the majority of her specific prophecies and horoscope readings missed their mark. Think about it. How many daily readings by astrologists have you read that predict a day of death or horrific accident for an individual? Yet, these events happen by the millions each day. With six billion souls existing on earth and any even distribution of birthdates throughout a 365-day year, more than 16 million individuals share common birthdays and approximately 500 million share common zodiac signs. How absurd, to think they all share common personal characteristics or futures, based on their birthdates.

Stefan Paulus spent a lot of time twisting Nostradamus's quatrains to fit known historical facts. Paulus then documented his findings in a 1997 book, which included the following Nostradamus prediction: "The year 1999, the seventh month from the sky there will come a great King of terror."[25] Paulus interpreted this to mean planet Earth was going to be impacted by a comet with a great loss of life and property. Obviously, the Nostradamus prophecy was in error. At least, most of us are unaware of any startling terror raining from the sky in July, 1999. Fanatical believers probably will come up with a cyclone or summer hail storm somewhere that would suffice, for them, to make the prediction accurate. Andy warns me against petty fictitiousness in my perceived sea of rationality, but *the point is* when soothsayers predict a specific event for a specific time they are no more accurate than any "good guesser." Edgar Cayce, who believed he was reincarnated and that Jesus had been reincarnated thirty times, foresaw the 1990s as a time of great geological upheaval. He predicted that by 1998, the American west and east coasts would be flooded, that Los Angeles and San Francisco would be destroyed by earthquakes, and that New York would be destroyed the same way shortly thereafter. He foresaw the great lakes draining into the Gulf of Mexico, and much of Japan submerged in water.[26] All of these events may and probably will happen—given enough time. Notwithstanding his prophetic successes,[27] the timing of these predictions were major misses.

Culver and Ianna (1984) surveyed 3,011 specific predictions made from 1974-1979 in U.S. Astrology magazines, such as *American Astrology*, and found that only 11 percent were correct. Many of these could be attributed to shrewd guesses, vagueness or insider information, so after allowing for chance there seemed to be nothing left for astrology to explain. After researching many such studies, Geoffrey Dean found all to achieve about the same results as the Culver and Ianna study.[28]

The majority of prophecies are a mixture of general "could bes" that aren't framed with enough specifics to be wrong, especially when they leave open-ended time tables and geography. Most of us can make intelligent guesses about future events. Some of us will be more accurate than others, because of a deeper understanding of nature, people, events in the arena of our guess, or we are plain lucky that random occurrences beyond our control and understanding align with our guesses. This, of course, does not make us prophets. Indeed, anyone reading these words probably has made a guess about some future event that proved to be accurate, but it turned out right for different reasons than the reasons used to support the uncertainty of the guess.

♭♭ Extrasensory Perception ♭♭

Speaking of uncertainties, extensive extrasensory perception (ESP)[29] studies have been conducted by J. B. Rhine of Duke University and others.[30] Most of these tests have been conducted under controlled conditions with the subjects required to guess the next card turned up in a five-card deck. These massive tests suggest that children are slightly more precognitive than adults and that intelligence and education are both negative precognitive influences. These tests did not prove with certainty that any single human has definitive, repetitive ESP capability; the tests only suggested that ESP capability may be a possibility. Millions of people appear to believe in at least some aspects of astrology, ESP or other mystic experiences, so these beliefs must fulfill a deep human need. Rational thinkers who are mystic disbelievers do not have conclusive answers on mysticism either. On such issues, one should hear others but listen to themselves. Often there is more than one correct answer to a question, but surely it is advantageous for individuals to be unable to foretell future events. Consider how debilitating it would be to worry about a certain fall and broken leg or a car wreck that injures or kills you or a loved one. Misfortune, if it has to happen, is terrible, but it is much better as a surprise than a preknown certainty. *Ah, sweet mysteries!*

♪♪ Reincarnation ♪♪

In a rigorous, searching investigation, Ian Wilson combined detailed historical research with psychological insights to unravel some of the mystery surrounding subjects who believe they were reincarnated.[31] In the process, he discovered a striking similarity between these oddities of the mind and those suffering from multiple personalities. Wilson focused his research on those documented cases where specifics of dates, names, and places in the alleged past life experiences were available. He looked closely at many reincarnation and multiple personality cases, including the famous Bridey Murphy case.[32]

In each case where there was sufficient evidence, he found substantial errors in details of the subjects' past lives or he found the main thrust of their past-life descriptions had come from something they had read, seen or been exposed to that took root in their subconscious and conspired with other facts and conditions of their memories to invent their past lives.

Another famous case history Wilson investigated was Chris Sizemore (*Three Faces of Eve*).[33] In each of the cases capable of an orderly investigation, he found that reincarnation was not real; rather the subjects were experiencing illusions. But, Wilson caveats his findings with a statement that he did not totally disprove the phenomenon of reincarnation. There were too many strange, but alleged, facts beyond his ability to verify or disprove.

The business of disproving something is often impossible. For example, it has been suggested that it is impossible to disprove conclusively that mushrooms are sensing devices placed on earth by aliens from outer space, though we know they aren't. And, even if they are, they sure taste good sauteed or in salads. Anyway, Wilson showed that in some cases the subjects' conscious minds were unaware of their past existences, which only surfaced under hypnotic regression. In other cases, the subjects' awareness of their past life was a part of their conscious state, although hypnotic regression heightened their understanding and recall of their alleged past lives. Subjects, when reverting or converting from their normal conscious identity to another identity, often acquire remarkable changes in appearance, language, voice, and personality.

♪♪ Conscious and Unconscious Memory ♪♪

There can be little doubt there is memory within our brain of which we have no conscious awareness. Wilson cites numerous, certifiable experiences that demonstrate this. For instance, in 1970 Professor Erika Fromm documented the case of a twenty-six-year-old Californian named Don whose parents, although racially Japanese, spoke only English at home.[34] Don grew up thinking he knew only a smattering of Japanese words–words like "good food" and "Thank you" that he had learned from his bilingual grandmother. However, hypnotically regressed to the age of three, Don spoke fluent Japanese, in a high-pitched child's voice. During World War II Don had been interned with his parents and other Japanese-Americans at an American "relocation center" where Japanese was the predominate language. When Don and his parents left the relocation center, his parents reverted to using English exclusively, and Don lost all conscious awareness that he had ever known the language. After the hypnosis session and when the tape of his Japanese was played, it was gibberish to him. He was unable to understand what he had spoken. Yet, linguists fluent in the Japanese language confirmed that Don's unconscious words preserved the language.

Julian Jaynes, American psychologist, provided a provocative twist when he described our subconsciousness, split consciousness, or whatever we choose to call that memory in our brain of which we have no conscious awareness as follows:[35]

> Consciousness is a much smaller part of our mental life than we are conscious of, because we cannot be conscious of what we are not conscious of. How simple that is to say, how difficult to appreciate! It is like asking a flashlight in a dark room to search around for something that does not have any light shining upon it. The flashlight, since there is light in whatever direction it turns, would have to conclude there is light everywhere. And so consciousness can seem to pervade all mentality when actually it does not.

It is easy to cite examples of how frequently we think we are conscious, in the sense of being self-aware, when really we are on autopilot, not imposing our consciousness on our thoughts and actions. If an accomplished pianist in the midst of playing a fast-paced piece became totally conscious of herself and her fingers, she would ruin her performance. Most athletes who have trained extensively know what it is like to be in a "zone" where their training takes over and their actions require little conscious thought. In fact, the less conscious thought the better their performance. This is a form of self-hypnosis. For example, any basketball player (even high school players) who has had an exceptional offensive game will tell you they were in a zone, meaning the brain subverted just about everything to their subconscious level—except the basketball and goal. A few exceptional athletes like Wayne Gretsky and Michael Jordan combined talent with practice until they consistently performed in a "zone."

There is no better illustration of a similar "zone" than the simple task of driving an automobile from Point A to Point B. If you have driven a car much, you have driven in traffic, stopped at traffic lights, changed lanes, and then realized you did it without thinking, not even knowing for sure how you got to Point B. And Point B may have not been your original destination, because you allowed habit to take you on a more familiar course. Yet during the process, you: listened to a radio program; scratched yourself a dozen times in a dozen different places; moved your foot from the accelerator to the brake a number of times; turned the steering wheel back and forth; watched traffic move to and fro; observed scenery and signs; repositioned your head, rump, arms and legs for comfort; rubbed your nose; squinted, opened and closed your eyes; exchanged friendly nods of "you-go-first" with fellow travelers; complained silently about the brightness of the sun; enjoyed the beauty of the day; whiffed a donut shop and pizza place; adjusted the air conditioner controls and rear view mirror; looked out the rear view mirror; talked on your cell phone; thought about dinner, friends, events, upcoming chores, enemies, sex and a zillion other things. During the short trek, your senses and neurons exercised frantically in countless ways, while working simultaneously and in series, parallel and series-parallel to control your actions and information retrieval. To detail all of the experiences would take a substantial computer hard drive. And, many of these experiences were imposed on, or performed by, your subconsciousness with no conscious awareness on your part.

We all have minds filled with information that we don't know we possess and may or may not ever use; we move, at times, in self-hypnotic states, and we exhibit changing personalities. The facts and personal experiences reveal this.

Our own unique combination of genetics and nurturing, causes each of us to focus, filter and react differently to the same stimulus. My wife and I can be puttering around the house with the radio playing in the background. When a commentator announces the professional or college game scores, my inner antenna perks up and I listen to the scores and can repeat what I've heard; my wife hears much better than I but couldn't repeat a single score. We can hear the same song and after a few times she will know many of the lyrics. While I enjoy music, I'm lucky if I learn the "hook line" after hearing it ten times. Our subconscious obviously has a measure of control over our mind's focus.

A good friend, Keith Jenkins, had such fond memories of sleeping, as a child, under a tin roof and listening to the soothing pitter-patter of rain that he went to a hardware store and bought an eight-foot section of galvanized tin. Keith was a music buff and owned a state-of-the art recording apparatus. When the next rain came, he placed the sheet of tin near a door and positioned his recorder to capture the sound of rain. Keith decided the pitter-patters were just right, so he engaged the recorder; he was ecstatic, knowing that he had captured and gained a wonderful sleep aid. But, to his great surprise and disappointment when he replayed his masterpiece of "pitter-pattering rain on tin," it was barely audible compared to the sounds of barking dogs, voices of neighbor youngsters playing in the rain, and passing automobiles. He replayed the tape for me and his only profit was a big laugh from both of us. Due to the strength of his desire and focus, these louder sounds had been subdued or filtered out of his conscious hearing. Ah, our mind is a mysterious, complicated, *vulnerable,* and essentially untapped dynamo.

For centuries, hallucinatory drugs have demonstrated how mysterious the mind is. These drugs can control our minds, hence our bodies and fantasies. With all of the well-publicized down sides and expense of alcohol, marijuana and narcotics like cocaine and opium, the feature that makes them such a valuable commodity in our human culture is their ability to alter our states of consciousness, allowing the users to temporarily escape from a wide range of perceived miseries. A host of drugs have been found that can override our conscious state, so it doesn't seem too strange that internal factors could jumble our vulnerable neuron activity, achieving the same sort of result.

Ian Wilson explains that one of the most persistent factors in past-life regressions is that the subjects do not recognize what has come from within them, and this has been fundamental in persuading so many participants in past-life regression experiments that what they have seen or experienced in a past-life must have been real. Wilson tells about a hardheaded, magazine assistant editor Brian Hitchen who, after being regressed to a life in the reign of King James II, remarked:

> When the recording of my regression was played back to me I found myself listening to a man I had never known. The voice was mine but the sentiments belonged to somebody else. Answers that I would have given consciously if I had tried to cheat were not coming out right. It was as if another part of me had taken over almost completely.[36]

After observing surgical operations performed with hypnosis as the only pain killer, Ernest Hilgard felt quite sure that during hypnosis the consciousness was in some way being switched off or dissociated. But, he also felt that while the conscious "I" was genuinely receiving no sensation of pain, something somewhere else in the mind was. Professor Hilgard called this the "hidden observer." A startling example of this "hidden observer" phenomenon, reported by Hilgard, occurred when E. A. Kaplan hypnotized a twenty-year-old student and suggested to him that his left hand was insensitive to pain. There was nothing new in this, but Kaplan also told the student that while his left hand remained insensitive, his right hand would be free to write automatically, without conscious awareness of what it was communicating. With the student in deep hypnosis, Kaplan pricked his left hand three times with a hypodermic needle. The student's hypnotically desensitized left hand showed no reaction. But, his right hand immediately and frantically scrawled, "Ouch, damn it, you're hurting me!" A few moments later the student asked Kaplan in all innocence when the experiment was going to begin, clearly consciously unaware of anything that had happened. But, obviously on some level his subconscious knew he had been hurt by the needle.[37]

Each time we pick up a newspaper or turn on the radio or television, we find examples of weird beliefs and behavior due to altered states of consciousness. Drugs, emotional conditions, beliefs in causes or prophets who can induce hypnotic states, and fantasies that become enmeshed in the minds of individuals so that they appear to be reality can alter the state of an individual's consciousness, resulting in murders, suicides, wild hallucinations and a wide range of delusions and irrational acts. No act in my memory is more bizarre or irrational than the Guyana tragedy, in which 912 followers of the religious "prophet" James Jones committed mass suicide in 1979 at Jamestown, Guyana. A little known fact of this event is that one of the last instructions to the group was made by one of Jones's aides, Don Macelvane. This is Macelvane's appeal:

> Uh–what I used to do before I came here, uh, let me tell you about it: it might make a lot of you feel a little more comfortable. Sit down and be quiet, please! One of the things I used to do, I used to be a therapist; and the kind of therapy that I did had to do with reincarnation and past-life situations. And every time anybody had the experience of going into a past life, I was fortunate through Father (James Jones) to be able to let them experience all the way through their deaths, so to speak. And everybody was so happy when they made that step to the other side.[38]

With that assurance 912 men, women, and children drank Kool-Aid laced with cyanide and went to their deaths in the Guyana clearing under Jones's tragically mocking placard which read, "Those who do not remember the past are condemned to repeat it."

What difference does it make if we realize and understand the true interplay between our genetic makeup, our environment, our will and the mysteries of our age? An answer is that it can alter our self-view, increasing our self-esteem and peace-of-mind by better understanding the basis of our wants, behaviors, and responses that make us who we are. In the process it will confirm that mysteries in many cases serve us better than their solutions would and that it is in our best interest to listen to our inner-self. It is difficult to believe 912 individuals, no matter how wretched their existence, listening to themselves, would agree to commit mass suicide.

William Wright believes "you and I were 'born that way' and it is not necessary to see ourselves as walking good-evil battlefields, but just as collections of countless genetic impulses—some good, some evil, some depressing, some joyous, some altruistic, some selfish, some prudish, some bawdy, some sad, some hilarious, some wise, some silly—all those unconnected neurons that we call a personality firing at different times and with different intensity in each of us."[39]

The Minnesota Twin Study[40] and other research projects have revealed major genetic components to social attitudes, political leanings and rigidly held positions on such diverse subjects as: gun control, capital punishment, gay rights, abortion, choice of hobbies, art, wardrobes, racial attitudes, and personality tendencies such as aggressiveness and emotional control.

Thomas Bouchard, professor of psychology at the University of Minnesota, led the landmark Minnesota Twin Study. When this invaluable study was in full swing, he had a professional staff of eighteen—psychologists, psychiatrists, ophthalmologists, cardiologists, pathologists, and geneticists. They studied 375 pairs of twins. Of these, forty-four pairs were identical twins raised in different homes, and 331 were twins reared together—217 of these twins were identical and 114 were fraternal twins. Late in 1986 the twin study results were released.[41] For most of the traits measured, more than 50 percent of the variability was found to be due to heredity, leaving less than half determined by the influence of parents, home environment and other experiences in life. The box score follows: social potency (61 percent due to heredity); traditionalism (60 percent); stress reaction, absorption, alienation, well-being and harm avoidance (all between 50-60 percent); aggression, achievement, control (between 40-50 percent) and social closeness (33 percent). The general study conclusions were that personality differences are more influenced by genetic diversity than environmental diversity and that shared family environments have a negligible effect on personality. Social closeness was the only trait that appeared to be mainly a product of family environment. The twin study also showed that intelligence was 70 percent due to heredity. These remarkable findings sent those (and there were many) who believed that our actions were primarily products of our culture, scurrying to review previous findings and positions.

Behavioral geneticists' current priorities are concerned with acute problems like addictions and mental illnesses, rather than links between genetics and attitudes. But, evidence to date suggests there are many, many links waiting to be discovered between our genes and our personal behavior and attitudes. It remains to be seen whether behavioral genetics and evolutionary psychology find the specific causes of explicit behavior. But already, their research has shown, as William Wright succinctly writes, that in addition to being seen as products of culture we can also be seen as blinking switchboards of gene-fired impulses, some perhaps older than our species, some weak, others powerful, some ever-present, others sporadic—but all waiting for their moment to take charge and move us to an action that evolution has decided increases our chance of survival. In short, the twenty-three pairs of chromosomes that produced our bodies also play an important role in every aspect of our behavior.

Brain function research by Michael Gazzaniga[42] has shown there is a center in the left hemisphere that processes and makes sense out of the impulses constantly flowing from all other areas of both brain hemispheres. Gazzaniga calls this region of the brain "the interpreter." The interpreter has been found to be a remarkable, but not totally honest processor of information. In verified experiments, testers gave instructions to the right side of a subject's brain whose left hemisphere was severed from the right, then asked the left or "interpreter" side why the subject performed the requested action. Ignorant of the real reason, the subject's interpreter ad-libbed an answer. Gazzaniga describes the interpreter's job as explaining and making sense of actions decided on by other brain segments—for reasons it may not know. And, when it doesn't know it may ad-lib an incorrect answer that we believe correct with all our heart. *Because we can't believe an answer provided by our own brain would deliberately hoodwink ourself.*

There is little doubt that genetic and cultural factors[43] are the major causes, perhaps as a number of scientists believe the only causes, in determining how we feel and act. It would seem, if these are the only factors, individually we have no control over our actions and are powerless to deviate from a destiny not of our own making. If we believe an illusion is reality or commit an evil act, we couldn't help it any more than we could stop ourselves from an act of kindness. Hello *free will*, where are you?

♬ Free Will ♬

Any serious discussion of the mind should include a go at free will. Science continually erodes away at the concept of free will, because each cause of action it has clarified to date is either cultural or genetic. But, science has no way of handling the uncaused notion that underlies the concept of free will. Steven Pinker reconciles this conflict by believing that science and the ethics of free will are two different self-contained systems involving the same entities, just as poker and bridge are different games played with the same fifty-two card deck. Science and morality are separate spheres of reasoning. While there are countless mysteries and problems left to resolve in the cultural and genetic arenas, the deepest, unproved mysteries of man lie in the arena of free will. Pinker, wisely, advises us that science with its mechanical stance allows us to understand what makes us tick and how we fit into the physical universe. When these discussions wind down for the day, we can resume talking about each other as free and dignified human beings.[44]

Most of us choose to believe we are the final arbitrators of our will. In other words, after our minds assimilate all the input inserted there from our nurture and nature, we are free to choose what we will do. Said another way, we have free will. According to many with a scientific viewpoint, there is simply no such thing as free will. Everything we do is a product of nurture and nature which broadly includes events we are exposed to by random chance. Dr. Francis Crick's astonishing hypothesis is "You, your joys and your sorrows, your memories and your ambitions, your sense of personal identity and free will, are in fact no more than the behavior of a vast assembly of nerve cells and their associated molecules."[45] Perhaps the most astonishing thing about this hypothesis is that a scientist of Crick's stature would presume a search for free will and our soul.

Crick's focus for outlining the plausibility of his hypothesis is the interrelation of the visual system and brain. Crick informs us that the language of the brain is based on neurons. He makes no pretense that his hypothesis is contaminated by certainty. Rather, he is trying to persuade scientists involved with the study of the brain to take consciousness seriously which means they need to experiment with, study and think in terms of neuron activity. In so doing they are more likely to grasp the overall performance of our brains with explanations that will replace the fuzzy folk notions we have today. He even postulates that the position of our "unfree" free will and soul is hardwired near the brain's anterior cingulate (right side, near the top and toward the front, inside surface; the surface you would see if the brain were cut in half). This postulation is based on patients who appear to have lost their will when this area of the brain was damaged.

No one, including the individuals who believe it, enjoys the thought that what we do depends on processes we do not understand or cannot control. We refuse to accept there are neurons or agents lurking in our minds that we do not control and that render us little more than preprogramed robots. So we invent free will, which lies beyond the constraint of both nurture and nature. The proof of free will, like the proof of God's existence, lies beyond the present and past capabilities of man. To believe in free will, like other mysteries, requires intuition and faith, because experience and reason have failed to prove it. But, as Andy Wright is quick to remind us, neither has science disproved it.

Free will, then, exists in the domain of unanswerable questions such as "Is there a God?" or "What is the true purpose of life?" These questions are different, but they share a circular quality. One question always begs another question, like "What God made God?" So one never finds the ultimate answer and they can only circle about the question. When children keep asking, "Why?" adults learn to stop this by saying, "Just because!" And the child soon tires of the circle. What stops adults from dwelling on such questions? A partial answer is "They don't." Unanswerable questions keep bubbling up in our consciousness, but Marvin Minsky believes that human cultures have found special ways to deal with these questions.[46] One way is to brand them with shame and taboo; another way is to cloak them in awe or mystery; both methods make the questions less debatable. Consensus, as with social styles and trends, is the simplest way to resolve our quest for answers, wherein we each accept as true whatever others in our culture do. Human cultures evolve institutions of religion and philosophy that adopt specific answers to circular questions. One might complain that such establishments substitute dogma for reason and truth. But in exchange, they spare whole populations from wasting time in search of answers to unanswerable questions. Minds can be more productive when working on problems that can be solved. The twenty-first century with its freer flow of information and knowledge between cultures will help strip away taboos, awe, mystery and, yes, religions and philosophies, allowing us to hammer away at our mysteries with renewed vigor.

It would seem the answer to the question of free will is within man's reach and that Francis Crick is correct in his assessment that the scientific community needs to apply their minds and resources to this question. Until science provides more information, my choice is to believe we have a measure of free will floating around in that mixture of chemical soup and nerve cells that form our minds. The only disagreement I have with Andy on free will is that I believe we have a small measure of it, while he knows we have an abundance of free will. Plus Andy knows exactly what it is and I don't. *Ah, sweet mystery.*

Mark Thornton suggests the two key features of free will are autonomy and the existence of alternatives. His extensive study of the subject has led him to postulate that the positions on free will can be broken down into three groups: Hard Determinism (everything we do is predetermined by our genetics and environment, so there is no free will); Libertarianism (free will and no determinism); and Compatibilism (where all human activity is determined via neurophysiological states of the brain and central nervous system). Thornton believes Compatibilism is the answer. Here, acting in concert yet independent of this physiological determinism is psychological freedom, unbound by physiological determinism. Thus, Thornton declares that we have good reasons for believing that we have free will. Even from the physiologist's standpoint, if we are deterministic mechanisms, this does not preclude our also being rational, free-willed creatures.[47] This seems analogous to Pinker's explanation that you can play more than one game with a single deck of cards. Neither explanation seems to hold together all that well, but I will continue to cast my lot with the notion that we have a measure of free will until the deterministic crowd produces a lot more proof. Proof that is unlikely to unfold during my earthly journey. Meanwhile Andy wonders what all this gumming and fuss are about? To him, it is evident to any rational, God-fearing person that free will is present in all of us; those who exercise it properly will join Jesus in Heaven and those who do not are headed for Hell.

Minsky correctly teaches that human thought is not based on any single and uniform kind of logic, but upon a myriad of processes, scripts, stereotypes, critics and censors, analogies and metaphors.[48] Some are acquired through the operation of our genes, others are learned from our environments; yet others we construct for ourselves. But even inside the mind, no one really learns alone, since every step employs many things we've learned before, from language, family, and friends—as well as from our former selves. Without each stage to teach the next, no one could construct anything as complex as a developed mind. Many social principles that each of us regards as personal are really "long-term memories," in which our cultures store what they have learned across the centuries. At every step, the choices we make depend on what we have become. We've all heard from parents or mentors the truthful cliches: "You are what you eat," "You are what you read," "You are who you associate with," etc. Our scientific and artistic skills or moralistic views do not originate from detached ideals of truth, beauty, or virtue, but stem partly from our endeavors to placate or please the images established in earlier years. Thus, our adult dispositions evolve from impulses that have been transformed or sublimated in our subconsciousness.

♭♭ Neural Activity ♭♭

In the past decade, cognitive scientists in a flurry of activity and with the use of sophisticated instrumentation have shown that each cognitive act, from thinking about a chess solution, to reading, to imagining a face, activates a distinctive network of neural activity in the human brain.[49] We've been discussing different aspects of consciousness, when in reality, as Daniel C. Dennett reminds us, we don't truly know what consciousness is. Dennett has some intriguing ideas on the subject.[50] Dennett, a philosopher with a mind deeply steeped in science, thinks we should discard the faulty dualistic Cartesian thinking that somewhere there is a single center in our brain, controlling all of our thoughts and actions. Dennett believes the evidence supports a multitude of centers that are all working simultaneously in our brains in parallel, series, and series-parallel arrangements waiting to be discovered.[51] Scientists know they are just beginning to make inroads into the mysteries of the mind and believe this century will produce significant progress. It appears that the twenty-first century will be a busy and exciting time of discovery for those studying the mind.

Billions of humans have come and gone; billions still reside on earth; and trillions more, hopefully, will come and go. Considering the complexity of the human mind, which we have just scratched the surface,[52] and the countless variations in genetic and cultural inputs imposed on each of us, there is little wonder that the diversities of our brains encompass a broad spectrum and that these diversities include people who firmly believe they have participated in or observed, first hand, every conceivable kind of miracle or mystery—people who sometimes hear songs that are just their own; songs unheard by others. That fact is no stranger than the genetic and cultural roll-of-the-dice that results in some of us being idiots; some geniuses; some child prodigies; and some bright, yet without enough common sense to protect themselves from bad weather or from punishing their bodies and minds with food or drugs. On reflection, the strangest fact is that so many of us develop into rational, generally intelligent humans—humans who understand that our sensory systems and our minds are capable of being hoodwinked by magicians, hypnotists, natural events, circumstances and, last but not least, ***ourselves***.

Chapter Notes

1. Lyrics from the Grateful Dead's "Eyes of the World." Words by Robert Hunter; music by Jerry Garcia; published by Ice Nine Publishing. The word "mind" was substituted for "heart" in the lyrics shown here. The Grateful Dead grew out of the California drug culture in 1966 and continued to play their music until the death of Garcia in 1996. Hunter, through his lyrics and poetry, vividly depicts the depth and the influence of life's mysteries.

2. Christopher Cerf and Victor Navasky, *The Experts Speak,* (New York, NY: Villard Books, 1998).

3. David Hume, *An Enquiry Concerning Human Understanding*, *Harvard Classics, Volume 37,* (New York, NY: P.F. Collier & Son, 1920, originally published in England: 1748). Hume states that a wise man proportions his belief to the evidence and that a miracle is a violation of the laws of nature.

4. Steven Pinker, *How the Mind Works*, (New York, NY: W. W. Norton & Co, 1997).

5. Norman Geschwind and Albert Galaburda, *Cerebral Lateralization*, (Cambridge, MA: MIT Press, 1987).

6. Terry Armstrong and Nicole C. Rust, *Brain Topics: A Handbook for Teachers & Parents,* "Chapter 1. The Unique Brain: Evidence and Implications," 1996. http://Oscar.ed.vidaho.edu/brain.

7. Steven Pinker, *How the Mind Works*, (New York, NY: W. W. Norton & Co., 1997). The Minnesota Twin Study is the principal basis for these conclusions and will be discussed in more detail later.

8. Ibid.

9. Judith Harris, *The Nurture Assumption*, (New York, NY: Touchstone Books, 1998).

10. Khalil Gibran, *The Prophet*, (New York, NY: Alfred A. Knopf, 1923). Message to parents: "You are the bows from which your children as living arrows are sent forth."

11. Lise Eliot, PhD., *What's Going On In There?*, (New York, NY: Bantam Books, 1999).

12. John McCrone, *The Myth of Irrationality,* (New York, NY: Carroll & Graf, 1994). McCrone, in his chapter, "Wolf Children and the Bifold Mind," lists fifteen references, each giving detailed accounts of wild children, including accounts of Indian wild children written by Col. William Sleeman.

13. Ibid.

14. Joseph Singh and Robert Zing, *Wolf Children and Feral Man*, (New York, NY: Harper, 1942).

15. Harlan Lane, *The Wild Boy of Aveyron*, (Cambridge, MA: Harvard University Press, 1976).

16. Andy Wright chimes in with "Amen, you have faith not first-hand knowledge of facts that may in fact not be facts."

17. Charles Sell, *Unfinished Business*, (Portland, OR: Multnomah, 1989). Sell reports on the results of Rene Spitz's study.

18. Joel Charon, *Sociology: A Brief Introduction*, (New York, NY: Longman, 1997).

19. Robert Fulgham, *All I Ever Really Needed to Know I Learned in Kindergarten*, (New York, NY: Ivy Books, 1993).

20. Matt Ridley, *The Red Queen*, (Baltimore, MA: Penguin Books, 1995).

21. Charles Mackay, *Extraordinary Popular Delusions and the Madness of Crowds*, (London: Richard Bentley Publishers, 1841).

22. Henry C. Roberts, translator, *The Complete Prophecies of Nostradamus*, (Oyster Bay, NY: Nostradamus Co., 45th printing, 1981).

23. Richard Lewinsohn, *Science, Prophecy and Prediction*, (New York, NY: Bell Publishing Company, Inc., 1961).

24. http://www.fadetoblack.com/horoscopes.

25. Stefan Paulus, *Nostradamus, 1999*, (St. Paul, MN: Llewellyn Publications, 1997).

26. http://www.globalpsychics.com/prophecy.

27. Ibid. GlobalPsychics, Inc. website reports that idiots, without any scientific basis, claim that Cayce's work is an illusion. GlobalPsychics claims that Cayce's prophecies are 90% accurate and there is an 85% probability that his prediction of a reversal of the North and South Pole magnetic fields will take place by 2002. So we will soon see if he missed that prediction, like he missed his schedule for the flooding of western California and New York.

28. Kendrick Frazier, Editor, *The Hundredth Monkey and Other Paradigms of the Paranormal,* (Buffalo, NY: Prometheus Books, 1991). "Does Astrology need to Be True? Part 1: A Look at the Real Thing," by Geofrey Dean.

29. ESP is alleged phenomena such as telepathy (mind reading), clairvoyance (ability to perceive things not in sight), and precognition (knowledge of future events).

30. Robert Todd Carroll, *The Skeptic's Dictionary*, http:/skepdic.com.

31. Ian Wilson, *All in the Mind*, (Garden City, NY: Doubleday & Co, 1982).

32. Morey Bernstein, *The Search for Bridey Murphy*, (New York, NY: Doubleday & Co, 1956). This case was big news with claims that it proved reincarnation was real and counterclaims of hoax. It involved the hypnotic regression sessions of 29 year-old Virginia Tighe where she recalled many details of a past life as Bridey Murphy—an Irish lass named Bridget Kathleen Murphy, born on December 20, 1798 near the town of Cork, Ireland.

33. Corbett H. Thigpen and Hervey M. Cleckley, *The Three Faces of Eve,* (New York, NY: McGraw-Hill, 1957). This was a best selling book and a popular movie that documented the split personalities of Chris Costner. She was: Chris Costner, coarse speaking and sexually provocative; Chris White, soft spoken, restrained, and self effacing; and Jane Doe, poised and cultured with an impressive voice and diction. Later, it was learned she had at least seven other personalities.

34. Dr. Erika Fromm, "Age Regression with Unexpected Reappearance of a Regressed Childhood Language," *International Journal of Clinical and Experimental Hypnosis*, *Vol. 18*, 1970.

35. Dr. Julian Jaynes, Princeton University, *The Origins of Consciousness in the Breakdown of the Bicameral Mind,* (Boston, MA: Houghton Mifflin, 1976).

36. Ian Wilson, see Note 31.

37. Professor Ernest R. Hilgard, *Divided Consciousness*, (New York, NY: John Wiley, 1977).

38. These notes were tape-recorded at the time and published by David Blundy, "The Jonestown Tape," *Sunday Time Magazine*, November 25, 1979.

39. William Wright, *Born That Way*, (New York, NY: Alfred A. Knopf, Inc., 1998).

40. Lead article in the December 2, 1986 issue of *New York Times* "Science Times."

41. Ibid.

42. Michael Gazzaniga, *Nature's Mind*, (New York, NY: Basic Books, 1992).

43. Here genetic and cultural factors are used in the broad sense where genetics includes the total ancestry of our bodies and minds, and cultural embodies the family, society, location and events experienced in our lives.

44. Steven Pinker, see Note 7.

45. Francis Crick, *The Astonishing Hypothesis, The Scientific Search for the Soul*, (New York, NY: Charles Scribner's Sons,1994). Francis Crick, Nobel Laureate, along with James Watson, made history with the discovery of the structure of DNA. This discovery forever changed our understanding of life and opened the door for ongoing and future research that will continue to alter our understanding of life, as perhaps no other discovery has done.

46. Marvin Minsky, *The Society of Mind*, (New York, NY: Simon & Schuster Inc., 1988). Marvin Minsky is Professor of Science at MIT where he cofounded the Artificial Intelligence Laboratory.

47. Mark Thornton, *Do We Have Free Will*, (New York, NY: St Martin's Press, 1989).

48. Marvin Minsky, see Note 46.

49. Robert L. Solso, Editor, *Mind and Brain Sciences in the 21ˢᵗ Century*, (Cambridge, MA: MIT Press, 1997).

50. Daniel C. Dennett, *Consciousness Explained*, (Boston, MA: Little, Brown and Company, 1991).

51. It is presumptuous to paraphrase the thrust of Dennett's work in a few words. Hopefully, none of the cited works in this book have been misrepresented. Anyone interested in this subject should read the references and make their own judgements.

52. "Scratch the surface," means in relationship to the combined output of all scientists and thinkers; not merely the output of this abridged discussion.

♭♭ Three ♭♭

On a Hill Far Away[1]

(Religion)

O n a hill far away stood an old rugged cross, the emblem of suffering and shame. How many times have we heard the beautiful, haunting words of old Christian hymns as they waft from the mouths of believers? Words inspired by the Bible that provide answers for things we can't understand, absolution from our misdeeds, inner-peace on our earthly journey, and eternal salvation in paradise for embracing the Christian religion and following Christian rules. As my young grandson would say, "Wow-wee!" Me? I think Christianity is a wonderful faith-based belief system rooted from the fantasies of mortal men. A belief system that trumpets four of mankind's most important concepts—*Love, Hope, Charity and Faith*. Belief systems and fantasies sustain us by soothing, motivating and entertaining, so they are important—one might reason they are essential to our individual and collective well being, especially our spiritual well being. But, also, it is important to differentiate between a firmly held opinion that may be fantasy based and fact-driven reality.

Walter Alston, longtime manager of the old Brooklyn Dodgers baseball team, once posed a question to a group of sportswriters that went something like this. "The score is tied, it's the last of the ninth, there is one out and we have an outstanding base stealer on first and a speedy three-hundred hitter at the plate who is also an excellent bunter. Do you baseball experts believe I should flash (a) the steal sign, (b) the hit and run, or (c) the bunt signal?" About one-third of the sportswriters voted for (a), about a third voted for (b) and about one-third voted for (c). Alston then declared "You see, no matter which decision I make about two-thirds of you think I've made the wrong one."

𝄞𝄞 Choice of Religion 𝄞𝄞

From a simplistic, but interesting humanistic point of view, choice of one's religion is similar to the baseball manager's quandary. And that is no matter what one's choice of religion is, they will have a much larger segment of the world's population in disagreement with them. Presently there are approximately two-billion Christians in the world, making it the largest religious population.[2] Since the world's population is approximately six-billion, this means (like Walter Alston's problem) two-thirds of the people disagree that Christianity is the correct religious choice. Even among Christians there is major divisiveness, slightly over one-half of Christians are Roman Catholics, more than 360-million are Protestants of many different denominations and the remaining 500-plus million are Orthodox, Anglicans and other Christians.

Christianity is by no means the dominant religious preference of mankind. There are more than a billion Muslims, more than three-fourths of a billion Hindus, more than three-fourths of a billion who claim no religion, more than 360-million Buddhists (approximately the same number as Protestants) and more than 360-million Chinese folk religionists. There are more than 150-million Atheists and the remaining billion-plus religious preferences are scattered among a host of minor religions. Despite the disproportionate share of the world's religious-related publicity pro and con, Judaism is a very minor religion, having only 14.6-million adherents. Whether there are a few or many who share our beliefs doesn't make our beliefs right or wrong, but the divisions of religious beliefs does enlighten us and demonstrate that religious belief systems of all kinds abound.

Experience, throughout history, has shown that most individuals want and need religion. We need something to explain the unexplainable, something to guide us and something to give us eternal hope. The above statistics confirm this. And, to date, for most of mankind, that something has been religion. So what is the proper religious choice? Mind you, no choice is a choice! Like so many contradictions in life, I am convinced the correct answer is all of the religions or none of them, if practicing the religious belief doesn't harm or infringe on the rights of others. It depends on you and me and what our genetic makeup, study and life experiences have led us to comfortably believe. Said another way, you should listen to you and I should listen to me. What can be so bad about an individual having the comfort of a belief system (even though it may be fantasy based) that eases the hardships of their life and holds the promise of a "golden-dream-like" world after death? Answer: It isn't bad, particularly when such a belief promotes social interchange and provides guidelines that help control man's seemingly natural propensity for self-gain, self-gratification, and retribution against or at the expense of others.

Even as a youngster raised in a Protestant environment, I had problems accepting that Christ rose from His grave, the virgin birth, and other tenants of the Christian church as undeniable truths. These problems surfaced at about the time I realized Santa couldn't be everywhere at once. Still, when asked as a young adult, I called myself a Protestant, but refused the specific cloak of a Baptist, Methodist, etc. This stance exposed me to many well-meaning attempts by various Christians to persuade me to identify with "their" church.

Finally, due to social pressure and, in measure, giving up on my own ability to decipher the truth, I, an adult with a family and in full possession of my faculties, publicly confessed my acceptance of Christ, was baptized and accepted into The Disciples of Christ Church in Clearwater, Florida. For the better part of a year, I was a friend and supporter of the minister and a diligent working member of the church, although I knew on some level of my consciousness that I was in the midst of a personal charade.

A vivid memory of this church experience was the uproar and emotion our church members had over the question of whether one was truly baptized if they were baptized by sprinkling water as opposed to being fully immersed in water. Anyone baptized in our church was fully immersed, but over the years many had been accepted in the church by letters from other churches where they had been baptized by a minister sprinkling water on them. This baptismal issue became so important to many of the parishioners that a special membership-at-large meeting was held to discuss the matter, after a regular Sunday worship. At first the meeting dialogue was heated but civil, then it became increasingly angry and ugly. The meeting culminated with about 40 percent of the church members walking out, withdrawing their membership and starting a new church of their own. The only issue in question that split this church was an interpretation over the acceptable use of water for baptizing.

It wasn't long after this experience and further study that I realized I was a religious agnostic. Thomas Huxley coined this word or doctrine in 1870. He derived it from the Greek word agnõstos, meaning unknown or unknowable. An agnostic is a person who believes that the human mind cannot know whether there is a God or an ultimate cause.[3] An agnostic may hope and suspect there is a God based on the order of the universe or other rationale, but he cannot know with certainty, because it is beyond his ability to know. And, that's my conclusion. Although, at times, when my thinking is fuzzy, I am closer to being ignostic.[4] Andy Wright believes or at least hopes that when he dies he will go to Heaven, and he suggests that when I die I am headed for a place called "The Great Perhaps."

Still, I am confident that (no matter how powerful man's intellect,[5] no matter how broad his experience, no matter what time period he has lived in, no matter how spiritually inclined or trained, no matter how diligently he throws off the materialistic robes of mankind, no matter the matter) man cannot know there is a God. By all means, he can assume there is a God and accept that as fact bordering on knowledge through faith. In spite of the importance of knowledge, many men believe faith is more important than knowledge. But, for me, *Uncle Reason* and his *Cousin Experience* are more important than *Aunt Faith* and her *Cousin Intuition*. John Locke correctly tells us nothing that is contrary to, and inconsistent with the clear and self-evident dictates of reason, has a right to be assented to as a matter of faith.[6]

Faith means one believes with complete trust, confidence, or reliance. Faith is faith, whether the basis for it is a trusted friend's advice, a lifetime of concentrated study, or some numinous experience.[7]

Charles Stewart, a student and teacher of Judaism and Christianity, in his book, *A Search for Original Christianity,* tells this story from a California high school philosophy course he taught. "We had read and were discussing Thoreau's *Civil Disobedience* and *Walden*. I mentioned that I felt many of Thoreau's thoughts came from the *Book of Ecclesiastes* and I suggested that we study that book to discover possible relationships. One of the classes' streetwise kids, Ricardo, spoke up vehemently, 'The Bible ain't shit!' Stewart said, "That's not a valid statement. Have you ever read the Bible or the *Book of Ecclesiastes*?" 'No,' Ricardo replied. Stewart then suggested that Ricardo read the *Book of Ecclesiastes* before he could accept Ricardo's opinion as valid.[8]

Stewart's experience illustrates that, to some extent, we are all Ricardos. In this world of six-billion people, not many of us have the luxury, much less the intellectual curiosity, to devote our lives to the study of the *Bible, Quran,*[9] *Torah,*[10] or other sacred texts. Thus, we must depend on the sources available to us that we trust to aid in our religious-belief decision-making process, whether we are Socrates, St. Paul, Ghandi or Ricardo. It's little wonder that not many Buddhists spring from the southern United States' bible-belt area. The youth of that area are largely Protestant, because they adopt the religion, Christianity, from their trusted sources. Likewise, not many Christians can be found in Bagdad, Iraq, because the trustworthy sources there are mostly Muslims.

The practice and, to a large extent, the problem of basing our assent on the opinions of our friends, political parties, clergymen, neighbors, or leaders without fully applying our own reasoning are universal and timeless. Still, if one *believes* their religious choice is best for them, then it is. And that has little to do with how many direct hours the individual spent pursuing the question of faith nor how learned, ardent, or persuasive are those who disagree with them. One should sleep peacefully knowing they've done their best under their life circumstances to make a proper choice.

Everybody acts not only under external compulsion but also in accordance with an inner necessity that wells up from their genetic makeup and their environmental history. Schopenhauer articulated this premise in an excellent way when he said, "A man can do as he will, but not will as he will."[11] No less a person than Albert Einstein advised us that this deterministic feeling espoused by Schopenhauer mercifully mitigates the sense of responsibility, which so easily becomes paralyzing, and helps prevent us from taking ourselves and other people too seriously.

No one using reason and experience as their foundation knows that dire afterlife consequences await those having different views of God and religion. If you have strong religious beliefs, while living in the midst of those whose beliefs differ, then you are sure to have negative (mostly social) "this-world" consequences. Those who need to draw lines and stake out ironclad, immovable positions shouldn't choose their religion as the position to defend, because reason, at some point, will desert their argument. It goes without saying that each of us should take every opportunity to learn about and strengthen our personal beliefs. Like the Army recruiting ad recommends, we should, "Be all we can be." Certainly, if our religious choice involves harm or persecution of others, or taking away the rights of those who disagree with us, we should expect earthly retribution.

The choice of religion didn't come easy for my college professor of religion, the Reverend David Linge. Rev. Linge devoted thousands of hours in his search for religious truth. The lives of those exposed to his knowledge have been enriched by his dedicated effort. Linge came down, personally, on the side of Christianity, but not without a deep understanding and appreciation for alternate views. For others, like my dear wife's father, the Reverend Curtis Cockman, a Methodist minister for almost seventy years, the choice of Christianity was easy. He knew, without a doubt, at the age of thirteen, that Christianity was the correct choice, and spent his lifetime in honest, honorable service to all those he touched, studying and preaching the gospel as he interpreted it from the Bible. Does the study and dedication of these fine gentlemen make their choice of Christianity correct? For them, the answer is a resounding yes! But, for billions of others having alternate choices of religions, their choices also deserve affirmation.

How can a beautiful child of the Islamic faith or a fair-minded, peace-loving African-adult Sikh be banned from the Kingdom of Heaven because they failed to profess Jesus Christ as the Son of God? Ricardo's answer to a religious question, while uneducated and crude, is as good for Ricardo as that of a learned Christian minster's articulate, well-meaning and sophisticated "tap dancing" around conflicts in the Bible.

With the exception of certain Fundamentalist or Orthodox religionists, relatively few people in the twenty-first century consider the Bible as totally factual or entirely the word of God. Those that do tell us that to properly understand any specific biblical doctrine that appears to be contradictory or in error, it is first necessary to comprehend the entirety of all biblical doctrines. Yet, it is impossible to comprehend the entirety of all biblical doctrines, until one understands the specific biblical doctrines separately. There is an *essential interdependence* between biblical doctrines. Each must be understood in light of all the others. But, how can we comprehend the Bible if we must understand all the doctrines before we can understand any one, and we cannot understand all the doctrines until we understand the sum total of each individual one? And, until we doubters understand it all, we falsely interpret passages as erroneous and inconsistent. The only solution to this paradox, the faithful tell us, is through God's Holy Spirit and by diligent, dedicated Bible study. In short, the error is not in the Bible, but it is in our interpretation.

Others insist the Bible speaks in three types of language—literal, symbolic, and figurative. If a word or passage of Scripture is literal, associated scriptural comparisons will prove that it is literal. If a word or passage of Scripture is symbolic, related scriptural comparisons will prove that it is symbolic. If a word or passage of Scripture is figurative, affiliated scriptural comparisons will prove that it is figurative. By keeping this in mind and not reading passages out of context, one will find there are no errors in the Bible. Again, the error is not in the Bible, but in our interpretation.

The majority of people whom I know and deeply respect, because of their wisdom and integrity are Christians who believe in the basic integrity of the Bible. There is no way I can or would impugn the sincerity or correctness of their judgement; however, there are many biblical passages that require serious Christian "jitterbugging" to defend.

♪♪ Biblical Conflicts[12] ♪♪

In Genesis 1:2, earth comes into existence on the first day, completely underwater. Only by the third day were waters of the deep collected, and dry land formed. But in Genesis 2:4-6, earth on the first day was dry land.

The first story reports that trees were made on the third day and man was formed three days later, Genesis 1:12-13 and 26-31. In the second version man was made before trees, Genesis 2:7, 9. If Genesis 1 is true, then fowls were created before man. If Genesis 2 is true, then they were created after man.

In Genesis 1:20-21, living creatures are brought forth from the waters, including winged fowl. But in Genesis 2:19 God brings forth *"every beast of the field and every fowl of the air"* from the ground.

Genesis 1:25, 27 teaches that man was created after all beasts. Genesis 2:7, 19 clearly states that Adam was created before beasts.

God commanded Noah to take two of all animals and two of all birds, Genesis 6:19-20. But in Genesis 7:1-3 the Lord commanded Noah to take seven pairs of the clean and one pair of the unclean animals and seven pairs of birds both clean and unclean.

In version one, Genesis 1:27, man and woman are created simultaneously. In version two, Genesis 2:7, 20-22, man and woman are separate acts of creation.

Whoa! This is not a good start for the perfect word of God. But these are *minor flaws* compared to what follows. Some tell us the number of problems, errors and inconsistencies in the Bible approach 50,000.[13] That may be a high estimate, but there are many,[14, 15, 16] and one would think that a single error is too many to be God's own and only true book. Nevertheless, the flaws do exist and this shouldn't be a surprise, considering the Bible was written by men who had little understanding of our planet and the Universe,[17] and it has undergone many translations—translations crossing the barriers of time and many different human minds, hands, and languages.

More biblical passages that appear to be errors, contradictions or problems include the following:[18]

In Exodus 33:20, God says, *"Thou canst not see my face; for there shall be no man see me and live."* God must have been mistaken, or changed his mind, because in Genesis 32:30 Jacob sees God "face to face" and lives. The same for Moses, Aaron, Nadab, Abihu and seventy elders, who saw God, ate and drank with Him in Exodus 24:9-11—and they continued to live. But not so, says John 1:18: *"No man hath seen God at any time."*

The genealogy of Christ from Abraham presented in Matthew 1:2-15 differs substantially from Christ's genealogy presented in Luke 3:23-32.

2 Samuel 24:1 says that the Lord incited David, saying, *"Go and take a census of Israel and Judah"* and 2 Samuel 24:9 says that Joab reported the number of the fighting men to the king: In Israel there were eight-hundred-thousand and in Judah five-hundred-thousand. While 1 Chronicles 21:1 says that Satan (not Christ) incited David to take a census of Israel and 1 Chronicles 21:5 says that Joab reported the number of fighting men in Israel as one-million one-hundred-thousand men and in Judah four-hundred-and-seventy-thousand.

Of the forty-two numbers listed in Ezra 5:3-60, eighteen differ from the corresponding numbers in Nehemiah 7.

There are two demon-possessed men in Matthew 8:28-34 versus one such man in Mark 5:1-20. Likewise, Matthew 20:30 tells of two blind men at Jericho, whereas Mark 10:46 and Luke 18:35 say there was one.

In 1 Kings 16:6, 8 the King of Israel, Baasha, dies, replaced by his son Elah during the twenty-sixth year of Asa's (King of Judah) reign. But in 2 Chronicles 16:1 Baasha, King of Israel, goes against Judah during Asa's thirty-sixth year, a decade after the earlier account.

In Genesis 9:3: *"Every moving thing that liveth shall be meat"* for Noah. But Deuteronomy 14:7-21 later gives a list of animals, birds and fish that must not be eaten.

Abraham had two sons, Ishmael and Isaac (Genesis 16:15 and 21:3) but Isaac was Abraham's "only" son (Genesis 22:2,12 and Hebrews 11:17).

Matthew 19:26 quotes Jesus, *"with God all things are possible."* Did Matthew or Jesus forget something? In Judges 1:19, God is not almighty, as he helped rid Judah of inhabitants of the mountain, yet could not drive out those in the valley *"because they had chariots of iron."*

In Exodus 31:17, like a man, God rests and is "refreshed." Isaiah scorns such contemptible weakness. In Exodus 40:28 he insists God, creator of the *"ends of the earth, fainteth not, neither is weary."* An infinite God can neither tire nor need to be refreshed.

In the Bible the earth isn't described as "spherical." For example in Revelation 7:1 it states: *". . . four angels standing on the four corners of the earth."*

James 1:17 says *God has no variableness*. But, in Jonah 3:10, God "repented" and changed his mind about smiting Nineveh's people. Numbers 23:19 states, *"God is not a man . . . neither the son of man, that he should repent."* Yet, God volunteers in Jeremiah 15:6, *"I am weary with repenting."*

In Deuteronomy 4:24 *"God is jealous and a consuming fire."* He's *"the God of Peace"* in Romans 15:33, but in Exodus 15:3 *"the Lord is a man of war."* But, He is not called a man in Numbers 23:19.

God is *"just and right"* in Deuteronomy 32:4, yet in an earlier passage, Deuteronomy 14:21, He advises that what you can't eat as unclean may be given *"unto the stranger . . . or thou mayest sell it unto an alien."*

"Now go and smite Amelek and utterly destroy all that they have, and spare them not; but slay both man and woman, infant and suckling, ox and sheep, camel and ass." In 1 Samuel 15:3 that was Samuel's order for Saul originating from the Lord. Mass murder is again condoned in Exodus 32:27; in Deuteronomy 2:15-16 and 34-36 and 3:6. In Ezekiel 9:5-6, the Lord said, *"Go through the city, and smite: let not your eye spare, neither have you pity. Slay utterly old and young, both maids and little children, and women."* In Numbers 31:17-18, Moses said, *"Have you saved all the women alive? Now kill every male among the little ones and kill every woman that has known a man by lying with him, but all the young girls who have not known a man by lying with him keep alive for yourselves."*

No "just and right" God of peace and love could order the massacre of innocent people. Yet, the God of the Bible ordered or supported this behavior.

God said in Isaiah 45:7 *"I make peace and create evil,"* a contradiction in one holy breath!

In Romans 14:5 the Sabbath is required to be kept as holy, but we can make up our own minds about it in Exodus 20:8.

Children will suffer for the sins of the parents in Exodus 20:5. Yet, in Ezekiel 18:20 no one will bear sins other than their own.

In Matthew 5:32, there's but one acceptable reason, adultery, to divorce your wife. However, in Deuteronomy 21:l4 and 24:1-3 divorce can be for any reason. In Deuteronomy a divorced woman can marry again without sin, but in Matthew, a divorced woman that remarries is guilty of adultery. In Leviticus 20:10 a divorced woman that remarries deserves death of both her and her new husband.

"No evil shall happen to the just" we're told in Proverbs l2:21. Yet, in Job 2:3-7, Job, about whom God said no one else on earth was nearly as good, is nevertheless handed over, by God, to Satan for torture.

If Eve was created from Adam's rib, it's little wonder that the Bible values women less than men, as in Leviticus 27:3-7, where a man's value in shekels is double that of a woman. l Corinthians 11:9 tells us *"Neither was man created for woman but woman for man."* The Bible is filled with examples where brawn and might are favored over weakness and where females (physically the weaker sex) are of less value and subservient to the male.

One of the biblical "miracles" was, according to 2 Kings 2:12-13, Elijah ascending into heaven in a flaming chariot. Another was Enoch departing to heaven, Hebrews 11:5. In John 3:13, *"No man hath ascended up to heaven who didn't come from heaven."* So the Bible itself presents evidence against the miracle of ascension. Indeed, in many of its own words, what the Bible claims in one passage it denies in another, and what it upholds there, it condemns here. My good friend, Stanley (Stan) Wallen, believes one doesn't have to torture the Bible too much to prove just about anything they choose.[19] In Ecclesiastes 8:15, the preacher tells us *"A man hath no better thing under the sun, than to eat, and to drink, and to be merry."* So let's party!

In Exodus the *"Just and right"* God approves a questionable double standard. In Exodus 21:15, adultery or just hitting your parents deserves death, but in Exodus 21:21 a master beating a servant or maid to death with a rod shall only *"be punished"* in a nonlethal manner. Here, the master can remain unpunished for beating servants daily because the servant *"is his money."* Exodus 21:2, 7 condones the possession and sale of human beings.

Not only is slavery condoned in the Old Testament, but in the New Testament, too: 1 Timothy 6:1 states those *"under the yoke"* (i.e., slaves) shall give *"all honour"* to their masters. Again in Ephesians 6:5, obedience to masters by servants is said to be just like obedient worship given Christ.

1 Timothy 6:10 preaches *"love of money is the root of all evil,"* but this idea is denied by Proverbs 10:15.

The evening of Christ's resurrection is the time of ascension for Luke in Luke 24:1-59; however, Acts 1:3 dates it forty days later. After resurrecting, Jesus met the disciples in Galilee, says Matthew in Matthew 28:16-17. But Luke 24:33-36 says it was in Jerusalem, merely one-hundred miles distant.

"I and my Father are One" in John 10:30. But, *"My Father is greater than I"* in John 14:28. Then *"My God, why hast thou forsaken me?"* in Matthew 27:46.

Leviticus 11:1-12 lists unclean animals that are forbidden foods, including rabbits, pigs, shellfish, oysters, shrimp, lobsters, crabs, clams, and others. These foods are called *"abominations."* Today, very few Christians adhere to these laws. Probably, few even know about them, and the majority who do, dismiss them as unimportant! Why are these laws less important than any other laws of the Bible? Answer: Because of individual interpretations.

The Bible does little to explain which of its teachings have precedence and which should or should not be followed. Also, as illustrated here, it is clear there are numerous errors, contradictions, and cruel vindictive activities that are condoned in the Bible. As well, there are many parables and much confusion that lead to an unbelievable range of interpretations. One only needs to look at the large number of splintered Christian churches to understand the breadth and range of interpretations. It's doubtful that a perfect God with an iota of interest in the well-being of humans would riddle us with parables and the book of Revelation as a form of guidance.

♪♪ Man and His Religions ♪♪

Little is known by this writer about the *Koran* (*Qur'an*), *Tripitaka*, *Veda*, *Torah*, *Talmund*, or other sacred texts. But, it is suspected these sacred texts representing systems of faith and religion have their own errors, inconsistencies, and can be interpreted to condone meanspirited or senseless activities. They must have problems because, like the Bible, they were formed and interpreted by the hands and minds of mortal, prejudiced and error-prone men. An interesting fact is that Abraham is the father of the Christian, Islamic, and Jewish faiths. Thus, over one-half of the worlds population (three billion plus) have this common religious denominator. One would think the brotherhood of man could build on this common heritage to promote greater peace and understanding.

Yet, Islamic terrorists struck terror, disbelief, and the deepest sorrow and sadness in the hearts of billions with their, September 11, 2001, use of hijacked airliners to destroy American landmarks and kill thousands of innocent men, women and children. To presume that a small handful of suicidal fanatics represents the mainstream of Islamic religious thought and goals is preposterous. The five pillars of the Islamic faith are (1) *shahada* or profession of their faith that there is but one God—Allah, (2) *salat* or worship that includes the duty to pray five times daily, (3) *zakat* or almsgiving to those less fortunate, (4) *sawm* or fasting which is at once a time of penance and a celebration of their free will, and (5) *hajj* or holy pilgrimage to Mecca, the place where God created the first man—Adam. The greater *jihad* is struggling to worship God in accordance with these pillars and the holy Scriptures of the Qur'an, while the lesser *jihad* justifies the use of arms and killing to fight oppression of Islam. It is hardline-fundamentalist-fanatics' narrow interpretation of oppression that provides the basis of their *jihad* or Holy war against the West. This warring faction does not represent the mainstream of the Islamic faith whose wish, like the mainstream of those of other faiths, is to worship God in peace. Islam is not poised for world domination. The true Islamic believers would say, "What need is there when Allah is the Lord of all Creation?"[20] Holy wars are not unique. Non-Islamic civilizations have fought more Holy wars and killed more people, in the name of religion, than Islamic civilizations. The Islamic terrorists have used poverty and ignorance in their attempt to promote a *jihad* version of a "Holy War." Time will show their major success was to awaken a slumbering world—a world that will no longer tolerate terrorism under the banner of a religion. But, a wide-awake world can never stamp-out terrorism until stark poverty and all crazed individuals are eliminated from the face of the earth. And, who has a *workable plan* to achieve this lofty goal? The answer is, of course, no individual, government, or institution; certainly not a fantasy-based religion!

My declaration of religious disbelief is not meant to condemn those who believe otherwise; they have equal right to their beliefs and fantasies. A Christian friend once commented that it must be lonely to miss out on religious and spiritual experiences. Not so. I've had many religious experiences. My first memory as a child of about three-years old was a religious experience. It was early spring and I was playing in a wooded area adjacent to our house where I picked up a rock. Spellbound, I watched as amazingly a beautiful violet slowly unfurled and greeted me. The wonder to my young eyes and mind left a lasting impression. When I peer into the clear night sky and see the immensity of the heavens filled with countless stars that dwarf our hidden sun, a feeling of unbounded admiration sweeps over me, taking my breath away and mesmerizing my spirit; because, I know I am witnessing a mystery formed by a mystery beyond my comprehension. This same type of spiritual experience occurs when I stand on the seashore at the break of dawn, listening to the swishing sounds of the tide as the mighty Atlantic ocean breathes in and out while watching the huge golden, orange orb of the sun sneak then burst onto the eastern horizon. When I stood on the crest of White Mountain, California, and touched an 8,680-year-old living Bristlecone Pine, I had a profoundly, deep religious experience. The thought and reality of touching that tree which was alive more than six-thousand years before Jesus Christ was a twinkle in God's eyes overwhelmed me. The birth and development of my children exposed me to countless religious experiences. Almost every day that I open my eyes and mind to nature (an evolving nature) I have a religious experience that cannot be equaled by the words or ideas of man.

Humbly, I kneel in awe of the magnitude of order in the universe and our planet, of space's immensity, and of the complexity, scope, and beauty of the natural resources and life forms on this planet. To a lesser degree, I stand in awe of the inherent goodness of most individuals I've met in my life. And, without knowing how, precisely when, or why; I know all these things have been created and science has shown they have evolved and are still evolving. So it would seem there is a creator we can label God, although to date we have no way of knowing precisely how to separate the created and evolved components. Also, we can't know if our creator (HE , SHE or IT) was in turn created by a still more omnipotent creator or committee of creators. Using the design of nature as a reasoning springboard for a deity or creator called God is not new; it's a compelling argument that men have used for centuries.[21,22] On this basis, I suspect and hope there is an Almighty God; however, this is an assumption that is distant from certainty. We pick and choose the basis for our actions and beliefs, but to me other proofs of God based on the incessant religious patter of prophets, philosophers and priests (while often imaginative and ingenious) circle the truth and are failures. Some of these proofs, when closely analyzed, are merely restatements or manifestations of the design of nature.[23]

Blaise Pascal, the mid-seventeenth century French mathematical genius who invented the calculating machine, had an interesting view on why we should believe in God. Pascal, deeply religious, withdrew from worldly life to devote himself entirely to spiritual studies. Still, his thoughts returned to the concept of mathematical probability, so much that he attempted to solve the most intricate religious problems by probability theory—this in spite of his faith in miracles! But Pascal's rationalism competed strongly with his inner trend toward mysticism. When asked whether it was worthwhile working for eternal salvation, Pascal replied that man must take a gamble for or against God. If we wager on God, our chances of success are greater than the risks we run, since, however small our chances of attaining eternal bliss, the reward is out of all proportion to the stakes. Thus, no reasonable man would refuse to contract such a wager. Pascal's rationale should persuade the gamblers among us.[24]

It seems ridiculous to claim that one knows their creator by knowing something about the things created. That's like looking at your dinner fork and being able to describe the person or persons who created it. We can't know the answer to that simple question without research beyond our reach. I defy you to track down and identify the individuals or machines that mined, smelted, processed, and transported the clump of ore in your dinner fork. While it's contrary to reason to claim certain knowledge of our creator, it is more unbelievable that we set up rules of morals and behavior based on the creator's desires as communicated via his supposed prophets. The rules for morals and behavior that guide us in our day-to-day living are best set up through our needs and our systems of government and laws. While imperfect, this process allows for changes in our varying cultures and is superior to a rigid set of religious rules based on a two-thousand-year-old culture.

Perhaps the most important passage in the Bible is Jesus's instruction in Matthew 7:12 and Luke 6:31: ***"All things whatsoever ye would that men should do to you, do ye even so to them."*** If this instruction was obeyed by all, it would eliminate most of our earthly problems associated with getting along with others. But, this important passage wasn't original. It is a restatement from the

Mahabharata, circa 800 B.C., which says "Deal with others as thou wouldst thyself be dealt by. Do nothing to thy neighbor which thou wouldst not have him to thee."[25] More than three centuries before Matthew and Luke penned their passages, Plato, in his eleventh law wrote "Do to others as I would that they should do to me."[26]

As Thomas Paine articulated in the eighteenth century, "Creation speaks the universal language, independent of human language and independent of the will of man. The wonder of creation preaches to all nations and to all men, and reveals to man all that he can know or is necessary for him to know."[27] With the current scientific information available, Paine surely would recognize the truth of evolution, which too is a part of nature.

The creationist view that man has not evolved, but was created in his present form, opposes what science has taught us. But, neither has science provided ironclad proof that man evolved from a cellular seed incubated in the ocean depths. Therefore our public schools should acknowledge that alternate opinions to evolution, such as the creationist view, exist and that further proof is required before knowledge of our genesis approaches certainty.[28] The marriage of science and the creationist view is argued by Dr. Gerald L. Schroeder, but he makes an unconvincing stretch when he interprets that the days defined in Genesis have varying lengths. The first days before Adam were hundreds-of-millions of years in length, while after the creation of Adam the days were in line with our known twenty-four hour day. This, according to Dr. Schroeder, is the truth. Therefore, the time-line of the Bible equates closely to the scientifically known ancient age of earth and the short history of man.[29]

One can't examine religion without finding the state or government wrapped around it like a suffocating blanket. *Separation of state and religion* is a buzz phrase that's another fantasy. Jody McCloud, principal of a public high school in Kingston, Tennessee, illustrated the extent of federal government meddling with religion when, preceding a Kingston, Tennessee, high-school football game, she read the following statement:

> It has always been the custom at Roane County High School football games to say a prayer and play the National Anthem to honor God and Country. Due to a recent ruling by the Supreme Court, I am told that saying a prayer is a violation of Federal Case Law.
>
> As I understand the law at this time, I can use this public facility to approve of sexual perversion and call it an alternate lifestyle, and if someone is offended, that's OK. I can use it to condone sexual promiscuity by dispensing condoms and calling it safe sex. If someone is offended, that's OK. I can even use this public facility to present the merits of killing an unborn baby as a viable means of birth control. If someone is offended, no problem. I can designate a school day as earth day and involve students in activities to religiously worship and praise the Goddess, Mother Earth, and call it ecology.
>
> I can use literature, videos and presentations in the classroom that depict people with strong, traditional, Christian convictions as simple minded and ignorant, and call it enlightenment. However, if anyone uses this facility to honor God and ask Him to bless this event with safety and good sportsmanship, Federal Case Law is violated.
>
> This appears to be inconsistent at best, and at worst, diabolical. Apparently, we are to be tolerant of everything and anyone except God and His Commandments. Nevertheless, as a school principal, I frequently ask staff and students to abide by rules which they do not necessarily agree. For me to do otherwise would be inconsistent at best, and at worst, hypocritical. I suffer from that affliction enough unintentionally. I certainly do not need to add an intentional transgression. For this reason, I shall, "Render unto Caesar that which is Caesar's," and refrain from praying at this time. However, if you feel inspired to honor, praise and thank God, and ask Him in the name of Jesus to bless this event, please feel free to do so. As far as I know, that's not against the law—yet.

AND . . . one by one, the people in the stands bowed their heads, held hands with one another, and began to pray. They prayed in the stands. They prayed in the team huddles. They prayed at the concession stand. And they prayed in the announcer's box.[30]

Applause! Applause! Well said, High School Principal, Ms Jody McCloud! And, God Bless America! The federal government has no business trying to control prayer in our public schools. The final decision about what should be taught in a local school should be determined by the local population. And, if the local majority wants Christian prayer in their school system, they should have it. Surely those with a minority religious view can maintain silence and respect while the majority take a few moments to pray together. Too much government is an abomination of the highest order and will be the subject of chapter five.

Nature's revelations to man are ongoing. The combined knowledge gleaned and achievements of mankind during the last several-thousand years are awesome. In the last millennium, we've learned that the planet earth is but a minor speck in the cosmos made up of billions of galaxies. We've learned the earliest manlike creature walked on earth more than 3-million years ago,[31] and we've learned that our earth was formed about 4.6-billion years ago.[32] Advancements in agriculture, physics, science, communications, transportation, medicine, computers, genetics, and most fields of man's endeavor have been amazing. These advancements were gained through science and the "sweat of man's brow," not through religious proclamations or mysticism.

The systems of religion that have taken root on earth are morally good in many respects, but a true religion must be *one with creation, evolution, and truth.* Prophets and mystics do not have a monopoly on truth, morality, or what life after death holds for their followers or anyone else. Any serious student of early religions will recognize that numerous ideas and rites of present-day religions, including Christianity, are warmed over myths and practices of the ancient pagans. Based on the preceding rationale, the Christian system of faith in some ways contradicts creation, evolution, and truth, and it defines the unknowable as known.

In this Chapter, Christianity has been attacked.[33] While I may not understand why an enquiring mind could accept many of its fundamental premises and teachings, it is clear that Christianity and other religions have satisfied a deep spiritual need for billions of people throughout the centuries. Also, who can deny the staggering amount of good work accomplished by individuals driven by their religious faith and basic goodness?

A number of problems with the Bible have been cited here, but there is no other book that contains more beautiful and meaningful passages. For example, love is such an important but elusive concept. And, nowhere is there a better definition of love than 1 Corinthians, which states *"Love is patient, love is kind. It does not envy, it does not boast, it is not proud. It is not rude, it is not self-seeking, it is not easily angered, it keeps no record of wrongs. Love does not delight in evil but rejoices with the truth. It always protects, always trusts, always hopes, always perseveres. Love never fails."*

Cardinal Prefect Joseph Ratzinger profoundly concludes that history is the struggle between love and the refusal of love. To the often asked question, *'And what does God really want from us?,'* Cardinal Ratzinger answers "That we become loving persons, for then we are His images. For He is, as Saint John tells us, love itself, and He wants there to be creatures who are similar to Him and who thus, out of the freedom of their own loving, become like Him and belong in His company and thus, as it were, spread the radiance that is His."[34]

Edward O. Wilson is a world-class scientist, two-time Pulitzer prize winner and long-time Harvard professor, who, as a boy, attended the Southern Baptist Church. Edward Wilson's view on religion, like most scientists,[35] has been tempered by years of intellectual pursuits, seeking scientific answers to difficult questions.

Dr. Wilson shares this experience with us. In January 1984, at which time he hadn't sat through a Protestant service for forty years, he attended a Protestant service conducted by Martin Luther King Sr. at Harvard's Memorial Church. At the end of the service, a choir of African-American Harvard students surprised him by singing a medley of old-time gospel hymns, such as he had heard in the churches of his youth. Dr. Wilson said, "To my even greater surprise, I wept quietly as I listened. My people, I thought. My people. And what else lay hidden deep within my soul?"[36]

I've had the privilege of listening to the wonderful Christian gospel music of the John Cockman Family.[37] Through their music and commitment to Christ, they are earnest, sincere, articulate messengers of their faith who touch the hearts of Christians and unbelievers. My kind of people, I think. My people. And what else lies hidden deep within my soul? When the basic elements of the human genetic code are eventually unraveled and decoded, it may be found that a trace of Christianity has evolved and been embedded in many of us.

Although I am uncertain of God's existence, Christians may have Him accurately pegged. On one level of my consciousness I hope they do. Using Aristotle's logic that predates Christ by several-hundred years, they may have drawn true conclusions based on false premises. Either way, Christians have the same right to their beliefs and fantasies as I have to mine. I believe Christians are blinded to the truth by their faith. Andy Wright is quick to point out that I am blinded to the truth by my lack of faith. "Touché!!"

It is easy to cast disparaging remarks and difficult to offer constructive alternatives. But, no alternate religions are needed; already there are more than enough to go around. The point of the arguments made here is that we need to develop a tolerance for other viewpoints, because our own viewpoint, concerning our religious beliefs, may be based on erroneous premises. Premises conjured up by the imagination and fantasies of mortals, attempting to assign absolutes to variables and answer questions beyond their ken.

Religious leaders of all Christian denominations should recognize that religious truth did not begin or end with Abraham, Moses or the birth and death of Christ. Pious scholars have lived in every age, including our own. Man knew lying, murder, stealing, and adultery were sins against one another long before Moses's supposed encounter with God on Mount Sinai. Christian leaders should enjoin an ecumenical council to update the Bible to remove all of the obvious errors, inconsistencies and hate verbiage. Jesus Christ, like Socrates, was too wise to produce written errors, so the corrections would be to man's fallible hand. What a daunting task this would be, but what a wonderful gift for Christianity.

Without religion, this would be a dull, uninspired world for most people. Religions' message of love, hope, charity and faith shrouds many with a calming, healing wind of purpose and forgiveness. However, true understanding of our creator (whether holy, solely by evolutionary processes, or some combination) is like the old Christian hymn—*On A Hill Far Away*. This knowledge is so far away that man has little hope of ever finding satisfactory answers. Few consider this, but we might not be able to handle the truth near as well as we handle the mystery. Besides, there is great value and satisfaction for many souls in the seeking process. *Ah, sweet mystery!* But, the probability of us finding and then universally understanding the answer to this sweet mystery is less than that of us finding a grasshopper that can perform brain surgery on an alien from another galaxy. *Amen!*

♪♪♪♪

Chapter Notes

1. James and Albert Morehead, *Best Loved Songs & Hymns*, (New York, NY: Funk & Wagnalls, 1965). This is the well-known opening line for the Christian hymn, "The Old Rugged Cross" by George Bennard. Within thirty years of its publication, more than twenty-million copies of this hymn had been sold—more than any other musical composition in all history.

2. Religious affiliation populations are rounded-off figures obtained from *The World Almanac and Book of Facts, 2000*.

3. God is an euphemism for the omnificent Creator of Heaven and earth and all that resides within. Other words meaning the same thing include: Yahweh, Lord, Elohim, Allah, Adonai, Jehovah, etc. Interestingly, Jehovah is a word coined by a scholar thought to have been Petrus Galatinus, A.D. 1520. Galatinus made the word by combining the consonants from JHWH (ancient Hebrew word meaning God) and the vowels from Adonai. Jehovah is an artificial word for God that through its use in the *King James Version of the Bible* has become a popular word for God.

4. Rabbi Morris Adler of Detroit, Michigan's Temple Beth El in discussing the Creator created a new word—*ignostic*. Rabbi Adler explained: "An atheist says, 'I know what you are talking about and I don't believe you.' An agnostic says, 'I know what you are talking about, but I'm not sure I believe you.' An *ignostic* says, 'I don't know what you are talking about and I am not sure I believe you.'" This word neatly summarizes the paradox of man's finite relation to the infinite.

5. One of the greatest intellects of all time, Albert Einstein, wrote "I cannot conceive of a God who rewards and punishes his creatures, or has a will of the type of which we are conscious in ourselves...Enough for me the mystery of the eternity of life, and the inkling of the marvelous structure of reality, together with the single-hearted endeavor to comprehend a portion, be it ever so tiny, of the reason that manifests itself in nature." Albert Einstein, *The World As I See It*, (New York, NY: Wisdom Library, 1949).

6. John Locke, *Essay Concerning Human Understanding; With Notes of the Author,* (England: Dutton, 1909). Lock (1632-1704) believed that man wants proof, so there is certainty in our knowledge. Where certainty isn't

possible we want probability to guide us. We need to determine the importance between reason and faith as the basis for our knowledge. Locke found that religion gladly makes use of reason until it fails them, then they cry out, "It is a matter of faith and above reason." Thus, as Locke said "until we can determine the relative value of reason versus faith there is no way we can dispute matters of faith and we will in vain dispute and never be able to convince one another in matters of religion."

7. Dr. Rudolf Otto, *The Idea of the Holy*, translated by John W. Harvey, (Oxford: Oxford University Press, 1923, second edition 1950). Otto (1869-1937) introduced the concept of numinosity which is the quality of holy objects, persons, or religious experiences. For example, one might dream there is a God and the dream is so real that through this numinous or religious experience they are certain there is a God.

8. Charles Stewart, *A Search for Original Christianity*, (Knoxville, TN: Tennessee Valley Publishing, 1998).

9. Dr. Rashad Khalifa, *Quran, Hadith & Islam*, (Tucson, AZ: Masjid, 1992). Islam's Word of God: *(Qur'an) Sunna*, collections of *Adth*, describing what the prophet Muhammad said or did.

10. The Ben Ish Hai, *The Power of Torah*, translated by Daniel Levy, (Nanuet, NY: Feldheim Publishing, 2001). *Torah* of Moses is the basic source of Jewish teachings. The five books of Moses constitute the written *Torah*. Special sanctity is assigned other writings of the Hebrew Bible—teachings of oral *Torah* are recorded in the *Talmud*, in the *Midrash*, and various other commentaries.

11. Arthur Schopenhauer, (German philosopher, 1788-1860), *The World as Will and Representation*, translated by E.F.J. Payne, (Mineola, NY: Dover Publications, 1969). This book was originally published in 1819, then reprinted in 1851.

12. *King James Version of Bible*, set forth in 1611, (New York: American Bible Society, 1980).

13. Jehovah Witnesses say the Bible contains about 50,000 errors. *Awake Magazine*, 8 September 1957.

14. Thomas Paine, *Age of Reason I* and *II*, printouts of Paine's work is available online at http://www.ushistory.org/paine/reason. Paine wrote his scathing indictments of the Bible in the late eighteenth century.

15. Marshall Gauvin, *Struggle Between Science and Religion*, (Keli, Montana: Kessinger Publishing, authorized reprint, original published in 1923). Gauvin cites many biblical errors.

16. Robin Lane Fox, *The Unauthorized Version*, (New York, NY: Viking/Penquin, 1992). Current listings of many more biblical errors can be found on the Internet at http://www.answering-Christianity.com.

17. Moses began the first five books of the Bible (Genesis, Exodus, Leviticus, Numbers, and Deuteronomy) before 1400 B.C., and the apostle John penned the last book of the Bible, Revelations, about A.D. 95. During the 1,500 years between the writing of the first and last books of the Bible, forty-four writers made contributions. They lived at different times and were strangers to one another. They were businessmen, traders, shepherds, fishermen, soldiers, physicians, preachers, and kings. They served under different governments, and lived within contrasting cultures and systems of philosophy. Antiquated and erroneous Babylonian astronomy is evident throughout the Bible. The great Christian scholar Saint Augustine (354-430 A.D.) and others continued the traditional denial of the earth's roundness, claiming, if round, rain would "fall upward" in places.

18. *King James Version of Bible,* see Note 12. Many Christians close their minds to these problems, believing they are misinterpretations, trivial, or that questioning them is the work of the devil.

19. Stanley Wallen, PhD., New York University, is a student and teacher of religion, science and history. Stan's willingness to share his knowledge and extensive library, on these subjects, with the author has been a blessing.

20. Frances Gumley and Brian Redhead, *The Pillars of Islam*, (London: BBC Books, 1990).

21. Aristotle and scores of philosophers, theologists and thinkers, including William Pauley in his 1802 book *Natural Theology,* tell us that design in nature proves God's existence.

22. Wernher von Braun (1912-1977), the twentieth century rocket scientist who entering a room lit it up with his energy and charisma wrote, "One cannot be exposed to the law and order of the universe without concluding there must be a design and purpose behind it."

23. St. Thomas Aquinas (1225-1274), Italian master and teacher of theology, was a wonderful Christian writer who embodied many of Aristotle's ideas and logic in his teachings and writings. Aquinas tells us in *The Summa Theologica* there are five proofs for God's existence. (1) Motion: Many things in the world are in motion. There must have been a first mover (God) to set and maintain motion. (2) Efficient Cause: Every effect has a cause and if we trace back to the first cause it must be God. (3) Possibility and Necessity: In nature we find things that are not only possible but necessary for existence. Therefore there must be a being (God) having of itself its own necessity, and not receiving it from another, rather causing in others their necessity. (4) Graduation of things: Among beings there are some more or less good. There must be something (God) which is to all beings the cause of their goodness and perfection. (5) Governance of things: Things that lack knowledge act in intelligent ways. They achieve their end not by chance, but by design. Therefore some intelligent being (God) exists by whom all natural things are ordered to their end.

24. Richard Lewinsohn, *Science, Prophecy and Prediction*, (New York, NY: Bell Publishing Company, 1961).

25. The Mahabharata is a narrative of the fratricidal struggle between two branches of a royal family. Indian mythology dates the original events at 3102 B.C. but modern historians are more comfortable with a date nearer fifteenth century B.C. The epic was passed on for generations in an oral form, doubtless tweaked and tuned along the way. It is believed to have been written down, in Sanskrit, sometime between 200 B.C. and 200 A.D. http://www.geocities. com/Tokyo/Bridge/1771/Desh/Mb/node4.html.

26. Robert Maynard Hutchins, Editor In Chief, *Plato*, (Chicago, London, Toronto: Encyclopaedia Britannica, Inc., 1952).

27. Paine, *Age of Reason*, see Note 14.

28. Robert Pennock, *Tower of Babel*, (Boston, MA: MIT Press, 1999). The evidence against the New Creationism is outlined in Pennock's book.

29. Gerald L. Schroeder, PhD., *Genesis and the Big Bang*, (New York, NY: Bantam Books, 1990).

30. Life Issues Institute, *Radio Transcript 2496*, (Cincinnati, OH: 01/29/01).

31. Donald Johanson, Lenora Johanson with Blake Edgar, *Ancestors, In Search of Human Origins*, (New York, NY: Villard Books, 1994). Lucy, an early hominid was found by Donald Johanson and Tom Gray during November, 1974, at the site of Hadar in Ethiopia. Lucy is 3.18 million years old and is the earliest known ancestor of mankind.

32. Dr. Preston Cloud, *Oasis In Space*, (New York, NY: W. W. Norton & Company, 1988). Cloud reports that the accepted estimates for the age of earth has risen from the Biblical estimates of 6,000 to 10,000 years in the seventeenth century to 4.6-billion years. Geologists and naturalists, through their study of rock formations, earth layering, and fossils were among the first scientific investigators to understand that the biblical account was way off base. Darwin, in the late nineteenth century estimated that the earth was 400-million years. The development of instrumentation (especially the mass spectrometer) and understanding of material decay rates (especially the transmutation of uranium to lead) led to increasingly refined and greater estimates that leveled off at about 4.6-billion years in the late twentieth century.

33. Andy Wright tells me, with dripping sarcasm, that the institution of Christianity is trembling from the rigor and force of this attack.

34. Joseph Ratzinger, Cardinal Prefect, *To Look On Christ: Exercises in Faith, Hope and Love*, (1991).

35. A survey of National Academy of Science (NAS) members found more than 90% were atheistic or agnostic. Many leading scientists are members of NAS. E.J. Larson and L. Witham, 'Leading scientists still reject God,' *Nature* 394(6691):313, 23 July 1998.

36. Dr. Edward O. Wilson, *Naturalist*, (Washington, D.C.: Island Press, 1994). This is a marvelous book by a great twentieth-century American.

37. The Cockman Family music (tapes, cds, videos) can be obtained at their address: P.O. Box 63, Sherrills Ford, NC 28673 or Fax 1-828-478-4306.

♪♪ Four ♪♪

When Johnny Comes Marching Home

(War and Killing)

It seems like someone somewhere always is singing "When Johnny Comes Marching Home, Hurrah, Hurrah"[1] because of war and killing. Unfortunately, the hurrahs are small consolation for those killed or maimed and their families and frriends. History shows mankind not only needs religion but, apparently, also war and killing. In an effort to understand this phenomenon, we will search world history for facts, information and statistics, focusing on our own "peace-loving" country—the United States of America.

♪♪ Facts, Facts, Facts ♪♪

Statistics and historical facts (or at least proximity of facts) are measures of human experience and prop up our reasoning on solid ground, much as the results of laboratory experiments buttress a scientific principle. Mark Twain advised us, "Get your facts first, and then you can distort them as much as you please." Andy Wright tells me I am a statistic-and-fact drunk and since I can't know that historical facts are accurate, they can't be knowledge. Here, then I become a two-faced drunk, relying on the *faith* of my facts rather than *reason* that was trumpeted as the fountainhead of knowledge in the previous chapter on religion. Ah, hah! How often there is a clash between those two giant pedestals of understanding and knowledge—*faith* and *reason*. But, as the old English proverb goes, "Facts are stubborn things and they need to be reckoned with whether we like them or not." Even if boring historical facts and statistics are correct, Andy reminds us that the environment and human conditions can change so the facts of history are worthless as aids to drawing meaningful conclusions about the present and the future. While his points are valid, there are sober and important lessons to be learned from a close examination of the past. Andy, in turn, needs to be reminded that no human possesses the absolute truth. And those few who think they do are absolute fools.

Not being absolute fools, the best we can do is assign the highest degree of probability to a particular judgement, at a particular time, based on our own genetics and learning. None of us can do any better, although we may learn something later that alters our judgement. We should listen to the voices of others and analyze their views. But, when all the available facts and judgements are in, the most important voice to heed on the most important questions is our own.

At no time in history has mankind had more access to meaningful information about the past and present than we have in the new millennium. In 1833, Thomas Carlyle's master of philosophy, Herr Teufelsdröckh, sat at the highest point in the city where he had the visibility of the whole "life-circulation" to properly hone his conclusions.[2] Teufelsdröckh told us no biped stood so high as he looked down into that "wasp-nest" or "bee hive" and witnessed their wax-laying and honey-making and poison-brewing. He could see that living flood, pouring through the streets, of all qualities and ages, none knowing where they came from nor where they were going. He could see it all. He told us that he was observing the living link which interweaves all Being, and warned us "to watch well, or it will be past thee, and seen no more."

While Carlyle was a shrewd hombre, almost two additional centuries of discoveries by thousands of individuals, coupled with the information explosion whose Sirius is the Internet, permit us to stand and observe from a vantage point that was incomprehensible to his Teufelsdröckh and the great thinkers of past generations, such as Plato and Confucius. Although we can't build a linear extrapolation of past deeds to future trends from historical data, it's the best building block we have for educated choices and projections. So, we will press on with an examination of available facts about war and killing.

♬ Early War and Killing ♬

War exists when a group—a state or nation, but often a political, social, or an economic faction within some political group—seeks to impose its beliefs or control on a rival group through the use of violent force.

Ancient weapons, cave paintings, and skeletal remains preserved by archaeologists reveal that a killer instinct was present in prehistoric man. It would seem this instinct to be aggressive and defend ourselves, at all cost, is biologically embedded in man's makeup. This inborn pattern of behavior has helped man survive and to an extent master the earth and its other creatures, but not ourselves. The earliest civilizations along the Nile had warfare. But warfare was not new; it had been practiced in prehistoric times.

When the Sumarians learned to write more than five thousand years ago, they already had wars to describe. The most reliable count of total battles and sieges to date is 4,345.[3] That is a lot of wars and killing, but it is not near the number claimed by another supposedly reliable source that stated in 1960 a Norwegian statistician found there were 14,531 wars over the past 5,560 years resulting in the killing of three-billion-six-hundred-and-forty-million people. In checking the reference, these numbers were found to be figments of a newspaper reporter's imagination that were misused, and reported as fact in many books and popular magazines such as the New York Times Magazine in 1963 and the Time Magazine in 1965. This is what Andy (Mr. Wright) was warning me about. No matter how careful one is about the source of their so-called facts, at best they are estimates and sometimes outright fabrications. Still, the overall accuracy of historical data provides valuable lessons.

In ancient days, war was limited to small-scale battles. The increase in the scope of war parallels: the growth of populations; the growth of political organizations into cities, states, and countries; and the growth of economics, religion, and nationalism. The innate aggressiveness of man seems to be a constant among variable causes of war. Geoffrey Blainey suggests the following seven factors are the principal causes of war: military strength and the ability to apply that strength efficiently; predictions on how outside nations would behave; perceptions of internal unity and of the unity or discord of the enemy; memory or forgetfulness of the realities and sufferings of war; perceptions of prosperity and ability to sustain the kind of war envisaged; nationalism and ideology; and the personality and mental qualities of the leaders who weighed the evidence and decided for peace or war.[4]

War has been dramatically influenced by technological change. The development of weapons from the bow and arrow to chemical, biological, and nuclear weapons has expanded the reach and consequences of armed conflict. But whether war is local, regional, worldwide, all-out or limited by an agreement among participants, the results are death and mayhem. The major difference is in the number of people killed or maimed.

Before the beginning of the sixteenth century, North America was populated by approximately ten-million Indians scattered across the continent. Little knowledge exists of their activities, but we can deduce from surviving artifacts that war and killing frequently occurred. During the sixteenth and seventeenth centuries, there was consistent, ongoing armed conflict between the English, Dutch,

Spanish and French and various Indian tribes as the exploration and settlement of America were initiated by different European factions. Ponce de Leon explored Florida in 1513, Giovanni da Verrazano led a French expedition along the east coast, from the Carolinas to Maine in 1524, and Pedro Menendez founded St. Augustine, Florida, which was attacked and destroyed by Francis Drake in 1586.

Eloy Gallegos, in his series of books, traces the early history of America, showing the Spanish had a much greater impact and influence in the early settlement of America than our school history books typically show. The results of Gallegos's research confirm there was constant warfare and killing between the Spanish and others, as they competed for the land and riches of early America.[5]

In 1664 three-hundred British troops seized New Netherlands from the Dutch and renamed it New York. The Dutch recaptured the colony in 1673, only to cede it to the British in 1674. In 1676, Nathaniel Bacon led planters in a revolt against the British and burned Jamestown, Virginia. In the same year, a bloody Indian War in New England ended with the killing of the Wampanoag chief and many Narragansett Indians.

In the eighteenth and nineteenth centuries, with settlers continuing to pour into America and the early European settlers having secured footholds all along the eastern coast, along the Mississippi River, and other parts of the country, minor and major skirmishes increased. These skirmishes were commonplace. Some of these events are shown and further illustrate that America's early history was pockmarked with war and killing.

1701-1713	British-Colonial troops fought the French in Queen Anne's War.
1744-1748	King George's War pitted British and colonials against French Colonials.
1754-1763	French and Indian War; the French lost Canada and the American Midwest to the British as a result of this war.

1775-1781	Revolutionary War. George Washington disbanded the Army in 1783.
1812-1815	War of 1812 with British (2,000 killed).
1846-1848	Mexican War (13,000 killed).
1861-1865	Civil War (498,000 killed).

A reasonable estimate for the total number of people killed in wars during these four centuries (sixteenth through nineteenth) in America is approximately one million.[6] These numbers from a less-civilized time represent a drop-in-the-bucket compared to the twentieth-century blood letting from war and killing. If you don't already know the facts, you will find them horrendous, incomprehensible and unbelievable!

♪♪ Twentieth-Century War and Killing ♪♪

The following summarizes our significant death statistics for twentieth-century wars: Spanish American War (11,000 Americans killed); World War I (126,000 Americans killed—total 9,000,000 killed); World War II (500,000 Americans killed—total 15,000,000 killed); Korean War (37,000 Americans killed); Vietnam War (58,000 Americans killed); and less than 300 Americans were killed in the Grenada, Panama, Persian Gulf and Somalia Wars combined.

These statistics reveal that the twentieth century was noted for its bloody wars. World War I (the war to end all wars) saw 9-million people killed in battle, an incredible record that was far surpassed within a few decades by 15-million World War II battle deaths. In total the twentieth century's death toll in all its international and domestic wars, revolutions, and violent conflicts was about 35,654,000. From a killing standpoint this atrocious number is the good news. *Yes, good news!* The bad news is that many more people in the twentieth century were killed by absolutist governments than in all the wars combined. This shocking, and largely unknown, fact is well documented by Dr. Rudolph J. Rummel and others.[7]

Dr. Rummel has prepared a table (shown below) that provides the approximate total number of killings and classifies them by country and time spans. This killing is apart from the pursuit of any ongoing military action or campaign. For example, the Jews that Hitler slaughtered during World War II would be counted, since their merciless killing was unrelated to Hitler's pursuit of the war. The number of Jews killed by the Nazis was not counted in the 15-million World War II battle deaths shown above. The mass killing has been so immense that Dr. Rummel coined a new term—"democide." His definition of democide is all of those killed by: Genocide (killing of people by a government because of their group membership [race, ethnicity, religion, language]); Politicide (murder of persons by a government because of their political purposes); and Mass Murder (the indiscriminate killing of any person or people by a government).

Twentieth Century Democide Statistics
by Dr. Rudolph Rummel

USSR	1900-1987	61,911,000
China (PRC)	1917-1987	35,236,000
Germany	1933-1945	20,946,000
China (KMT)	1928-1949	10,075,000
Japan	1936-1945	5,964,000
China (Mao Soviets)	1923-1949	3,466,000
Miscellaneous Others	1900-1987	2,792,000
Cambodia	1975-1979	2,035,000
Turkey	1909-1918	1,883,000
Vietnam	1945-1987	1,670,000
Poland	1945-1948	1,585,000
Pakistan	1958-1987	1,503,000
Yugoslavia (Tito)	1944-1987	1,072,000
North Korea	1948-1987	1,663,000
Mexico	1900-1920	1,417,000
Russia	1900-1917	1,066,000
China (War Lords)	1917-1949	910,000
Turkey	1919-1923	878,000
United Kingdom	1900-1987	816,000
Portugal	1926-1982	741,000
Indonesia	1965-1987	729,000
Total		158,358,000

A portion of Dr. Rummel's explanation and discussion of the more than 158-million democides in the above table follows:[8]

> The totals in the table are based on a nation-by-nation assessment and are absolute minimal figures that may underestimate the true total by 10 percent or more. Moreover, these figures do not even include the 1921-1922 and 1958-1961 famines in the Soviet Union and China which caused about four million and 27 million dead, respectively. The former famine was mainly due to the imposition of a command agricultural economy, forced requisitions of food by the Soviets, and the liquidation campaigns of the Cheka; the latter was wholly caused by Mao's agriculturally destructive Great Leap Forward and collectivization. Had these people all been shot, the Soviet and Chinese governments' moral responsibility could be no greater....

> From 1918 to 1953, the Soviet government executed, slaughtered, starved, beat or tortured to death, or otherwise killed 39,500,000 of its own people (my best estimate among figures ranging from a minimum of twenty million killed by Stalin to a total over the whole communist period of eighty-three million). For China under Mao Tse-tung, the communist government eliminated, as an average figure between estimates, 45,000,000 Chinese. The number killed for just these two nations, during this period, is about 84,500,000 human beings, or a lethality of 252 percent more than both World Wars together.

> Yet, have the world community and intellectuals generally shown anything like the same horror, the same outrage, the same out pouring of anti-killing literature, over these Soviet and Chinese megakillings as has been directed at the much less deadly World Wars? As can be seen from the table, communist governments are overall almost four times more lethal to their citizens than non-communist ones, and in per capita terms nearly twice as lethal (even considering the huge populations of the USSR and China).

> From the table, we can see that the more freedom in a nation, the fewer people killed by government. Freedom acts to brake the use

of a governing elite's power over life and death to pursue their policies and ensure their rule. In no case have I found a democratic government carrying out massacres, genocide, and mass executions of its own citizens; nor have I found a case where such a government's policies have knowingly and directly resulted in the large scale deaths of its people though privation, torture, beatings, and the like. Absolutism is not only many times deadlier than war, but itself is the major factor causing war and other forms of violent conflict. It is a major cause of militarism. Indeed, absolutism, not war, is mankind's deadliest scourge of all. In light of all this, the peaceful, nonviolent, pursuit and fostering of civil liberties and political rights must be made mankind's highest humanitarian goal. Not simply to give the greatest number the greatest happiness, not simply to obey the moral imperative of individual rights, not simply to further the efficiency and productivity of a free society, but also and mainly because freedom preserves peace and life.[9]

♣♣ Horrors Residing in Statistics ♣♣

Let's look inside these grim statistics and get a feel for the horror lurking there. Horror that no words can describe adequately, so there is little need to protract a description of grim reality—broken and crushed bodies; bloated, rotted, and burned carcasses; the unceasing stench of fear and death; and the unimaginable atrocities committed by men against men. Without experiencing it, how can we know the stark terror of waiting for the soldiers, the attacks, the shells, the mines, the bombs, or violent death? So this will be a short visit; limited to scenes from the two world wars of the twentieth century. But, we should not forget that the full measure of this horror has been dealt to each of the approximately 200-million men and women represented by the cold statistics just presented. There is no way to comprehend these numbers, but they approximate the total 1950 population of the United States of America. If my arithmetic is correct and the earth was dry land, we could lay the dead bodies end-to-end and walk completely around the earth's circumference about ten times, stepping on nothing but dead bodies. And, the statistics we have dealt with are deaths, typically in war there are more wounded than killed and no one can hazard an intelligent guess as to the number psychologically damaged (both military and civilian). All of these human beings received their measure of war and killing on our "so-called" twentieth-century-civilized earth.

One of the defining characteristics of World War I was its trenches. More than 1,000 miles of trenches were dug.[10] There were major blood baths at Somme, Verdun, Ypres, Saint-Miel, Argonne, Sedan and other battle sites. Hearing the names of these towns sent shivers down the spines of those who fought and survived World War I. There are 5 liters or about 1.32 gallons of blood in the average body. Multiply this number by 9-million men killed and one calculates almost 12-million gallons of blood. That is plenty of blood to qualify these battles as "blood baths."

By the end of 1914, gigantic gashes had been carved across the face of Europe from the North Sea to the Alps, stretching 475 miles. Two opposing lines of trenches had been dug, and crouching inside them on one side were the armies of England, France and their allies, while German soldiers and their central power allies crouched in the opposing trenches. In places these trenches were only thirty or forty feet apart. These armies faced each other in deadly combat. They would remain there for more than three years. The soldiers died by the millions in senseless battles, while the survivors lived like rats in oppressive heat, numbing cold, filth and mud.

The most dreaded order a soldier in World War I could receive was "over the top." The soldiers in the trenches knew that these words, sending them over the trench wall to no-man's land, were a death sentence for most of the first wave of infantry.

The night before an attack, the men tried to take their minds off of the next day. Yet, all the preparations reminded them of pending death. Each man wrote a letter home, which was given to an officer to be mailed if the writer was killed. The letters informed loved ones that the writer was dead. Each man also wrote a last will in an official booklet that recorded army pay due him.

A German soldier described the scene as he waited in a reserve trench for the order to attack: "There we lay the whole day, crouching in the narrow trench on a thin layer of straw, in an overpowering din of shelling which never ceased all day or the greater part of the night—the whole ground trembling and shaking. Attacks generally came at dawn."[11]

Robert Graves, an English officer, wrote of a platoon that went over the top only to throw themselves to the ground immediately to avoid machine-gun fire. When the officer blew his whistle to signal advance again, no one moved. "You bloody cowards," he called "are you leaving me to go on alone?" The platoon sergeant lifted himself on a shattered arm and said, "Not cowards, sir. Willing enough, but they're all fucking dead."[12]

Patrick MacGill, a member of a British medical unit, described some of his war experiences as follows: "The smoke and noise caused men to lose their way. They might run along the barbed wire, looking for a place to get through. Out in no-man's land you saw men and bits of men lying all over the place. A leg, an arm, then again a leg, cut off at the hip. I stopped to bandage a man. A big high-explosive shell flew over our heads and dropped fifty yards away in a little hollow where seven or eight figures in khaki lay prostrate, faces to the ground. The shell burst and the wounded and dead rose slowly into the air to a height of six or seven yards and dropped slowly again, looking for all the world like puppets worked by wires."[13]

"A huge Prussian was fighting three little Tommies. The bayonet from the Hun's rifle was gone, and he was clutching the barrel in both hands and swinging the butt around his head. The Tommy nearest me," wrote Guy Empey, "received the butt of the German's rifle in a smashing blow below the right temple. It smashed his head like an eggshell. He pitched forward on his side and a convulsive shudder ran through his body. Meanwhile, the other Tommy had gained the rear of the Prussian. Suddenly about four inches of bayonet protruded from the throat of the Hun, who staggered forward and fell. I will never forget the look of blank astonishment that came over his face."[14]

In muddy, shell-blasted areas like Ypres and the Somme, many of the wounded bled to death where they fell. The unburied dead, after a day or two in the sun, began to stink and were health hazards. "Do not ask about the fate of the wounded!" a German soldier wrote home. "Anybody who was incapable of walking to the doctor had to die a miserable death . . . a dog, dying in the poorest hovel at home, is enviable by comparison."[15]

"A wounded officer lay groaning in no-man's land. Several men tried to rescue him, only to be hit themselves. The officer sent word back that he was dying, and that no more rescue attempts were to be made. He sent his apologies to the company for making such a noise. Graves went out at dusk, and found the man hit in 17 places. I found that he had forced his knuckles into his mouth to stop himself crying out and attracting any more men to their death."[16]

A typical day in the trenches varied from one place to another, but usually, the day was turned upside down, with most of the work being done at night, because darkness gave greater cover and safety to men moving about. At dusk, after the evening meal, the command was given to "stand to." The men on duty mounted the fire step with their rifles' ready. It was a drill, repeated at dusk and dawn. When the order was given to "stand down," the real work of the night began.[17]

The main work in the trenches was digging. Damage done by shellfire or raid had to be repaired. New trenches were constantly being built. Water had to be pumped out of the trench, using hand pumps, and mud shoveled over the edge of the trench. There were sandbags, endless sandbags, to be refilled and replaced. It was dull work, backbreaking work, work carried out under danger of death at any time.

"We stooped and crouched and we scratched at the earth on our knees. We toiled and turned like men in nightmares. The earth is muddy and sticky and hangs on our tools like glue. The men slept in mud, washed in mud, ate mud and dreamed mud. I still shudder at the memory of the smell of burnt and poisoned mud—for months on end—the stink of corrupting human flesh." And wet, bone-chilling winters were worse.[18]

Supplies for the front trenches were also brought up at night. Everything had to be carried by hand through the network of communication trenches. This included food, ammunition, tools, timbers, barbed wire, pumps, mail, medical supplies—all carried by that beast of burden, the common soldier.

Word would be passed down the line: "ten minutes to go." Ten minutes to live was a common thought among the soldiers. "There you have a brave young chap," wrote a French officer. "It was his first show. He was sweating with fear, shaking with fear. He gripped his rifle, he threw himself forward, and he went because he had to go. He was afraid of nothing so much as showing his fear. *All men have some restraining influence to help them in hours of trial, some principle or some illusion. Duty, patriotism, vanity, and dreams come to the help of men in the trenches, all illusions probably, ephemeral and fleeting. But for a man who is as ephemeral and fleeting as his illusions are, he can lay his back against them and defy death and the terrors of the world.*"[19]

These are some of the recollections of men who were there. We can be thankful that we were not. Most gave their lives, not for their flag, religion, or other high-sounding cause. Rather they sacrificied their lives for their comrades-in-arms whom destiny had cast as their brothers. More than 90,000 of the Allied forces killed were gassed to death, a new form of killing. Also, this was the first war with air-to-air combat—another new way to die. But, for really sophisticated air-to-air, air-to-ground, and ground-to-air combat let's move to World War II. During World War II, twice as many Army Air Force officers died in battle than officers in all the rest of the Army.[20]

During the 1990-2000 decade, the surviving American veterans of World War II became old men and mortality shrunk their numbers faster than the German and Japanese armies could. Many of these veterans wrote memoirs about their war experiences and couldn't get them published because the market was saturated with these stories. As an editor during this period, I read a number of these stories, which were marked by the veteran's attention to detail, their dogged determination to get it right without sounding like a hero, and the accounts of amazing, unbelievable things that happen in combat. A couple of their stories are repeated here that illustrate truth, indeed, is stranger than fiction.[21]

Words of James C. Wilson
World War II Air Force Bomber Pilot and Prisoner of War[22]

We were awakened at 0230 and briefed at 0330 for an oil target north of Vienna. It was my second mission so I was flying copilot for Bert Stodden but the rest of the men were my regular crew. Van was acting as navigator as well as bombardier, so Dutch was not assigned that day. Bruce, my copilot, was with another crew. Our plane was assigned to position Number 5 of the last flight, the well known "Purple Heart Corner." Take off was about 0530 on 26 June 1944. Things went along quite smoothly until we passed the Platten Sea in Hungary. Here our combat wing was attacked by Me-109's. The two planes ahead of us were left with smoking engines, but we were untouched. Our P-51 escort drove off the enemy fighters and shot down several. One hit the mountain just below us in a beautiful splash of orange flame. As we approached the I.P. the flack began and we were hit again by fighters. A Me-110 made a head-on attack right down our formation and got our Number 3 engine. The oil pressure dropped toward zero, so we feathered the engine and increased power on the other three. The supercharger amplifier on Number 4 went out, dropping the power, and the R.P.M. on Number 2 stuck at 2700.

Paquet, our engineer, came out of the top turret and replaced the amplifier. We were still not able to keep up with the formation. We made our run on the target, but Van could not get the bombs to release. Paquet pulled the salvo release, and we got our bombs in the target area. The flack began to sound like hail on the plane. The formation was out of sight and we were being attacked by Me-109's. Stodden headed for the deck to shake the fighters. We flew right over a fighter field at about 150 feet altitude. Ground M.G's and light flack fired on us. Our waist gunners strafed back. More fighters took after us. Paquet reported the bomb bay on fire.

Our interphone was out, but Stodden gave the order to crash land as we were right on the deck. We were able to level out the plane, but we hit with power on doing about 180 mph. We landed in an open field, skidded across a road, and came to a stop about 100 feet from a row of houses in Strassburg, Austria. The plane broke open on the pilot's side. Stodden was crushed. I crawled out 'the hole' over him. Paquet's chute had popped, and he was caught in the hole. Lush came out thru plexiglass in the nose turret. He helped me get Paquet out. The plane was burning all over, and the ammunition began to explode. We expected the fuel tanks to go any time, so we helped Paquet away from the plane.

A man ran out and motioned us to come into the walled courtyard by his house. He was a member of the Land Guard. We were checked for weapons, but had none. Van came crawling out of the nose. He seemed dazed but came into the court when we called. He was the last man to get out of the plane. He could hardly walk, and Paquet needed help to get around. Lush and I were practically unhurt. We were trying to decide whether we should go off and leave the two injured men when some German Luftwaffe soldiers arrived and decided the matter. The local families were quite excited when the fuel exploded and the 50 cal. ammunition kept popping, but they seemed friendly enough and brought us water. Our plane crumpled at the waist windows on landing and completely burned, so we never expected to see the rest of the crew again.

The Luftwaffe guards walked us up town to the Burgermeister's office. Here we were thoroughly searched and relieved of all our possessions except clothing. We were quite decently treated by the officials, but a Nazi civilian came in and did much yelling, spitting, and threw a steel helmet at Van. A Luftwaffe non-com with a four-man guard picked us up at the Burgermeister's in a Ford truck. He spent the afternoon going from one town to another collecting members of other crews who had been shot down and captured. By late afternoon there were portions of four or five crews in the truck. None were seriously injured, but most everybody was bloody and had torn or burnt clothing.

We were taken to Haus Udet Field in Wiener-Neoustadt. The Messerschmidt factory there was completely bombed out, but some of the Luftwaffe barracks and administration buildings were only partially damaged. Here we were searched again, and all possessions including my ring, watch, and jacket were taken away. At the headquarters, to my great surprise, I saw Ellis, Czarnecki, and Lipczynski. Lippy's ankle was broken. The other two were unhurt. They had jumped out of the plane while we were flying at less than 200 feet shortly after we flew over the fighter field. They said the plane was melting apart just aft of the bomb bay. The interphone being out, they had jumped without orders. Shorty Lyons had been hit by 20mm, before leaving the tail. He jumped first. His chute opened, but the Germans said that he was found dead.

Words of Fred Nichol[23]
(Fred was a young P-38 pilot, flying his first combat mission)

Our job was to keep the German fighters from attacking the B-26's. German fighters liked to attack firstly from the rear, and secondly, from out of the sun. Since almost all of the missions flown by the medium size bombers, B-25's and B-26's were scheduled, by our top brass, for a target time of 1200 hours high noon, the Germans could anticipate our arrival. Although they never knew the exact target of the day, they knew in general that the bombers would hit, and on nearing the Italian coast, the German fighters would position themselves high, and then they were well situated for their attack, either from the rear or out of the sun. A second bunch of attacking fighters, would stay higher, and when the opportunity presented itself, would dive straight down through the bomber formation and then back up, straight through them again firing all the way. They were known to us as the Yo-Yo boys.

Our leaders spotted the first enemy fighters when we were north of Naples and just over the shoreline heading inward. At our present altitude of 13,000 feet the haze was well beneath us. The morning sky was crystal clear and the visibility was truly unlimited. This time it was a fact and not just a catchy weatherman's phrase. We had been on top of our bombers for about ten to fifteen minutes, weaving back and forth, and I was busy flying formation on my leader. I tried to look around a little, but it was enough for me to keep check on my cockpit instruments and stay off Pappy's wing at the same time. Then came the little crack of static in the earphones, signaling that somebody had pushed his mike button, "Six at ten o'clock high." And then another static break, "Four at two o'clock high." Then Pappy's voice came over loud and clear, "Petdog squadron, prepare to drop tanks." Now I had to find those switches, flip the safety covers up, arm the dropping mechanism, turn on the gun-sight switch, turn on the gun switch, the canon switch and the camera switch. Increase the RPM's on both engines—get them even—synchronize them so they won't vibrate to pieces. Increase the mixture control. Stay in formation. Then slip a peek into the sky. See if you can spot any of those fighters.

I was starting to sweat profusely. Up until now, I just had wet arm pits, but now it was flowing. I could smell it. It didn't smell normal. It was a smell different than any I had ever smelled before. The sweat of fear has an odor all its own. And even with the oxygen mask on, I could smell it. Pappy's voice broke the silence again. "Petdog squadron, drop tanks." That was all he needed to say. All the other tasks were automatic and understood. If you hadn't completed them by now, you had better get your ass in gear. Pappy turned and glanced at me on his wing. He motioned me back a little then stuck a gloved thumb up at me. I think he was smiling under his oxygen mask.

Then Cragmore and Springcap squadrons started calling out more locations of fighters. I couldn't count them all, and I couldn't tell how many might be duplicated. All I could really think about, other than the present peril, was that five days ago the group sent 36 P-38's up here to escort some B-26's and only 24 of them made it back. The radio cracked again. Then the voice, "Petdog red-flight, there's a bunch at three o'clock high starting in, get ready to break right—get ready—break-k-k now!" All four of us flipped our planes to the right at about 45 degrees, and hauled back on the controls causing a violent and screaming right-hand climbing turn that caught the oncoming Me-109's off guard.

I did a pretty good sharp right turn, climbing and staying with my leader, but I panicked. When I hauled back on the wheel, I squeezed everything that was at fingers reach. The guns fired, the cannon went off, the mike came alive, and tracer bullets roared out from the front of my plane and sprayed the air above the top of Pappy's cockpit. I saw Pappy's head turn for a split second, and as I came off the mike button, I heard the last part of "Jesus Christ, Nick!" and then everyone was firing at the oncoming Me-109's. Some Me-109's tried to veer off, some couldn't as they had fully committed themselves. One Me-109 exploded—another belched flame and smoke—and then it was all over. In the time frame of three to five seconds, a mini air battle had commenced—had been fought —and had ended. And then it was all over. Our flight was rapidly turning back to join the other two flights and form a more basic squadron pattern over the B-26's. We could hear the lead squadron, Cragmore, who was flying a little higher than us, having an affair with a bunch of Folk-Wolf 190's; and all this time the B-26's beneath us were lumbering on their path, climbing a little, trying to get in a little better formation for their final turn onto the bombing-run leg.

I didn't know how to estimate the number of enemy fighters that were in the area. Everyplace I looked there were little black dots moving around in small groups. Most of the time they weren't bothering anybody, just trying to get in a position where they could make a pass that would be more advantageous to them than to us. We were stuck with our escort duties and couldn't chase and attack them. We had to wait until they made a pass, and then we still waited, waited until they fully committed themselves before making our play. That way, we could lure them in close enough to fire a few short bursts at them. It was a cat and mouse sort of game. And it took clever technique and experience on the part of our leaders to play the game well.

In a way, it was the pros versus us amateurs. But anyway you looked at it—it was the only game in town. A few of them would come straight down—through us and the bombers below—their yellow noses glistening in the morning sun—and their machine guns blinking at us like lights on a Christmas tree. When the Herman Goring yo-yo boys had completed their first attack of down through and back up, they coordinated their next attack on the flanks and to the rear of our bombers. There was no attempt at radio silence at this stage. There were so many screams calling out attacking fighters, and leaders calling tactical maneuvers that I could hardly distinguish between squadrons.

I tried to program my mind to screen out everything that didn't sound like "Petdog Red Flight." The fight developed into a true dog-fight—there were fighters everywhere—and Pappy was turning and firing and turning, trying to ward-off incoming fighters. Then the tactics changed. Where before, we waited until they came in so close, that they had fully committed themselves, so we could fire at them; now we were just trying to ward them off of the bombers. And we didn't give a damn if we got a good shot in or not. In this nightmarish turmoil of a dog-fight, which seemed to never end—I learned one thing—and that was that our leaders had their priorities straight. They wanted those bombers to fly that approach leg as safely and unmolested as possible so they could drop their bombs accurately. At this stage of the mission, it was better to ward off four fighters than it was to shoot one down.

It seemed to me that the flak was fairly heavy in the target area. And this is another thing I learned on my first mission—where and when the flak is the heaviest, the German fighters would hold back and keep a safe distance. This also gives the escorting fighters a breathing spell and a chance to get back in proper formation to cover the bombers on their departure from the target. During this short breathing spell, the bombers did their damage. They dropped 500 and 1,000 pound bombs by the dozens, and on each drop, their planes would pop up twenty to fifty feet as this deadly shackle of weight was released from their bellies.

James Wilson and Fred Nichol were just two of the millions of young men, who were frightened out of their wits as they drove, sailed, and flew their complex fighting machines. World War II had its share of hand-to-hand fighting that was so prevalent in World War I, but by the 1940s technology had made man's weapons of war more complex, thus many of the battles were machine-to-machine rather than eyeball-to-eyeball. This diminished personal contact in battles whether they were on land or sea, or in the air. But, when the shell or bomb hit the results were the same—mutilation, death, and destruction. The only significant difference was the body count. Fifteen-million battle deaths! The weapon that ended World War II was the most horrific weapon ever developed and deployed—*the atomic bomb.*

♪♪ The Atomic Bomb ♪♪

America's use of the atomic bomb was surrounded by ethical and moral questions, because of its immense destructive power. These questions seem to gain momentum as time passes, and some historical revisionists paint America's decision to use the atomic bomb as the action of a demon nation. Say what you will, in 1945 most citizens of the world, friend and foe alike, were happy to see the end of World War II and felt like the death and destruction caused by exploding atomic bombs over Hiroshima and Nagasaki were small prices to pay for a much larger gain.

Ray Zuker provides well-researched, astute answers to the revisionists, by discussing the use of the atomic bomb and the consequences of that action in his 1994 booklet entitled, *Pearl Harbor Remembered*. Zuker, a decorated bomber pilot of World War II is a free-lance writer, author of several books, and a long-time activist in retired Eighth Air Force Association affairs. Excerpts from Zuker's commentary follow; it is abridged with his permission.[24]

A half-century has passed since the end of World War II, and memories are dimming now for the combat survivors. Some choose to forget, but certain irrefutable facts remain. Yet, two events planned for 1995, fifty years after the war officially ended, if demonstrated as planned, distort the facts and will be the ultimate disservice to those who participated in the war. These two events are (1) a Japanese Bell and (2) the denigration of the role the B-29 "Enola Gay" bomber played in ending World War II by the Smithsonian Institute's Air & Space Museum.

A seven-foot high, 8,000 pound Japanese designed bell is to be installed in the city of Oak Ridge, Tennessee. Oak Ridge is the home of the secret Manhattan Project, established early in World War II. This so called "Freedom Bell" is to be rung on August 6th, 1995 and each year thereafter. By any definition, this event will be a gesture of "atonement" for our using the atomic bombs that finally ended World War II.

Millions of persons survived World War II, because of the action taken by Harry Truman in 1945 to use the atomic bomb. To complete the perspective after the bombing of Hiroshima and Nagasaki, we must consider what assuredly would have happened if the Emperor of Japan had not overruled his warlords who would have had the war continue.

Nine atomic bombs were built and at least four of these bombs were made ready to use if the Japanese had chosen to ignore the terms of the Potsdam Declaration (The unconditional surrender of Japan). Japan then would have been faced with much greater destruction.

In July, 1945, President Truman approved the plans for "Operation Downfall." This plan called for the invasion of the Japanese home islands of Kyushu and Honshu by mainly United States military forces.

An important factor in our planning was the abysmal lack of intelligence, as to the deployment of Japanese military forces in the home islands. We would find that we had grossly underestimated these forces, only after the occupation began.

Another, enormously important factor was the weather. In an area plagued with typhoons, planning had to take this fact into consideration. Considering weather, late fall or early spring was the best time for the invasions. Even so, unseasonable storms devastated the area on September 15th and October 9-12, 1945. Only the largest naval vessels at sea would have survived the high seas of typhoon winds. Assault craft and troop ships would not have survived.

Not only were the Japanese planning their defense, they were praying to the Shinto gods for deliverance from their enemy. In the year 1281 the Chinese put more than 3,000 ships to sea, filled with warriors. Their intention was to invade the Japanese islands. As if in answer to Japanese prayers, a typhoon came out of the China Sea toward the island of Kyushu, where the Chinese fleet rode at anchor. When the winds died away, the Chinese fleet had been destroyed. In 1945, the Japanese again would pray for the Kamikaze (Divine Wind).

Few are aware of the plans that had been prepared for the American invasion of the Japanese home islands. "Operation Downfall" called for two military invasions to be carried out in succession. In the first invasion, American combat troops would be landed by amphibious assault on November 1, 1945, on Japan itself. On March 1, 1946, the second invasion, would send 22 more American combat divisions to assault the main island of Honshu against one million Japanese defenders.

"Operation Downfall" was to be an American operation. A total of 4.5 million American servicemen, more than 40% of all servicemen in uniform in 1945, were to be a part of the invasions. Casualties were expected to be extremely heavy. General Charles Willoughby, Chief of Army Intelligence, estimated that American casualties from the operation would be one million men. As part of the gruesome logistics, the U.S. military ordered 250,000 body bags. This was preparation for bringing many of our American servicemen home.

Our military leaders were deathly afraid of the Japanese "Kamikaze" and with good cause. The Kamikazes were unique in military history. Adhering to the code of Bushido (code of the warrior), Japanese military men were prepared to die in suicide attacks. This stemmed from the Japanese ideal of "The Path of Eternal Duty;" the belief that family and individual welfare were not important when compared to the long history of the Empire.

The Kamikazes or "sacred warriors" participated in the battles of Leyte, Iwo Jima and Okinawa. Kamikaze operations at Okinawa werc the fiercest of the war. More than 1,900 suicides attacks took place. Suicide planes killed 4,900 American sailors and wounded more than 4,800. These were the heaviest losses incurred in any naval campaign in World War II.

The Japanese defense plan against attack of their mainland called for a four-fold aerial strike. While American ships were approaching Japan, but still in the open seas, an initial force of 2,000 army and navy fighters were to fight to the death in order to control the skies over Kyushu. A second force of 330 specially trained Navy combat pilots were to take off and attack the main body of the task force.

While these two forces were engaged, a third force of 825 suicide planes was to hit the American transports in the open seas. As the troop convoys approached their anchorages, another 2,000 suicide planes were to be detailed in waves of 200 to 300, to be used in hour-by-hour attacks.

The Japanese had more plans for invaders. Attempting to sink our troop-carrying transports would be almost 300 *Kairyu* suicide submarines. These two-man subs carried 1,320 pound bombs in their nose. Especially feared by our Navy, were the *Kaitens*, which were to be used against our invasion fleet just off the beaches. These *Kaitens* were human manned torpedoes over 60 feet long, each carried a warhead of more than 3,500 pounds and each was capable of sinking ships as large as an aircraft carrier. The last line of maritime defense was the Japanese suicide "frogmen," called "*Fukuryu.*" These were divers armed with mines, each capable of sinking a landing craft up to 950 tons. These divers, numbering in the thousands, could stay submerged for up to ten hours, and were to thrust their explosive charges into the bottom of the landing craft and, in effect, serve as human mines.

The invasion of Japan never became a reality because on August 6, 1945 the entire nature of war changed when the first atomic bomb was exploded over Hiroshima. On August 9, 1945, a second bomb was exploded over Nagasaki, and within days the war with Japan was at a close.

As thorough as plans for "Operation Downfall" had been made, the estimates of United States and Japanese casualties were not realistic. Our planners did not fully comprehend the magnitude of the resolve of the Japanese defenders. It is reasonable now to make an estimate of more than one million military casualties, especially if the loss of life is added that would have occurred had our men been at sea when typhoons hit the area on September 15, 1945 and again on October 11, 1945.

These facts were part of the *reality of the time.* Our Congress and citizenry were weary of war. Gold stars in windows across the country were sad reminders of the cost of the war in American lives. The country was in no mood to suffer further causalities. The will of the country was "*to end the war and send the troops home.*"

It was not the Divine Wind that saved the Japanese culture. Rather, it was a man-made device that served its purpose. The Japanese made the major contribution to the atomic bombs when they forged the triggers for those bombs on December 7, 1941. Remember Pearl Harbor?[25]

Ray Zuker's words reflect the truth of the time, and because of his efforts and the efforts of thousands of other veterans, the Smithsonian Institute softened their revisionist rhetoric and modified their B-29 "Enola Gay" bomber display, but the Japanese-Oak Ridge Freedom Bell project was not derailed.

World War II is often referred to as the "big one." From a moralistic standpoint, an excellent case could be made also for calling this war the "most justified" in America's history. We were standing, clearly, against aggressor nations who struck the first blows and whose unquestionable aim was world dominance. The Allies were victorious, but time has clouded over the closeness of the outcome. A few different scenarios, such as the Japanese attacking Eastern Russia instead of the United States or lucky breaks here and there and the Axis powers would have defeated the Allies. Accurate historians know that such a "what-if" assessment is nonproductive, but it is realistic.

♩♩ Despots of War ♩♩

Earlier we noted the causes of war include: man's inherent aggression; growth of population; growth of political organizations into cities, states, and countries; and the expanding reach of economics, religion, and nationalism. It is interesting to see how these causes intermingle in the rise to power of a despot. In the twentieth century, no despot comes to mind before Adolph Hitler, although Stalin and Mao undoubtedly were responsible for more deaths.

A despotic leader like Hitler receives all the bad press throughout history after the failure of their ambitions, but despots are only the polarizer of a population—a population filled with aggression, frustration, national pride and the desire to obtain comforts for themselves and their children at the expense of, in their collective opinion, less deserving populations. Hitler's edicts were applauded by a large majority of the German population, each guilty to a large extent of the same sins as their leader. Hitler, in World War II, never personally killed a single Allied soldier. Yet, millions were killed by those supporting his agenda.

Few leaders begin with an offensive war against other nations on their minds. Rather their cries, as one, are for large defensive armies—armies that can protect and preserve peace. As their armies grow and situations develop, they envision the possibilities of further expansion and then convince or order their followers to act out their evolving plans for expansion. In 1936 a book, *Adolph Hitler*, was published that provides an intimate look at Hitler's rise to power. The book has a number of photographs, some obviously staged, but many which clearly show the look of admiration and pride on the faces of the German citizenry in the presence of their Führer, Adolph Hitler. Dr. Joseph Goebbels wrote the foreword of the book, in a brown-nosing braggart's voice, telling readers that the high art of propaganda was key to the success of the German National Socialist Party.[26]

Some of the text is presented here verbatim and some slightly abridged for brevity. This text shows Hitler's interests and activities three years prior to the start of World War II. War is often mentioned in this book, but it is their past war—World War I. The emphasis throughout *Adolph Hitler* is on "National Unity," "Peace," "A Defensive Army," "Full Employment" and "Prosperity" for the German people; not war and killing. The words sound familiar, don't they? They should, because they are the universal language of politicians, parroting the desires of most populations.

Excerpts from the Foreword of *Adolph Hitler*:[27]

In the whole world and even in Germany today there are enormous misconceptions concerning the term 'propaganda' which are difficult to explain since they are mostly based on prejudices. And this is the case, although the German people have enjoyed first-hand lessons in this respect, since the end of the war, lessons that could not have been any better or more powerful. During this relatively short historic period in Germany, propaganda has proven to be a first-rate political force, for today there is no longer a need to prove that Imperial Germany was overthrown under the influence of Marxist propaganda, and that the Marxist-democratic regime could only be eliminated because not only National Socialist ideas but also National Socialist propaganda opposed it with a superior new order and skill.

Not only did National Socialism and its main representatives bring with them a natural talent for the art of propaganda but they also learned to increasingly fine-tune and apply this art. The Führer himself was the great teacher in this. It is a little known fact that the office he held in the early days of the Party was none other than that of propaganda chief, and that through his ingenious mastery and command of this office he put the true spiritual, organizational, and political stamp on the Party.

Today the whole globe recognizes the Führer as the creator of the National Socialist doctrine and the National Socialist State. Thus, he is the trailblazer of a new European order and the guide to peace and welfare of the nations. This knowledge is supported among untold millions in the whole world by an idea of the electrifying and fascinating phenomenon of Adolf Hitler, the man. The great simplicity and simple greatness that radiate from his person have a strong and convincing effect not only on every German but also on every foreigner with a healthy instinct. In the whole world today he can probably be called the one man who is rooted the most deeply in the thinking and feeling of our modern times and who, therefore, has the ability like no other to give a new shape to this time.

While this book drips with propaganda, it also captures the mentality and spirit of the German people. They believed that Hitler had solved their problems of economic chaos and restored their spirit of unity. To them, he was Germany's savior. A few more excerpts reveals the extent of this relationship.

Excerpts from "The Führer and the German People" chapter:[28]

Nowhere else in the world is there such a fanatic love of millions of people for one. No man ever got closer to the hearts of the people. Therefore the nation loves him, therefore the nation trusts him, therefore the nation is so unspeakably happy because it truly became itself in this man for the first time in history. This is the secret of the indestructibility of Adolf Hitler and his work, the assurance that the path he has chosen is unalterable. For it is not Adolf Hitler, the man, and it is not his work and not his path, but rather it is the German nation itself that expresses itself in him. In him it loves itself and in him it follows its most secret wishes, in him its boldest thoughts become reality. Each and every German feels this, and thus Adolf Hitler is a stranger to no one and no one is a stranger to the Führer. Workers and farmers, recipients of the Nobel prize and artists, fighters and dreamers, those that are happy and those that are in despair, they all speak with him and they all hear their own language, they understand and are understood. Every thing is unintentional and natural, and no one feels shy before this great man. No one is being commanded, no one is enticed, but everyone is being called as if he were called by his own conscience, and there is nothing he can do but follow, unless he wants to be guilty and unhappy in his own heart. Whatever is going to happen inevitably is already happening voluntarily and there is no nation on earth that is freer than the German nation...

Excerpts from "The Führer as a Statesman" chapter:[29]

All human greatness has its origin in the blood. Instinct is its guide and intuition is its great inspiration. Reason has only a limited part in the accomplishments of true genius; it is more occupied with tracing their direction and meaning and exposing them to the eye of the later observer. These laws are true, especially for art that is the highest and noblest activity of men and puts them close to their divine origin. Likewise they are of value and importance for the area of politics; for politics is indeed an art and contains all essential characteristics of artistic creation.

Geniuses topple worlds and build new worlds. They are the great beacons of the nations; the times orient themselves according to them. They set the course of history. The saying that there is a child hidden in every man is true especially of a genius; for he acts and creates uninhibited like a child and faces things with the natural self-confidence of a child.

The ingenious statesman dares to do that which is impossible in order to make that which is possible possible. His true strength is in simplifying contexts to which there is seemingly no solution... In 1933, the Führer assumed power, demonstrating his genius of statesmanship as he managed to bring about the miracle of staging a full-scale revolution without major bloodshed by reconciling with the true forces of tradition. Here once again is proof of the infallible instinct of a man of superior action. Within three years the German nation is once again able to protect its national life out of its own strength, has set the size of its own fleet in an honest treaty with England at a level commensurate with its own national dignity. A Nation which is today once again a global power among the other nations, which increasingly attracts the admiration or at least the envy of the whole world, and which is becoming more and more visible as an important element of world peace. All of this is the result of a political development, which led to the world power of the German Reich. An immense number of decisions is contained in this development. Together they form the image of a marvelous and fantastic rise [to power], which will no doubt be praised by later historians as the greatest political miracle of the twentieth century.

Excerpts from "Adolf Hitler and his Roads" chapter:[30]

The Führer derives a lot of joy from visiting a construction site or a completed stretch of road. Everything at the construction site is of interest to him: the organization, the buildings, the accommodations of the workers, and especially the routing of the road through the landscape. The Führer wants his roads to be bold and generous, but at the same time he wants them to be in harmony with the landscape. The workers are frequently very surprised when he suddenly steps among them. More than one dropped his pickaxe with surprise. But then their eye's light up with pure joy that the Führer is coming to see their work. One cannot imagine the feeling of happiness and joy at a construction site when hundreds of adult faces show an expression of joy such as is known only in children at the sight of the Christmas tree. The Führer told a seventy-year-old worker near Darmstadt, "If I live to be as old as you are I would like to be able to work as well as you do now." As the pyramids tell the history of the pharaohs, and the Roman roads testify to the might of the Roman emperors, thus the wonderful roads for automobiles will forever remind the German nation of the most unusual personality of its history.

> *What luck for rulers, that men do not think.*
> Adolph Hitler

Within a few years the brown-shirt Nazi soldiers, by the tens of thousands, were driving their war machines on these roads as they forged ahead to their destiny of killing and being killed. The German peoples' destiny clashed with, and changed, the destinies of hundreds of millions of people scattered around the world.

I was a lad of ten in 1943, living in a small railroad town in north-central Arkansas and remember well the total commitment of our community to the war effort. American propaganda worked too. Troop trains regularly stopped in our small town; I and other town urchins would sell candy, cigarettes and newspapers to the soldiers, who couldn't leave the train, for what seemed to us handsome profits. On many blocks in our rural community, there were flags with stars hanging in the windows of homes where sons and daughters were away fighting in the war. Our town suffered more than our share of casualties. Almost everybody participated in some way. Sugar, tires and gasoline were rationed. My family was "as poor as proverbial church mice," but I saved my dimes to buy ten-cent war stamps and rolled tinfoil wrappers to donate to the war effort. I can't recall how the tinfoil wrappers were collected, but I do remember proudly rolling the tinfoil into balls.

One of my vivid memories is standing outside a prison train with a few neighborhood friends, gawking as the American guards brought the prisoners out six at a time to stretch their legs and breathe some fresh air—which they immediately filled with cigarette smoke. To my unforgettable surprise, many of the prisoners were not much older than me. Those boys were dressed in the uniforms of German soldiers. They were German soldiers, puffing cigarettes and acting and being treated like men. I still remember the emotions of envy and admiration (not hate), surfacing in my mind for those blonde-headed boys. In retrospect, I think what a waste and what a burden to have placed on our soldiers who were men and had to kill some of these children in hand-to-hand combat. But, hey, as Andy just reminded me, that's a trivial downside of war.

♭♭ Paradox of Conflicts ♭♭

A strange paradox of wars and personal squabbles is that today's enemy may very well become tomorrow's ally or hero. Here is a first-hand example. After World War II, America brought Wernher von Braun and his team of rocket scientists, including Kurt Debus and Theodore Popple, to Redstone Arsenal near Huntsville, Alabama. Von Braun was one of Germany's young scientific stars, and he and his team were the architects of the notorious V-2 buzz bombs that reigned death and terror on England.

When President John F. Kennedy made his "man-on-the-moon-in-this-decade declaration," Von Braun and his team were given the authority and money to accomplish the task. Von Braun headed up the organization known as Marshall Spaceflight Center which developed the moon rocket. Kurt Debus moved to Florida and headed up the launch facilities now known as Kennedy Spaceflight Center.

As an electrical design engineer for launch support equipment in Theodore Popple's design division located in Huntsville, Alabama, I was a minor contributor to the effort, and was swept up, willingly and wholeheartedly, in the enthusiasm of what became known as America's great space race with Russia. In this capacity, I once had the opportunity to meet, and talk briefly with Wernher Von Braun. During the conversation, Von Braun flattered me by being interested in the details of my "worker-bee" tasks. Von Braun was slightly pudgy, but when he entered a room he lit it up with his energy, confidence and charisma. This man, who had shaken the hand of Adolf Hitler and who less than twenty years earlier was America's mortal enemy, was now a hero to me and many other Americans.

In the early 1960s our design group in Huntsville, Alabama, held a design review meeting which was attended by Kurt Debus and other operation's personnel from the Cape.[31] After the meeting, I and a few co-workers watched from a second-floor window, as Kurt Debus and our manager, Theodore Popple, on the street below, were engaged in an obvious personal and animated conversation. When they parted, they each stepped back, clicked their heels, and gave the Hiel Hitler salute—an upward flip of their right hands with palms out. It was a quick, unconscious, but obviously a deeply-seated act on their part. My colleagues and I looked at each other in surprise, disbelief and astonishment. Our work leaders, in 1963, were flashing in broad daylight on a public Huntsville, Alabama, street the hated Nazi salute of Hitler's Germany.

Notwithstanding the unpleasant facts associated with war and killing, another paradox is that one has to grudgingly admit there are many pluses for humanity derived from them. "War kills men, and men deplore the loss, but war also crushes bad principles and tyrants, and so saves societies."[32]

One of the greatest problems facing the world in the twenty-first century is overpopulation. This problem would be much worse today, if war and killing, over time, hadn't thinned our ranks by killing off millions, perhaps billions, of people. Darwin's followers might say war weeds out those more unfit in our world, but that seems unlikely. Most of those killed in war were young men between the ages of eighteen and thirty, perhaps the most physically fit group in their society. Those deaths don't seem to fit Darwin's theory. Rather, they are random facts of the dark side of man's nature and nurture.

A significant benefit of war is the creation of a booming economy and the stifling of unemployment. War is a certain way to heat up the wheels of a country's economy, because an endless supply of machines, vehicles, clothing, weapons, munitions, and supplies are required to support the war effort. Another advantage of war is the unity and pride built among a country's population as they band together in a well-defined activity that propaganda will convince them is necessary for their personal benefit, freedom and survival. Another benefit is the interchange of cultures and experiences of the war's participants who survive. Most veterans will agree that their military experience was a defining event in their lives. They and their comrades who survive are bonded together for a lifetime. Veterans' organizations by the tens of thousands and active participants in these organizations by the millions attest to this. Intermarriage of couples from different cultures, races and socioeconomic backgrounds is more common during war time, and is, probably, a long-term benefit to the diversity of mankind. Still another positive result of war is the rapid advancement of technology. During war time, participants work feverishly in their laboratories and factories to produce the best machines and products to wage and win war. Many of these technological changes improve the standards of living for those who survive the conflicts.

Most of us would vote to forego these benefits of war and killing or find suitable alternatives if we could exchange them for a lasting and true peace on earth.

Wars also help make heroes and presidents; i.e., George Washington, Andrew Jackson, William Henry Harrison, Zachary

Taylor, Ulysses S. Grant, Rutherford B. Hayes, James Garfield, Benjamin Harrison, William McKinley, Theodore Roosevelt, Dwight D. Eisenhower, John F. Kennedy, and George Bush. Other American presidents also served in the military.

General Colin Powell, if he chooses, has an excellent chance to one day be the first African American to be elected president of the United States. General Powell believes in the importance of the proper nurturing of our children as a fundamental way of achieving peace and prosperity. Before serving as Secretary of State, he demonstrated this belief by his role as leader of America's Promise.[33] America's Promise believes that the answer to a strong and caring country resides in the love and education of *all our children.*

♪♪ Factors of Aggression ♪♪

Back to war and killing! The facts of history reviewed here seem to demonstrate there is a characteristic of aggression inherent in mankind that leads to conflicts of needs, desires and ideas. These conflicts invariably proceed from disturbed feelings, to verbal assault between individuals and factions, on to bodily harm on a personal, local, regional, national and international basis. It starts with our nuclear family. You name me one extended family that doesn't have internal squabbles, and I'll predict that is a family you don't know as well as you think you do. We can't help ourselves. There just aren't enough things to satisfy all of our wants and expectations, and the winds of anger and fright seem to easily blow out our minds.

So, many of us need to compete and fight more than we need the sanctity of peace and the continued goodwill of our neighbors. In the last decade, in the United States of America we have averaged more than 20,000 murders per year. This same primordial characteristic is at work; apparently it is a characteristic locked in our DNA. Andy Wright tells me, "Yes, this is what the doctrine of Original Sin is all about. The Bible tells us man was conceived in sin, born in sin, lives in sin and dies a sinner." Andy's unshakable faith in the correctness of his views on issues like this infuriates me to the point that I question my own reasoning. Let's study this question further.

There are two basic factors that shape and control our actions—our genetic makeup (nature) and our environment (nurture). The question is how much of our aggression is learned in our environment and how much of it is innate. Many learned individuals come down on the side that man's aggressive nature is fundamentally innate. They feel man is born that way and is a killer waiting to be unleashed. Charles Darwin and Sigmund Freud seemed to believe this. And so do Konrad Lorenz, Robert Ardrey, Raymond Dart, and Desmond Morris. All of these gentlemen are important thinkers.[34,35,36,37,38,39]

Valid opposing viewpoints exist. Ashley Montagu supports the view that one's culture and learning experience is a much greater factor in human aggression than any hardwired genetic innateness. Montagu bases his findings primarily on documented research of various sociologists who have studied and documented nonaggressive cultures, including the Papagbo Indians, the Hopi, the Zuñi, the Pueblo, the Semai of Malaya, the Punan of Borneo, the Land Dayaks of Sarawak, the Polynesian Tikopin and Ifaluk of the Western Pacific, the Lepchas of Sikkim in the Himalayas, the Tahitians of French Polynesia, the Tibetians and the Lapps.[40]

Montagu writes that no specific human behavior, including aggressive behavior, is genetically determined. He believes the facts of history support that the kind of behavior a human being displays in any circumstance isn't determined by his genes, although there is a genetic component, but largely by the experience he has undergone during his life in interaction with those genes. Genetic influences alone cannot be responsible for aggressive behavior, and in most cases such aggressive behavior is largely dependent on interaction with environmental factors.

The essence of Montagu's conclusions and of like-minded thinkers is that the way people behave is not so much a reflection of their innate drives as it is a reflection of what happens to them. Montagu agrees that man has an innate capacity for aggression as he has an innate capacity for cooperation, kindness or other personal characteristics. When it comes to aggressive action the prime driving force is man's environment and not his innate capacity for aggression. Montagu then informs us there is an environmental solution to aggressive behavior. That solution is "Love." He tells us that we find no juvenile delinquents in "primitive nonaggressive" societies simply because the conditions for producing them are absent in such communities, whereas in "civilized" societies, especially in our large cities, those conditions abound. The juvenile delinquent is the product of a delinquent society, in which parents, teachers, and the community have forgotten, if they have ever known, what it is to be human and what the needs of a growing human being are, the need, especially, for love. No child who was ever adequately loved, he tells us, ever became a delinquent or a murderer. Through love we have the ability to make and shape ourselves as peaceful, cooperative individuals, not barbarians.[41]

Serial murderers are the most vicious barbarians. John Douglas believes manipulation, domination and control are the three watchwords for serial killers and low self esteem is at the core of their personal, tormented lives. He concludes there is no certainty, but he believes both their biological natures and nurture are major factors in their decisions to kill. Douglas has met, studied and helped catch more American serial killers than anybody in the world. Those killers include: Charles Manson, Richard Speck, David Berkowitz (Son of Sam), Ted Bundy, Ed Gein (who dressed himself in his victim's peeled skin), and Wayne Williams (the Atlanta child killer). Some common characteristics of serial killers include: terrible, abusive childhoods, (especially abusive, domineering mothers); bed wetting; tendency to mistreat and mutilate animals; speech impediments; fantasy development; and early rejections by the opposite sex. Most serial killers are males who prey on the weaker members of our society—children, old people, and women, especially prostitutes. Douglas tells us serial killers are, by definition, successful killers who learn from their experiences.[42]

With the approximately 200-million killed through war, democides and murders just discussed, have we covered all of the killing that has taken place in the twentieth century? Not by a long shot! In America alone, there have been more than 40-million abortions since the procedure was legalized in 1973 and records maintained. More than five-million abortions have occurred in England since it was legalized in the 1960s.[43] No one knows the twentieth century total, but based on the facts we do know the abortion totals worldwide in the twentieth century exceed 100 million and could approach 200 million or more. Undoubtedly, more lives have been terminated by abortion than by all combined military actions and killing sprees of serial killers.

Before the 1960s most people in the world believed that abortion was killing and, as a result, it was illegal. Now the issue is debated from a multitude of perspectives. According to the pro-abortion Center for Reproductive Law and Policy in New York, about sixty-one percent of the global population now live in the fifty-four countries that have laws authorizing abortion on broad social and economic grounds; the other thirty-nine percent are in the ninety-seven countries that generally, by law, forbid abortion. While terminating an unborn life is different from terminating a life after birth, there can be no doubt that it is a termination of life. And, those who practice and condone it (regardless of extenuating circumstances or fault) are looking out for their own well being, not that of a budding, defenseless life.

If aggressiveness and the will to kill our fellow man are truly overpowering innatenesses in mankind, then we might as well toss in the towel on reforms and remorse—and ride with the tide until the most aggressive kill each other off. Then, if anyone survives perhaps they will be the least aggressive (the cowards hiding and holding hands in holes), and mankind can start over evolving a less violence-prone population. But, who can hold with this scenario? Certainly not Andy Wright.

While we may have an innate capacity for aggressiveness, especially when threatened (a capacity that undoubtedly differs with each of our individual genetic makeups and environments that we were exposed to), assuredly we also have an innate capacity for cooperating with one another to achieve common goals. Most of us gladly lend a helping hand to complete strangers when we can do so without some threat to our own well being or to the well being of our loved ones.

So, it's difficult to accept the idea that all mankind is innately aggressive to the point we are "killing machines" just waiting for the right circumstances to bare our fangs and go for the jugular vein. Joan Baez asks a pertinent question on this subject, "If it's natural to kill why do men have to go into training to learn how?"[44]

In spite of all the war and killing in the preceding century, there is evidence that the worst of war and killing on this planet, at least in the near term, is behind us. This is so, despite the recent declaration of many world leaders to wage war on terrorists and the perpetual unrest between Israel and the Palestinians and other regional conflicts due to economical, ethnic and religious issues. Still, based on past history, wars seem certain to be a part of our future. But, if wholesale war and killing are in our immediate future, thank goodness it's unknown to us. *Ah, sweet mysteries!*

On the world scene, despots and the influence of communism have been replaced largely by democracies. This should mean more personal freedom and less democide in the world. Unfortunately, there are enough despots, warmongering fanatics and threats to world peace that America must maintain a strong military presence. But, we must recognize that preparation for war is one of the greatest obstacles to human progress and that it results in a vicious cycle of arms buildups, wars, violence and poverty. Every weapon made for war or prevention of war is a missed opportunity to feed starving children. As long as there are starving children, in the name of humanity, shame on us!

While our scientists work at unraveling the mysteries of our genetics, behavior, and natural world, the rest of us can work on strengthening the environment to deflate aggressive behavior. In this world we can have no higher calling than to help reclaim our youth, (every single one that we can!) from drugs, poverty, gangs, a steady diet of television and video games, disrespectful behavior, uncaring attitudes and idleness. Idleness (caused by adults allowing children to be lazy, or the lack of employment opportunities) is a major problem.

One thing we know, at the dawn of this new millennium, is that within seventy years or so, most of us who now are more than eighteen years of age will be dead.[45] Children are mankind's future and we need to band together in countries, cities, towns, races, cultures, and any other division and provide our children with love, education, and opportunity. We need to build their strength of character and challenge them by having high expectations of them. This is not an impossible dream nor on a hill so far away that it is an unreachable goal.

There are a number of organizations trying to achieve this in America such as America's Promise, The Points of Light Foundation, Volunteer Center National Network, Boy and Girl Scouts, Boys and Girls Clubs, Big Brothers and Big Sisters, and churches of all denominations. But they are barely holding back the flood of problems. The mainstream of American individuals needs to devote less time to their hobbies, recreation and TV viewing—and dedicate more time to helping a child or a group of children through constructive, character and hope-building activities. In other words give them love and encouragement, and help them sidestep activities that are harmful to them and our mutual society.

Despite mankind's warmongering history, we are not predestined to be aggressive killers. More important, we become mature humans, within our genetic limitations and environmental constraints, that we learn to be. We can provide a positive or negative influence on others as we all contribute to the composite environment. The choice within the limits of our nature and nurture is ours. If enough of us choose wisely, the refrain "When Johnny Comes Marching Home, Hurrah, Hurrah" can fade from our world.

♭♭♭♭

Chapter Notes

1. "When Johnny Comes Marching Home" is a lively World War I marching song, written by Louis Lambert, (Buffalo, NY: Montgomery Music, Inc., 1950).

2. Thomas Carlyle (1795-1881), *Sartor Resartus,* (England: Oxford University Press, World's Classic Series, 1987). Carlyle's ficticious genuis, Herr Teufelsdröckh (devil's dung) had seen it all and knew it all.

3. R. Ernest and Trevor N. Dupuy, *The Encyclopedia of Military History from 3500 BC to Present*, (New York, NY: Harper Collins, 1986).

4. Geoffrey Blainey, *The Causes of War*, (London: MacMillan Press Ltd., 1973).

5. Eloy Gallegos's books include: *Jacona, An Epic Story of the Spanish Southwest; Melungeons, The Pioneers of the Interior Southeastern United States 1526-1597*; *Santa Elena, Spanish Settlements on the Atlantic Seaboard from Florida to Virginia 1513 to 1607;* and *Spanish Pioneers in United States History,* (Knoxville, TN: Tennessee Valley Publishing ,1996-1999).

6. Statistics for early American wars are based on information provided by Our Wars and Our Veterans at http://www.computingcorner.com. Accurate death statistics from wars are difficult to produce, especially before the eighteenth century. While these statistics may not be precise, they help us comprehend the relative magnitude of killing.

7. Dr. Rudolph J. Rummel, Professor Emeritus of Political Science, is one of the foremost authorities on war and killing. Dr. Rummel spent many years studying the phenomena of war and mass killing. His research led to two books *Death by Government* and *Statistics of Democide*. His website is http://www2.hawaii.edu/~rummel.

8. This abridged discussion, which has been approved by Dr. Rummel, is only a brief example of his work. It represents the outstanding effort of a dedicated political scientist, who was a runner up for the Nobel Peace prize and has been recognized world wide for the depth and honesty of his

research. Approximately one-thousand references, supporting the accuracy of Dr. Rummel's table, are listed at his website—http://www2. hawaii.edu/~rummel.

9. Ibid.

10. Dorothy and Thomas Hoobler, *The Trenches*, (New York, NY: G.P. Putnam's Sons, 1978).

11. Ibid.

12. Robert Graves, *Good-Bye to All That*, (Garden City, NY: Doubleday Anchor Books, 1929).

13. Patrick MacGill, *The Great Push*, (New York, NY: Gosset and Dunlap, 1916).

14. Arthur G. Empey, *Over the Top*, (New York, NY: G.P. Putman's Sons, 1917).

15. Dorothy and Thomas Hoobler, *The Trenches*, (New York, NY: G.P. Putnam's Sons, 1978).

16. Robert Graves, *Good-Bye to All That*, (Garden City, NY: Doubleday Anchor Books, 1929).

17. Dorothy and Thomas Hoobler, *The Trenches*, (New York, NY: G.P. Putnam's Sons, 1978).

18. Henri Barbusse, *Under Fire*, (New York, NY: E. P. Dutton, 1917).

19. Patrick MacGill, *The Great Push*, (New York, NY: Gosset and Dunlap, 1916).

20. Stephen E. Ambrose, *The Wild Blue*, (New York, NY: Simon & Schuster, 2001).

21. During the World War I discussion, we focused on the foot soldiers. For the World War II discussion, we will focus on airmen.

22. Esther W. Bare, *The Ancestry and the Descendants of Walter Clement Wilson and Amanda Melvina Snethen Wilson,*(Knoxville, TN: Tennessee Valley Publishing, 1991).

23. Fred Nichol, *An Odyssey of a Young Fighter Pilot*, (Knoxville, TN: Tennessee Valley Publishing, 1998).

24. Ray Zuker, *Pearl Harbor Remembered*, (Knoxville, TN: Tennessee Valley Publishing, 1994). Ray Zuker passed away in 2001.

25. Ibid.

26. Col. Landon G. Cox, Sr. acquired a copy of *Adolph Hitler,* written in German, while stationed in Germany following World War II. Sanctioned by the German National Socialist Party, the book was published and printed in 1936, and became a bestseller in Germany. This historically fascinating book was preserved and translated into English in 1999 by the efforts of Gene McLin of Seymour, Tennessee. Information about *Adolph Hitler* is also available at http://www.calvinedu/academic.

27. Ibid.

28. Ibid.

29. Ibid.

30. Ibid.

31. The Cape (short for Cape Canaveral) is located on Florida's Atlantic coast and is now known as Kennedy Space Flight Center.

32. Quote by Charles Caleb Colton (1780-1832), *War and Peace, Principles and Death*, http://brightpath.hypermart.abx.

33. America's Promise is an alliance of 500 organizations and nearly 500 communities across America. Its' mission is to mobilize people from every part of American life to build the character and strengthen the competence of the nations' youth.

34. Charles R. Darwin, (1809-1882), *The Origin of Species*, (Chicago, IL: Encyclopaedia Britannica, Inc., 1952).

35. Sigmund Freud, (1856-1939), *The Major Works of Freud*, (Chicago, IL: Encyclopaedia Britannica, Inc., 1952).

36. Konrad Lorenz, *On Aggression*, (New York, NY: Harcourt, Brace & World, 1966).

37. Robert Ardrey, *African Genesis*, (New York, NY: Atheneum, 1961).

38. Raymond Dart, *Adventures with the Missing Link*, (New York, NY: Harper & Row, 1959).

39. Desmond Morris, *The Naked Ape*, (New York, NY: McGraw Hill, 1967).

40. Ashley Montagu, *The Nature of Human Aggression*, (England: Oxford University Press, 1976).

41. Ibid.

42. John Douglas and Mark Olshaker, *Mindhunter*, (New York, NY: Pocketbooks, 1995). During his twenty-five year FBI career, John Douglas was agent in charge of the FBI behavioral science and investigative unit. Douglas was instrumental in the apprehension of a number of serial killers. He was one of the first to use profiling techniques, using lessons learned from past killers.

43. Total abortions from 1973 through 1998 were 38,010,378. (Based on numbers and estimates reported by the Alan Guttmacher Institute 1973-1996, with NRLC estimates of 1,365,730 for 1997 and 1998).

44. Quote by Joan Baez at http://brainyquote.com/quotes.

45. Number derived from the U.S. Census Bureau's IDB Summary Demographic Data for countries of the world. Approximately 70% of the United States' population is now over 19 years of age. http://www.census.gov/cgi-bin/ipc/idbsum.

Five

Blowin' in the Wind[1]

(Government)

The answer my friend is blowin' in the wind. The winds of change constantly sweep across the face of our planet. They change our geography, our populations, our surroundings, our needs; indeed, our wants and our expectations. As a result, our governments require revision to keep pace. Even so, America's Declaration of Independence sings out as gloriously today, as it did when written over 200 years ago:

> We hold these Truths to be self-evident, that all men are created equal, that they are endowed by their Creator with certain unalienable Rights, that among these are Life, Liberty, and the Pursuit of Happiness—That to secure these Rights, Governments are instituted among Men, deriving their just Powers from the Consent of the Governed, that whenever any Form of Government becomes destructive of these Ends, it is the Right of the People to alter or to abolish it, and institute new Government, laying its Foundation on such Principles, and organizing its Powers in such Form, as to them shall seem most likely to effect their Safety and Happiness.

The phrase "all men are created equal" isn't accurate because each of us are created different not equal, although we are created with great similarities. In the sense that we all are endowed with certain unalienable rights,[2] we should be endowed equally even though the dumbest lout knows that we are not, and I suppose this is what Thomas Jefferson meant or hoped.

The twenty-first century ushers in an American federal government that badly needs revision. It is axiomatic that those least governed, *if* safe from their fellows and through their labor, their basic needs of food, water, air and shelter are met—most enjoy life, liberty, and the pursuit of happiness. This is so, in spite of the largeness of the "if" factor. Least governed is, in fact, synonymous with liberty. But, both of our major political parties (Democrat and Republican) have moved further and further away from the least governmental principle envisioned by our founding fathers and spelled out in our constitution. A brief review of world-government history, especially the hectic twentieth century that has been filled with wars and killing discussed in the previous chapter, will illustrate why America has evolved from a republic with minimal government to a liberal, almost socialistic democracy. A democracy where Uncle Sam or some government regulation controls so much of our lives and has us headed directly toward national bankruptcy.

♪♪ History of Government ♪♪

The six independent civilizations of early history [Babylon, Egypt, India, China, Mexico (Aztecs) and Peru (Incas)] were all ruled by a single despot who had absolute power over their subjects. By the time the twentieth century dawned there were about fifty sovereign nations,[3] but a number of these were empires (British, Russian, French, German, etc.) that controlled countries across the world. Monarchy had become the prevalent form of government, and most of the world was ruled from Europe where the kings were often related. In the previous century the number of sovereign states was reduced. These states had either joined larger nation-states or been conquered by an imperialist power. There were few places in the world that had not been gobbled up by an empire—at least on the maps. In 1900, 50 percent of the world's population was governed by monarchs, about 20 percent (mostly in our Western Hemisphere) were governed by democracies and 30 percent (mostly in Africa) had no central government or their governments were in transition.[4] While the *Communist Manifesto* was written in 1848 and the communist germ was being spread, before 1900, communism had not yet infected a single country.

The world order began to unravel during the second decade of the twentieth century. By 1912, the Emperor of China was replaced by a quasi-democratic coalition and the assassination of the Crown Prince of Austria-Hungary launched World War I. When the smoke cleared, the world had lost three more of its most powerful monarchies—Russia in 1917, then Germany and Austria in 1918. Other oppressed nationalities declared their independence during this decade, and democracies replaced monarchies as the dominant form of government among the world's sovereign nations. By 1920 approximately 25 percent of the world's population were governed by democracies, 10 percent were governed by communists, and only 5 percent were governed by monarchies. ***Thus, in the space of two decades, the world had transformed its governmental structure beyond recognition!***

Although democracy was now the leading form of world government, a couple of new forms of government emerged in the post-World War I era to challenge it. Russia interrupted years of chaos with a communist government that attempted to level the extremes of rich and poor by bringing the entire economy under state control. In Italy, the Fascist Party came to power on the promise of full employment while restoring the lost glories of the nation by subordinating the individual needs to the needs of all the people, the state and the leader.

The "sweet" promise of communism to the average person is to take wealth away from the rich and distribute it for the benefit of all. This includes: abolition of property in land and application of all rents of land to public purposes; a heavy progressive or graduated income tax; abolition of all rights of inheritance; confiscation of the property of all emigrants and rebels; centralization of credit in the banks of the state; equal obligation of all to work; and free education for all children in public schools.

The *Communist Manifesto* proclaims that when force and all production has been concentrated in the hands of the vast association of the whole nation, the public power will lose its political character. Political power is merely the organized power of one class for oppressing another. When the workers or proletariat during its contest with the bourgeoisie is compelled, by means of a revolution, to make itself the ruling class, (and, as such, sweeps away by force the old conditions of production), then it will, along with these conditions, have swept away the conditions for the existence of class antagonisms and of classes generally. Thereby, it will have abolished its own supremacy as a class. In place of the old bourgeois society, with its classes and class antagonisms, there will emerge an association in which the free development of each is the condition for the free development of all. To spice it up, free love is thrown in. This all sounds too good to be true and some very painful experiments in the world arena have shown the *Communist Manifesto* to be heavily permeated with "idealistic crap." The communist experiments have shown that it is impossible to legislate or command unequals to become equals. Their experiments also have demonstrated that the proletariat can't govern any better than the bourgeois.

When the global economy collapsed in 1929, well-established democracies survived the crisis by instituting subsidies and unemployment relief and by moving toward socialism. But, the collapse of the economy destroyed the credibility of democracy. Thus, voters in many countries turned toward parties with more radical agendas that promised employment and worker utopia like the Communists and the Fascists. In Germany, the corporate and military elites supported the Nazi Party as did a plurality of the voters; therefore in 1933, Adolf Hitler became Chancellor of Germany.

Speaking of corporate elites, the captains of industry, with their wealth and influence were the real power brokers of the twentieth century and most of them were not too concerned about allegiance to one country or government ideal. Their allegiance was to accumulating wealth and they were happy to sell their goods to either or all combatants of a conflict. For example, IBM had offices in Europe (including Germany) and continued to do business with the Third Reich, both before and long after the United States of America had declared war on Germany. Through the use of IBM automation and support, Hitler was able to facilitate the purge of the Jewish population.[5]

Imperialism steadily lost power across Asia and Africa. In 1931, the British reorganized their Empire into a newer Commonwealth which granted independence to the dominions. Then, in 1932 and 1936, respectively, the British set the ancient nations of Iraq and Egypt free. In 1935, after a mass protest campaign led by Mohandas Gandhi, the British also agreed to a larger measure of self-government for India.

Some countries had missed out on the nineteenth-century conquests and joined the territory-grabbing bullies. But, the civilized world was becoming more opposed to bully tactics, so when Japan invaded Manchuria (1931) the rest of the world condemned them with strong rhetoric. Unfortunately, there was little active support of Manchuria. But, when Germany started to overrun and absorb its smaller neighbors (Austria and Czechoslovakia in 1938 and Poland in 1939), the Western Powers realized the only way to stop Hitler was by force.

Once World War II was in full swing, nations quickly began to disappear. Between 1937 and 1942, fourteen nations lost their sovereignty. Ten nations—Austria, Belgium, Czechoslovakia, Denmark, France, Greece, the Netherlands, Norway, Poland and Yugoslavia—were conquered by the Germans. Albania was annexed by Italy, while Estonia, Latvia and Lithuania became part of the

Soviet Union. Almost one-fourth of the world's nations vanished for the duration of World War II!

At the end of World War II most of the conquered nations were restored, but their political structures were wrecked. In Eastern Europe, the nations which had been occupied by the Soviet Union attempted to establish multiparty democracies, but Soviet-sponsored communist parties promptly gained the upper hand.

War losses made it difficult for the Imperialists to keep their colonies under control. Also, because the winners of World War II had fought to preserve freedom, the Allied Imperialists seemed obligated to grant freedom to their own colonies. By 1950, almost twenty new nations had emerged, and imperialist colonialism was no longer a significant world-government force. The defeat of the Nazi's regime essentially eradicated Fascism. The western Allies organized a stable democracy in Western Germany; Japan was given a democratic constitution; and Italy's new government was democratic. In a few places, forms of fascism lingered under the likes of Franco (Spain) and Peron (Argentina).

For the second time in the twentieth century, the world had transformed its governmental structure beyond recognition! With the fall of Fascism, the rise of Communism and the independence of several major colonies, over half of humanity had made a decisive break with their past forms of government.

My friend and coconspirator, Andy Wright, a staunch liberal Democrat, tells me this "revolving-door soap opera" of past governments isn't brief, as advertised, and is beginning to bore him. Moreover, he believes it has little bearing on the governmental issues facing us in the twenty-first century. But, lessons of the past, even abbreviated ones, are important. So, we will continue retracing the essence of dynamic world governments for the last half of the twentieth century.

By the 1950s, Communism infected a third of humanity and democracy regained its prominence, governing almost one-half of the world's population. These competing philosophies of government dominated world politics for several decades. The Cold War between the superpowers, Russia and the United States, was in full swing. The competition dictated the world alliances that formed and the borders that divided countries like Germany, Korea and Vietnam.

Although there are isolated cases, such as the French fighting to hang onto Indochina and Algeria, imperialism continued to lose favor. In 1955, there were only five independent nations in the continent of Africa. In the 1960s, forty-five new nations emerged. Imperialism was, for all practical purposes, eliminated in Africa. In most cases, the colonial powers released control to new nations that weren't prepared to govern themselves. The general formula was: a new constitution; a quick election; a new flag; then an unsuccessful struggle to make the new government work. Next came a coup d'état from a military junta.

Surprisingly, democracy hit a twentieth-century low in the 1970s. Whether this decline is measured in percentages of countries or in terms of total population, the trend was a serious downturn for democracy. In terms of total population, the post-colonial low of about 20 percent occurred in 1977, after Indira Gandhi declared a state of emergency and suspended civil rights in India. What was happening? Many democracies failed due to military coups and communism. Wherever possible, communism was rammed down the throats of those not killed in bloody purges,[6] mostly in China, Russia, Korea, Cambodia, and Vietnam. In Africa, many of the new nations staggered from coup to coup under a brutal succession of military despots.

These despots rose to power based on local circumstances, but under the corrupting influence of the Cold War. During the Cold War, both the East and West preferred stable allies. However, it was better to have an armed despot as an ally, rather than have a despot aligned with the opposition. Although, the West may have had qualms about supporting despots, they knew communists didn't. This led to often strange, "few-questions-asked," blind support of Juntas by the superpowers.

Until 1989, the decade of the 1980s saw few changes in the distribution of the structure of world governments. In spite of a lot of "saber rattling," there were no significant changes in the communist-democracy balance of power. And, relatively speaking, there were very few major outbreaks of war. Then, in the final months of the decade, the communists surrendered power throughout eastern Europe. The collapse of the Soviet Union resulted in two surges of democracy, the first in the fall of 1989 when the communists surrendered their monopoly of power in their satellite nations, and the second in the summer of 1991 when the constituent republics of the Soviet Union seceded. There was a surge in the number of nations as four former communist countries—USSR, Czechoslovakia, Ethiopia and Yugoslavia—ballooned to more than twenty nations.

The communistic world was in shambles and had few resources to allocate, and the western world no longer needed anticommunist thugs. As a result, throughout the Third World, many petty tyrants relinquished their power. Some were killed while others pilfered their national treasuries and scurried like roaches into hiding or found new sanctuaries.

Most Americas were aware of world changes, but few realized that for the *third time in the twentieth century, the world had transformed its governmental structure beyond recognition*! By the late 1990s, four continents (North America, South America, Australia and Europe) were almost entirely democratic. Today democracies are riding high, having survived for the moment the test of time. And, by any measure, the twentieth century imposed a gargantuan test.

The many ups and downs of world governments during the twentieth century are confusing (even with the simplifications piled upon simplifications in this short piece). Figure 1 should help put the chaos of governmental swings into perspective. The data in Figure 1

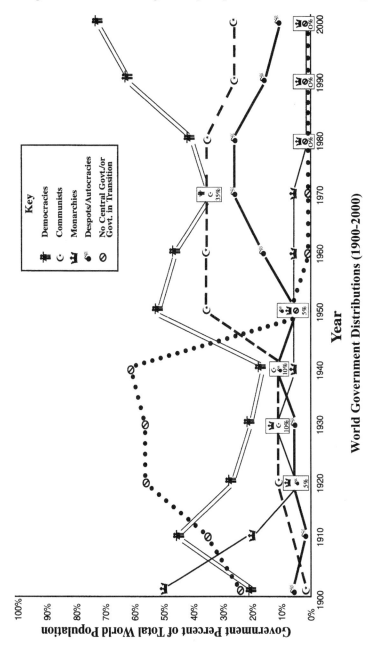

suggest that (1) monarchies are relics of the past; (2) in our era of improved communications not many populations will submit to the rule of an oppressive despot for any extended length of time; and (3) almost all of the countries around the world now have some form of central government. As Figure 1 illustrates, for much of the first half of the twentieth century, approximately 50 percent of the world's population had no stable central government. This was due, in large part, because of China's lack of central governments and their huge population. But The People's Republic of China was formally established by Mao Zedong on 1 October 1949. The communist "Liberation" of 1949 was welcomed by the majority of the *Chinese* people, because for the first time in decades China was ruled by a strong Chinese authority, which reunited the country and settled internal dissensions.[7] Figure 1 also shows that the communistic-government experiment has peaked and suffered a serious decline in terms of world influence. But, as long as China, with its population in excess of 1.2-billion people, remains communistic then communism will be a world force.[8]

As described in the previous chapter, the rise and decline of communism has been accomplished at the cost of many millions of lives and countless atrocities. Democracy in some form is now the choice of government for the majority of the world's six-billion people. Thus, the influence of Thomas Jefferson and America's founding fathers has found few boundaries on this planet. Democracy, the basic form of government in the United States of America since the country's birth, prevails. Approximately 75 percent of the world's sovereign nations, representing approximately two-thirds of the world's population, now have some form of democracy as their government.

Does this mean the best form of government for the world or America is settled? Of course, the answer is no. The winds of change and the complexities of life dictate the "no" answer. Thomas Carlyle[9] told us, correctly, that governments are like a suit of clothes that needs changing from time to time to keep up with the times. It's a marvel that democracy, so closely tailored by our constitution and forefathers, has withstood the sometimes violent winds of change for more than two centuries. And, still these clothes almost fit, wear well, and are nearly in fashion.

The abundant and rich natural resources of America and the character and attitude of our people would have allowed almost any non-oppressive form of government to work in this country, but *democracy has proven its merit*. On the other hand, many citizens of China are perfectly content and happy with their form of government—communism. Desmond Muirhead, who has traveled extensively throughout communist-held countries makes some interesting commentaries about a trip to Fukien, China:[10]

> Wan Tung, our waitress, was natural, graceful and feminine with a full mouth and sparkling eyes. After the long, tiring ride, it was nice to feel this warm and friendly atmosphere. Indeed I found the people of Fukien consistently attractive. The hotel help was clean, fresh-looking, well-dressed and coiffed with neat, attractive faces and a relaxed, uninhibited air about them. This is the indefinable quality induced by the non-competitive aspect of communism. I have also found it in East Germany, Czechoslovakia and parts of Russia. It is the upside of communism and it is too bad this quality of peaceful calm cannot be retained during the inevitable conversion to capitalism. There is none of the clawing greed and materialism we are becoming so used to in the West. A charming vulnerability, and the elusive family values so hollowly requested by our politicians are clearly evident here. There is a patient immobility on the part of a people bound to the land and living out their lives in one place. Home is real and permanent; human relationships widespread and rewarding; interlocking networks of friendships are pervasive. Why can't we get the best of both worlds, I wondered. Surely there is a decent middle way, a political and economic system which has the best of communism and capitalism.

Recently, at the first international conference of the Human Security and Global Governance (HUGG) Project, Mr. Majid Tehranian in his thought provoking speech stated:[11]

> We are at a critical juncture in human history in which the forces of globalization can tip us toward either more humane forms of governance or growing global gaps that will turn the world into islands of riches in oceans of structural poverty, resentment, and violence. The opening of a new century has always served as a symbolic turning point in human history. The twenty-first century is not an exception. The world stands at a historical juncture between the roads to self-destruction and self-renewal. On the one hand, an environmental catastrophe, a nuclear holocaust, a population explosion of unprecedented magnitude, a protracted terrorist war between the rich and poor, armed by conventional and unconventional weapons, a war among ethnic groups (as in the former Soviet Union, Yugoslavia, Iraq, and Lebanon), or among powerful regional blocs (fortress North America vs. fortress Western Europe vs. fortress East Asia), all seem to be distinct possibilities. On the other hand, human achievements in science, technology, telecommunication, education, and social organization have made possible new heights in human civilization. The conquest of ignorance, poverty, and suffering, the achievement of a new harmony among nations and between nature and humanity, and the development of a new sense of world community for the exploration of the outer and inner spaces all seem within reach.

Tehranian's comments neatly summarize the principal earthly challenges of twenty-first century humanity. No matter how strongly we in America feel the need to focus on our internal problems, we can not isolate ourselves from world affairs. Chance, destiny, nature, nurture and our collective will and makeup have made America a world power—the world power! There is no way we can turn our backs on this awesome honor and responsibility. This responsibility will be accommodated by our citizenry, even if eventually it proves to be a factor in our government's downfall.

♬ About Democracy ♬

Democracy, by definition, is a government in which the people hold the ruling power either directly or through elected representatives; i.e., rule by the ruled. Rule by the ruled or ruled by the people for the people becomes extremely complex and fraught with enormous basic problems of agreeing on common goals and administering the actions necessary to achieve these goals. The conditions are aggravated by uninformed voters, powerful special interest groups, world and natural events beyond our control, the biased and false spin of our politicians, and corrupt officials. The complexity often results in the paralysis of meaningful government action. Perhaps this is one of democracy's greatest strengths!

Plato, the wise Greek philosopher, clearly recognized the problems of popular rule and, as a result, favored autocratic rule.[12] But, history (as just outlined) shows that autocratic rule doesn't work over the long term, as well as democracy. A key problem of autocratic rule is that the transfer of power from one leader to the next often requires war. And, no matter how wise one individual is a group's collective wisdom is greater. Under autocratic rule, once a scoundrel is in office the only way to remove him from power is by war and killing. America's founding fathers recognized these fundamental problems of government and instituted some remarkable checks and balances, clearly spelled out in our Constitution. First, they placed handcuffs on our federal government by limiting its powers. Then by establishing the Judicial, Legislative and Executive branches of government, each with a measure of power over the other, they attempted to minimize the opportunity for a "run-away," corrupt governmental branch.

According to the Declaration of Independence we are entitled to "unalienable Rights of Life, Liberty, and the Pursuit of Happiness." To achieve these rights, the Constitution of the United States gave the following powers to congress:[13] collect taxes; borrow money; regulate commerce; establish Rule of Naturalization; establish uniform bankruptcy laws; coin money and provide for punishment of counterfeiters; establish Post Offices and post Roads; protect the rights of Authors and Inventors; Constitute Tribunals inferior to the supreme Court; define and punish Piracies and Felonies committed on the high Seas; declare war, as well as raise, maintain and control an army, navy and militia; and, finally, make laws needed to carry out these powers. Most of the remainder of the constitution deals with the structure and administration of the Judicial, Legislative and Executive branches of the government needed to carry out the foregoing powers and the delineation of State and individual rights.

America's Constitution reveals four basic aims for our federal government: (1) provide national defense; (2) preserve internal peace between states; (3) regulate trade between states and other countries; and (4) establish and maintain foreign relations. Our country adhered to these four aims reasonably well and based its economy and taxed its citizens accordingly, until the Great Depression. President Franklin D. Roosevelt's "New Deal," deservedly, was credited with breaking the Great Depression, but the New Deal also planted the ever-growing cancer of socialistic government spending.

The total economy is made up of two fundamental spending components: (1) federal, state and local government spending (called the government sector), and (2) private sector spending—the part from which growth of national productivity, savings and real incomes depend. Figure 2 shows an eighty-year history of the trends of these components. The government-spending sector has grown faster than the economy, while the private sector steadily has eroded. Now, at the dawn of the new millennium, America is a more socialistic, government-spending-dependent nation than ever before. As Michael Hodges suggests,[14] look carefully at this chart. It's quite easy to understand and tells a powerful story about government growth.

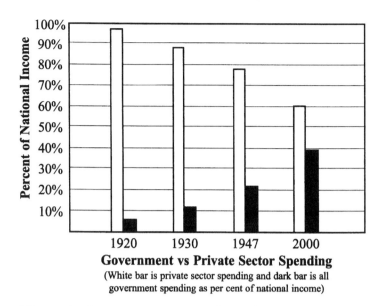

Government vs Private Sector Spending
(White bar is private sector spending and dark bar is all
government spending as per cent of national income)

Figure 2. Government and Private Spending Trends

Nowhere in America's Constitution does it suggest that the federal government should be involved in the education, medical care, establishment of unemployment or retirement funds, or other entitlements for its citizens. Yet, the three branches of our federal government have banded together to subvert the Constitution without changing it. This is so, notwithstanding all of the false rhetoric about close adherence to the Constitution by our politicians and court justices. When taking their oath of office, all American presidents, since Herbert Hoover, *have stretched the truth* when they swore to uphold the Constitution, because they have known America's Constitution does not give the federal government the power to tax its citizens or incur debt to provide general entitlements for education, medical care and retirement.

Regardless of the language of their constitutions,[15] governments should minimize the extremes between poverty and affluence within a population. If this isn't achieved or at least perceived as being achieved by the "have nots," at some point the "have nots" will rebel and take by force enough from the "haves" to meet their wants.[16]

Most assuredly this will happen when the "have nots" sufficiently outnumber the "haves" and an individual or group of organizers channel the dissension of the "have nots." This ebb and flow of wealth in every population and every government is as real and relentless as ocean tides. Without regard to the form of government, when the delicate economic balance swings too far, there is hell to pay in the form of civil disobedience, riots, resurrections, armed conflicts and war. The "haves" understand the fundamentals of this flow and attempt to share enough wealth to keep the "have nots" placated.

This gap in wealth that separates the rich and poor, according to David Landes, is the single greatest problem and danger facing the world of the third millennium; it supercedes the threat of nuclear war, overpopulation and environmental deterioration. Of course, all of these problem areas are interlaced. Landes believes that the disparity between rich and poor has increased significantly and continues to increase. His research shows the gap between income per head in the richest industrial nation, say Switzerland, and the poorest country, Mozambique, is about 400-to-1. Two hundred and fifty years ago the gap between the world's richest and poorest was about 5-to-1.[17]

The importance of economics and the equitable production, distribution and consumption of wealth cannot be overstated. This is the underpinning of societies. Most individuals who have enough wealth for themselves and their family to live comfortably now and in the foreseeable future, and who face no external threat to their wealth or well-being will reside happily under any form of government.

Look at the key words in America's Constitution's list of powers to congress: tax, coin money, borrow money, and regulate commerce. Our Constitution reveals the amazing insight and depth of understanding that our founding fathers had regarding the relationships between individuals and their government and wealth. They understood clearly that a reasonable degree of economic freedom and equality is essential to a civil society. The fair and equitable production of wealth and its distribution and consumption are the bedrock of any successful society or government.

As we enter the new millennium, America's economic plight is a confusing, frightening, seething minefield. Because of the intertwining relationship between economics and government, our government is also a frightening minefield. One wrongly exploded mine could cause a chain reaction that will make the Great Depression look like a *minor dent*. Debt, size of government, and fair distribution of wealth (citizen entitlements) are three of the most dangerous mines—all intermingled with a complexity that makes quantum mechanics seem simple. The financial minefield fundamentals cannot be controlled by the Federal Reserve, personified by Allen Greenspan, lowering or raising interest rates by a fraction of a percent here and there to coax soft landings. That's like trying to steer a field of icebergs with a piece of twine. This is an illusion that has worked only because the financial fundamentals and public acceptance have stayed within a range that perpetuates the illusion. One doesn't have to be Edgar Cayce (the psychic) to predict that big financial troubles await us in the twenty-first century. Our economic plight has not been caused by a series of natural and world disasters. Rather it has evolved through the selfishness of special interest groups, the enormous appetites of our citizens, the complexities of our internal and international responsibilities, the lack of vision and fortitude of our elected officials and our government (we the people) living beyond our collective means.

♭♭ Spend, Spend, Spend ♭♭

During the first 200 years of our nation's existence, we spent less than $350 billion on debt interest, but we have exceeded that amount annually since 1997. In fact, for the decade of the 1990s our annual national-debt interest payment averaged more than $300 billion. In 2000, the interest on our federal debt of $5,674,000,000,000 ($5.67 trillion) was $362.1 billion. Putting this in perspective, our 2000 gross-debt interest expenditure is more than 20 percent of our total outlay and exceeded the combined cost of our giant military, the Justice Department, the Labor Department, the Executive Office, the Commerce Department, the International Assistance Program (foreign aid), the Federal Communications Commission, the National Science Foundation and all independent agencies. Take away our medical and social security entitlements and Americans could finance our federal government with the money now spent on debt interest. Thomas Jefferson summarized his views on financial debt as follows: "I place economy among the first and most important virtues, and public debt as the greatest of dangers. To preserve our independence, we must not let our rulers load us with perpetual debt." In spite of this and countless other warnings, our leaders (with voter support) systematically have loaded us with a monstrous perpetual debt.

Fiscal year 2000 ended with the highest dollar debt in U.S. history, although there were incessant claims of a "surplus" by the Bill Clinton administration. Fiscal year 2001 ended with us $133 billion deeper in debt than fiscal year 2000. The big question is *How* can the federal government claim a surplus when the total federal debt increased to another record high? Michael Hodges has the answer:[18] By siphoning-off and spending trust fund surpluses which don't belong to the general government, just like a son spending his mother's retirement account for his own consumption while claiming he, himself, is running a surplus. Hodges elaborates further:

> Some political leaders bragged to the general public "we ran more than $100 billion budget surplus in both calendar year 1998 and 1999." We are misled to believe the federal government cut general spending and produced general government surpluses, reducing total federal debt. But, that's 'smoke & mirrors.' The truth is that they really ran an operational deficit (not a surplus) of $282 billion combined in those two years, since total federal debt increased $120 billion in calendar 1998 and increased another $162 billion in calendar year 1999. And, the data shows that again, in Fiscal Year 2000, the federal government further increased total debt to another record high, while of course again claiming a surplus.

One of the trust funds which we siphoned enough to clean it out was the Social Security Trust Fund, from which we got over half of the $428 billion we needed to cover operational deficits during 1998-1999. We recognize there are laws in every state against private sector firms siphoning-off their pension trust funds for non-pension spending for consumption and credit by companies, but our federal government plays by different rules.

So that extra FICA money workers are now paying is in effect a hidden income tax to enable the federal government to spend it on other stuff without counting that spending in the budget deficit calculations. In fact, if our Treasury Department's data are correct, to date the government has siphoned-off and consumed (on other stuff) $2 trillion from trusts, including from other trust funds such as highway trust, railroad trust, unemployment trust, etc.). On a per-capita basis, this works out to $7,500 per man, woman and child, or $30,000 per family of four.

But, our honest government officials have placed nonmarketable IOUs in the trusts for the record. The Federal Reserve Bank doesn't even recognize those internal IOUs as official debt because they are not marketable and because there is no plan to pay it off. If you borrowed against your own (or your mother's) private pension and spent it all to pay for your current lifestyle what would be available come old age? Well, that's what our federal government has done with our trust funds. (If a private firm did that to its employee pension fund its officers would go to jail—it's against the law in every state) And, our grandchildren are going to have to cope with the resulting mess.

You will note that I use the word "siphon-off" for spending trust fund surpluses for non-trust fund purposes, while Senator Ernest Hollings calls it "looting the trust," and Mr. Bartlett (formerly of Treasury) calls it "raiding the trust." Take your pick.

Therefore, while Clinton's liberal establishment was lauding three straight years of surpluses, they failed to tell Americans that this was a distortion of the books, because during this time the administration was raiding the government pension funds, a practice they learned from previous administrations—both Republicans and Democrats.

Our government economic system has evolved into an elaborate quazi-ponzi scheme. A ponzi scheme is an illegal investment scheme in which returns are paid to earlier investors, entirely out of money paid into the scheme by later investors.[19] A ponzi scheme ultimately fails because there is a finite and limited number of potential participants and no new wealth is created. Like early participants in a ponzi scheme, those Americans who have retired in the twentieth century with social security benefits far exceeding what they paid in, receive much of their benefits from later participants. As currently configured, there is little doubt that the social security system will self-destruct before the middle of the twenty-first century.

President Clinton's skill with language and the smooth spin of his liberal propaganda experts convinced millions that he—who by any measure of honesty or morality was a national disgrace—was good for this country. Under his leadership, there was a measure of prosperity, especially in the important areas of unemployment rates and inflation control, but the abysmal record shows that during his eight years in office the national debt ballooned another $1.26 trillion. While technological growth fueled part of this prosperity, too much of it was based on our government increasing the money supply and government and personal borrowing which history will show was false prosperity. Clinton added more national debt on his watch than all U.S. presidents from George Washington through Jimmy Carter combined. Although this didn't measure up to the red-ink ($3.4 trillion) of the preceding Reagan-Bush years, Reagan and Bush were pikers compared to Clinton when it came to raiding the trusts.

Notwithstanding the so-called economic boom, or perhaps because of it, both consumer borrowing and outstanding mortgage debt in the public sector rose more than 50 percent in the last five years of the Clinton administration, to a record $6.7 trillion and $1.6 trillion, respectively.[20] So, in addition to our government debt we

Americans started the new millennium burdened with tremendous personal debt. Even if we make a mockery of these statistics and back out the growth rate of the U.S. economy, there is still a debt increase exceeding the rate of economic expansion by more than 15 percent. According to the Federal Reserve, there is $4000 of consumer debt for each man, woman, and child in the United States. All of this debt adds up to a society that is saturated under the weight of things that we acquire today but plan to pay for in the future. It shouldn't be a surprise that the number of U.S. bankruptcy filings have also soared to new records during this time frame (1996-2000), averaging about 1.3 million per year. What is a surprising shame, is the number of bankruptcies during this period exceeded the number of college bachelor degrees awarded.[21] In the last decade of the twentieth century, more than eleven-million bankruptcies were declared by American citizens and businesses. This equates to a tremendous amount of psychological stress in the lives of millions of Americans.

Collectively, as of September 2001, we owed about $5.8 trillion in federal government debt.[22] But, to whom do we owe it? The largest portion, about 48%, is owed to the Federal Reserve Bank and to other government accounts. This part of the national debt is owed by one part of the government to another. These are the unmarketable IOUs that Michael Hodges clarified for us.[23] The remaining 52 percent of the debt, roughly $3 trillion, is privately held. About 57 percent of this privately held debt is scattered among American private and institutional owners (such as insurance companies), while about 43 percent of the private held debt ($1.2 trillion) is now owed to foreign or international investors. This is another disturbing trend, as only 5 percent of our privately held debt was in the hands of foreign interest in 1992.

Japanese investors now control about 28 percent of this foreign-held portion of America's national debt. Within fifty-five years after their World War II loss, Americans now owe the Japanese more than $330 billion and pay them an annual interest of approximately $24 billion, which is about five times more than America now pays for our military construction activities. This is an astounding financial turnabout that undoubtedly upsets the living veterans today who fought the Japanese in World War II. The joke that the Japanese couldn't whip Americans in war, so now they are "buying us" contains more reality than humor.

Interest payments on the national debt do not buy Americans much, as we know from our personal debts. These interest payments don't help us reduce poverty, maintain national highways, fund military or space exploration. What these payments do do (pun intended) is to line the pockets of individuals and financial institutions affluent enough to hold massive amounts of our federal bonds or fiduciaries. We must gain control of our runaway debt, before we can seriously begin the business of defusing the financial minefield.

While some public concern has been directed toward the growing national debt, much less attention has been devoted to the growing debts of state and local governments in America, which arc also at an all-time high of about $1.3 trillion. Constrained by federal tax laws and lower credit ratings, local government decision-makers have more trouble securing economical debt financing than their state and federal government counterparts.

Governments use debt financing to provide water and sewer lines, roads, bridges, power plants, and other needed infrastructure and economic development activities. Borrowing for long-term capital projects, such as these, is justified by the "pay-as-you-use" principle that holds those who receive the benefits of the projects should pay for their provision. Public debt issued by any government, as with individual debt, represents a shifting of financial burdens from one point in time to a later period. When borrowing is used to finance projects that will have long-lasting benefits stretching over the length of the repayment period, that seems a reasonable tradeoff. But, if the debt-servicing costs are greater than project benefits, or if the amortization schedule does not coincide with the project benefit schedule, then government officials are making risky decisions. Too often, policymakers resort to debt financing to provide for public projects rather than forego such projects or fund them on a "pay-as-you-go" or cash-reserve basis. In this way, public benefits may be delivered (or at least promised) in the short-run, while costs of the projects may be deferred until later when future taxpayers bear the burden of retiring the debt.

When any American enters the work force, he or she had better be prepared to "Saddle Up." And this doesn't mean putting a saddle on anyone except themselves, because they will carry a heavy-debt load. The age distribution of America's population shows that approximately 30 percent of our population is less than nineteen-years old and approximately 13 percent is more than sixty-five years old and retired.[24] Factor in an unemployment rate of approximately 5 percent and, at any point in time, about 6 percent for retirees and young people in the workforce. This leaves about 60 percent of our population working and carrying the government debt burdens.[25] Thus, when one becomes a member of this elite (gainfully employed and/or tax paying) group, they now shoulder the responsibility of $5.8-trillion national debt and $1.3-trillion state and local government liability. Based on these statistics, each American worker must shoulder approximately $43,000 in government debt, when they enter the workforce.[26] Andy Wright advises me that all this number crunching is so confusing that the point being made becomes lost. If it is, just remember two numbers—$5.8-trillion national debt and America's population which is approximately 275 million. Thus, each citizen of the United States of America: man, woman and child (including those in diapers) owes approximately $21,000 in federal government debt.[27]

Ross Perot, a successful businessman and U.S. presidential candidate in 1992 and 1996, proposed several methods of cutting federal expenditures that included: cutting the defense budget to meet its current mission which doesn't include the capability of fighting World War III; ending the subsidization of the rich; controlling run away entitlement costs; increasing tobacco and gasoline taxes; increasing IRS collections; and getting our allies to take on their fair share of the financial burden of the world's collective security.[28] Perot's vision for America's government was based on the underlying principles that all citizens are needed in the rebuilding of America, we can't keep living beyond our means, the size of government must be permanently reduced, and our greatest challenge is economic competition. Perhaps, Perot was not the "man of the hour," nor were his proposed solutions more than "band-aids." However, he had America's fundamental problems in focus and his recommended solutions were far more constructive than the spend and tax and raid-the-trusts policies of both the Republican and Democratic parties.

Controlling America's Democracy

The Democratic Party or the Republican Party has had uninterrupted control of the White House and Congress since 1852. For the past 150 years, the White House, Senate and House of Representatives have been battled for, traded back and forth and shared almost equally between these two parties.

Abraham Lincoln's Republican Party, when founded in 1854, stood for limited federal government. Republicans still contend that government should be decentralized and that the federal government must not get in the way of state and local officials, because local governments are much more capable of promoting the best interests of their constituents than a far-removed central government. Democrats, on the other hand, believe there are many endeavors which are beyond the capability of private citizens and local governments to perform efficiently and, therefore, the federal government should collect money from the people and accomplish these tasks. Democrats consistently affirm their support of underprivileged citizens i.e., the poor, minority groups, the elderly, and women. It is ironical that about 90 percent of the African-American population voted for the Democratic Party in our last election when it was the Republican Party, less than 150 years ago, that was formed to secure their emancipation. But, politics are noted for their unbounded flexibility and changing alliances, when the outcome of an election hangs in the balance. Because winning the election is how a party controls our democracy.

The two most prominent minor voices in the last presidential election were the Green Party and the Libertarian Party.[29,30] The Green Party believes that every issue must be seen from an ecological or environmental perspective. They promote a direct democracy rather than a representative one, a socialist-like redistribution of wealth, nonviolence and nonintervention in foreign affairs and the promotion of the poor and working classes to the point where self-government becomes the rule. The Libertarian Party embraces a free-market economy, personal freedom and civil liberties. The freedom of the individual from governmental interference is the foundation of the Libertarian movement, and it strongly opposes a large and powerful federal government. This party endorses large tax cuts for all Americans, placing control of and responsibility for lives of individuals in the hands of the citizens themselves. Libertarians also believe that people should have the freedom to conduct their lives however they wish, providing that they do not intrude on or violate the rights of others.

These and other minor voices are getting louder in America. And, they are on solid common ground since so much needs to be changed in our present form of democracy. Thoughtful Americans know there is a major need for changes in our country. They know, also, until some catastrophic event, comparable to the Great Depression occurs that change is not likely to take place in either the Democratic or Republican Party. Undoubtably, there is a large bloc of American voters who believe that things aren't yet broken, thus they are persuaded by the "if it ain't broke, don't fix or change it" philosophy.

But when a citizen now raises questions about the problems and conduct of our government, our representatives look around until they find someone to blame. On the federal level, the President blames

Congress, and Congress blames the President. Republicans blame Democrats, Democrats blame Republicans, and both parties blame the bureaucracy. This same process is repeated at the state and local levels.

William Simon, former U.S. Treasurer, reports that the businessman's standard of efficacy is a solution to the problem, and the more responsive he is to external reality, the better. The bureaucrat's standard procedure is obedience to the rules and respect for the vested interests of the hierarchy, however unyielding of a solution. That is why bureaucracies so often produce nothing but wastepaper and destroy the productive institutions they supervise. Bureaucrats are actually the first victims of their own regulations, the primary effect of which is to inhibit individual thought and personal responsibility.[31]

Access to government is overwhelming. There are at least 80,000 units of government in the United States and our Federal Government is only one. Other units in America include states, counties, cities, towns, villages, and districts with the independent ability to raise taxes and incur debt for schools, waters systems, sewer lines, roads, fire departments and similar functions. There are approximately 17-million public sector employees. At the appointed policy levels, there are another million individuals.[32] As Walter A. Burien, Jr. reports "growth in government over the last 30 years has been obscene. The composite liquid investment held by composite government is in excess of 35-trillion dollars. One-third held by federal and two-thirds held by state and local government. Gross composite government income for 1999 was about 8.5-trillion dollars while the entire pretax personal gross income for all Americans (Bill Gates to the paper boy, including all government employees) was about 8.2-trillion dollars."[33]

Andy Wright is screaming in my ear: "Stop, Stop, Stop! You're driving me crazy with doomsday slanted, big-number and boring statistics that prove nothing." Andy is partially correct. There are alternate ways of looking at every issue and every mystery. A number of very bright individuals believe our outrageous national debt is okay. They believe debt is harmless, even desirable, if it is successfully employed to achieve growth. They believe we should stop worrying and debating about debt and focus our energy on sustaining our true ally, which is our ***economic growth***.[34,35]

Steven Conover explains this concept in understandable language:[36]

Borrowing (or lending) money for good investments is sound financial practice; ask any banker. It's perfectly okay to borrow money for the following investments: the car that gets me to work, the new store that helps chain stores grow more profitable, the school that educates my kids, and the aircraft carrier that defends my country.

Good investments generate benefits into the future. My new car gets me to work for several years. A new store increases chain stores' profits for many years. A new school helps to educate our kids year after year. And, year after year, an aircraft carrier gives foreigners a big incentive not to try to take my car or other possessions away from me. All of these things are good investments, and borrowing for good investments is sound financial practice. Investment induces growth. Those are the two most important words in this discussion, so I'll repeat them: "INVESTMENT" and "GROWTH." Growth means to get wealthier. Investment is an attempt to induce growth.

All of us invest: I do, my city and county do, businesses do, and (last but not least) my federal government does. We all invest, attempting to make the future better than it would have been otherwise.

Some investment attempts succeed; those are the good investments. Some fail; those are the bad investments. Nobody's perfect—not me, not my local government, not businesses, not the feds—but if we all keep making more good investments than bad ones, we'll succeed in achieving growth in the aggregate.

Conover has assembled a number of stand-alone quotes from individuals that effectively support the position that growth is more important than debt. A few of these quotes follow:[37]

> Dr. Rick Boettger—Every single "luxury" we enjoy above the level of raw food and primitive shelter we owe to the natural concentration of work upon the most efficient producers, and the eventual re-employment of displaced workers on new, previously un-imagined projects.

> Steve Forbes—You can't cut your way to prosperity, you've got to grow the economy.

> George Gilder—Volatile and shifting ideas, not heavy and entrenched establishments, constitute the source of wealth.... Debt is dangerous only when assets are declining in value and income is shrinking.... The means of production of entrepreneurs are not land, labor, or capital, but minds and hearts. The single most important question for the future of America is how we treat our entrepreneurs. If we smear, harass, overtax, and over regulate them, our liberal politicians will be amazed how quickly the wealth of America flees to other countries.... The truly greedy seek comfort and security first. They seek goods and clout they have not earned. Because the best and safest way to gain unearned pay is to get the state to take it from others, greed leads, as by an invisible hand, toward ever more government action—to socialism, not capitalism.... The key to growth is quite simple: creative individuals with money. The cause of stagnation is similarly clear: depriving creative individuals of financial power.

> Soichiro Honda—We do not make something because the demand, the market is there. With our technology, we can create demand, we can create the market.

> Jane Jacob—Our ancestors expanded their economies by adding new kinds of work. So do we. Innovating economies expand and develop.... The emergence of new products in place of old ones is absolutely necessary to economic life; otherwise the planet would long since have been ruined from excessive, monotonous

exploitation of the same few resources.... Developing economies are all too ruthless to nature, but their depredations do not compare in destructiveness to those of stagnating and stagnant economies where people exploit too narrow a range of resources too heavily and monotonously for too long.... The primary economic conflict, I think, is between people whose interests are with already well-established economic activities, and those whose interests are with the emergence of new economic activities.... The only possible way to keep open the economic opportunities for new activities is for a "third force" to protect their weak and still incipient interests. Only governments can play this economic role.

Paul Zane Pilzer—Technology determines our supply of existing physical resources by determining both the efficiency with which we use resources and our ability to find, obtain, distribute, and store them.... Keynes was wrong in thinking that people's needs were basically fixed and absolute—that they were capable of eventually being met, at which point demand would be satiated.

Nathan Rosenberg—Growth is, of course, a form of change, and growth is impossible when change is not permitted. And successful change requires a large measure of freedom to experiment . . . The great majority of societies, past and present, have not allowed it. Nor have they escaped from poverty.

Ritter and Silber—Debt has to be viewed in context, in relation to the assets behind the debt and to the ability of debtors to service the debt.

Charles Van Doren—With all its stress, anxiety, and threat of dangers never before known, it is modern life that is simpler and easier, not the life of the past.

A final quote (and Andy Wright's favorite) of Conover's group is from the renowned philosopher and hall-of-fame, New York Yankee catcher, Yogi Berra, whose statement went far beyond debt, economic growth and government issues, when he said "I wish I had an answer to that, because I'm getting tired of answering that question."

So, the financial well-being of America boils down to a contest between perpetual debt and perpetual growth! If growth outpaces our debt and interest, then American prosperity can continue to tread the ever-deepening ocean of debt. Only the strongest proponent of growth, can, with any degree of comfort, claim that growth will continue indefinitely to outpace our staggering debt. Time and future circumstances will be the final arbitrator, because the answers lie beyond any man's knowledge. And, probably that is as it should be. *Sweet mystery!*

Notwithstanding, America's problems of debt, big government, unfair distribution of wealth, and the breakdown of family values, we Americans and our government(s) must be doing something right. If you ask most citizens of the world what country they would prefer to live in, the answer will be the *United States of America*. Why? Because on average compared to other countries Americans have: (1) more basic freedoms; (2) safer environments; (3) more opportunities for employment and advancement; (4) more community wealth in the form of roads, buildings and infrastructures; (5) friendlier people; and (6) a higher standard of living. Americans have more creature comforts than anyplace in the world (e.g., electricity, running water, air conditioning, heating and ventilating systems, televisions, radios, movies, cameras, computers, recorders, digital equipment of all kinds, automobiles, transportation and communication modes, housing, roads, appliances, tools, cds, dvds, and on-and-on). These are some key reasons why foreign investors with money to invest, such as the Japanese, are investing it in the United States.

♪♪ Problems with America's Democracy ♪♪

With a diverse group of people having diverse needs and expectations, there can be no perfect government. Conflicts of interest are inevitable. Solutions to these conflicts cannot satisfy everyone in the group. This is true with a group of three individuals and becomes even more true with each individual added to the mix. Certainly democracy is not a perfect system of government. In many respects it is a dismal failure.[38] After more than two centuries, democracy has failed to alleviate social inequalities such as substantial differences in wealth, education, health care and social status. These differences have persisted, and there is no indication these inequalities will ever disappear in democracies.

Some form of social inequality is inherent in democracy. In a democracy of 100 voters, a party of 51 voters can confiscate and divide the property of the other 49. A party of 80 is a better majority, but then there is much less to divide. A coalition of 60 percent can successfully disadvantage a minority of 40 percent. Every democracy is a temptation for the majorities to disadvantage the minorities.

So called fundamental rights guaranteed in a democracy do not prevent a low-status minority from being targeted, politically and socially. Those at the bottom of the social scale, in a democracy, can expect no significantly better conditions of life. There is no record that inequality of wealth and income has declined permanently in any democratic state. In spite of the great personal wealth evident in some democratic nations, millions of people (especially in Africa) live under conditions comparable to mediaeval European poverty. Democracy *does not* induce the rich to give their money to the poor: not individually, not locally, not nationally, and certainly not globally.

Globally, democracies limit immigration, because nationally they believe the stability of their political communities will be undermined. Democracies admit less immigrants than other nations and have installed more security and electronic surveillance systems at their borders, in attempts to limit immigration. Thus, democracy reinforces nationalism as a private state. This combination of the nation state, limited immigration and global inequality has created islands of wealth that coexist amid oceans of poverty. Although a few percent will break from the norm, those born in a rich society will continue to live in a rich society; whereas those born amid poverty will die in poverty.

Democracies develop stable party systems which, in a sense, are desirable. But, this makes it difficult to implement changes or innovations. In democracies, the difference in stated aims between major parties constantly shrinks, as they jockey for the votes of major interest groups within their boundaries. We have seen this in America, as the Republican and Democratic Party platforms have moved toward a common center—until now they are in agreement on most issues. Someone has said, with a measure of truth, the only difference between Republicans and Democrats is: Democrats want to tell you how to spend your money and Republicans want to tell you how to behave. Once political parties are entrenched in a democracy, they inhibit the formation of new political parties. About the best an upstart political party can hope to achieve is to persuade a major party to adopt some of their ideas.

Democracy doesn't exist separate from the so-called free market. They are joined at the hip. There are many injustices under the guises of tariffs, pricing, credit and fee arrangements. No entity is a bigger supporter of democracies than big business. Why? Because big businesses have found they can make more money and keep more of it with a democracy than any other system of government.

Elections legitimize a democracy. And the election decision made in accordance with democratic procedures and the rule of law (based on votes of the citizens) cannot be overthrown. This is enforced by the military and other policing agencies, such as the FBI and the IRS. A core principle of a democracy is *once in, never out*—the same as hoodlum gangs that we deplore. This principle was stated by Abraham Lincoln at the start of the American Civil War when he said *"A democratic government necessarily depends on the military power to sustain itself in office, and to prevent the unlimited secession of minorities . . . No guns, no democracy."*

Democracy cannot resolve most ethical issues— like abortion and euthanasia. Therefore, many people must live under laws they cannot accept in conscience. If a democracy allowed objections of conscience to dictate its decisions, then it would be reduced to little more than a debating society.

At best democracy is a system of government, no more! But the general assumption in democratic societies is that democracy represents the final truth about the political life of human beings. The consistent claim for the superiority of democracy is that living in a democracy is equivalent to "freedom." Have you checked your "freedom" lately? Does living in a democracy equate to true freedom? The answer is "NO," because the answer to each of the following questions is "no."

❑ Can you obtain compensation for election results which disadvantage you?
❑ Can you take legal action against voters or political parties to prevent them from voting for or advocating policies which harm you?
❑ Are all law abiding immigrants allowed to join the democracy?
❑ Is it legal to secede or promote secession, if you have moral objections to the democratically elected government, its values, or its policies?
❑ Is the population treated equally under the law?

Inside a democracy, social restrictions and the marketplace limit social and economic freedom, rather than the political regime. Most of us are limited to when and where we can visit by social, governmental, private enterprise and financial barriers. The same is true of where we live, what we eat, what we wear, and what we do. Increasingly, these barriers combine to limit our personal freedoms. Most of us like to believe that "nobody else has control over our lives," not a king, a despot, and not fellow-citizens either. Democracy does not give you the freedom to "control your own life," rather democracy gives most "control of your life" to different groups of your fellow-citizens. If one is free to go where they want and do as they choose, it is only because they choose to go and do whatever the democratic system (their fellow-citizens) allows.

If a present population makes a decision for a future population, the future population is excluded from the process. No political procedure can correct that exclusion. In this way, democracy allows the present population to "rule" the future population. This defect of democracy has permitted the last few generations of Americans with their "buy-now, have-now, pay-later" philosophy to place an onerous debt on their (our) children and children's children.

There are many reasons why Americans should want to change our present form of democracy, including the following:

❏ To reduce our debt to a manageable level;
❏ To minimize government's role in the entitlement business;
❏ To help return our parents to parenting;
❏ To minimize the waste of time and manpower in our present election processes;
❏ To prevent political gridlock from halting needed reforms;
❏ To prevent the uninformed from controlling our destiny;
❏ To provide more equitable balance of wealth among the haves and the have-nots;
❏ To end inequality, both in the United States and globally; and;
❏ To prevent or reverse morally wrong decisions.

On issues of government, like other important issues, we need to *hear what others say*, but when it comes time to voice our opinions and cast our votes *we should listen to ourselves*. Even if our choices prove wrong, history has shown we will survive bad governments. However, wrong choices will promote a more-painful existence, especially for those who follow us and have no say in decisions that affect their quality of life.

The answers to our problems of government are dynamic. Like Bob Dylan's song says, *"The answer my friend is blowin' in the wind."* Still, we need to collectively get our heads out of the sand and initiate corrective action to modify our government, so we can improve our chances of adequately addressing twenty-first century problems. The truth is—we cannot know where the roads of government lead! Our governments will continue to be in a state of perpetual change. They must continually evolve as we and our surroundings evolve. ***Ah, sweet mysteries!***

𝄞𝄞𝄞𝄞

Chapter Notes

1. "Blowin' in the Wind," words and music by Bob Dylan, composed in 1962. Copyrighted by Warner Bros, Inc. Renewed in 1990 by Bob Dylan.

2. William E. Simon, *A Time for Truth*, (New York, NY: Berkly Publishing Corp., 1979). Simon suggests that our founding fathers were in full rebellion against an almost unbroken human history of the divine right of kings and social tyranny rooted in hereditary privilege, so when they declared that "all men are created equal," they meant that men were equal before the law, that no legal chains forged by ancestry or caste should bind any individual to a permanent underclass. They meant that men should share an equal opportunity to face the challenges of life, each free to achieve what he could and rise to the level he could by his own wit, effort and merit.

3. *The World Almanac, Millennium Collector's Edition*, (New Jersey: World Almanac Books, 2001).

4. This information, plus parts of the ensuing discussion, were obtained from Matthew White's *Historical Atlas of the Twentieth Century*, dated June, 2000 at http://users.erols.com/mwhite28/warstats.htm. Anyone interested in the history of world government should visit this website.

5. Edmund Black, *IBM and the Holocaust*, (New York, NY: Crown Publishing, 2001). Black documents the dark, almost hidden role of IBM and its owner, Thomas Watson, in Hitler's massacre of the Jewish population in Europe. Watson's primary interest appears to have been profit.

6. These purges resulted in the majority of the 160-million deaths from democide discussed in the previous chapter.

7. Steven G. Haw, *A Traveler's History of China*, (Brooklyn, NY: Interlink Books, 1997).

8. This chart is a major simplification of an ever-changing world-governmental structure, but it helps sort out the most significant twentieth-century changes in world governments. Monarchies, constitutional and otherwise, are grouped together; communists of all persuasions are lumped

together; despots, autocracies, and fascists are grouped together and the "many shades" of democracy are all treated as one. Where countries are in a state of *central government* flux, no matter which way they are leaning, they are classified as no central government. The chart numbers are posted for the beginning of each decade, but where significant changes occurred within a few years of the decade start, the chart may reflect those changes. The basis for these numbers and much of the discussion comes from several sources: i.e., Matthew White's *Historical Atlas of the Twentieth Century*, dated June, 2000—http://users.erols.com/mwhite28/warstats.htm; *The World Almanac, Millennium Collector's Edition*, World Almanac Books, New Jersey, 2000; plus earlier versions of *The World Almanac*; and Freedom House's "Survey of Global Political Change in the 20th Century," http://www.freedomhouse.org. Any errors or oversimplifications of complex groupings are totally the responsibility of the author.

9. Thomas Carlyle (1795-1881), *Sartor Resartus,* (England: Oxford University Press, World's Classic Series, 1987).

10. Desmond Muirhead is a golf course architect; not a politician. His commentary can be found at his website. His address is P.O. Box 7607, Newport Beach, CA 92660.

11. Majid Tehranian's speech on "Power Shifts and Emerging Security Regimes," presented, April, 1997, at the University of Hawaii's Human Security and Global Governance Conference. The conference was sponsored by the Toda Institute for Global Peace and Policy Research; web site at http://www.toda.org/conferences.

12. Nineteenth-century romantic poet, Samuel Taylor Coleridge, once remarked "No matter what question I ask myself I find that Plato has already been there," or words similar that conveyed this meaning. Plato, who lived about 2400 years ago, is one of history's greatest thinkers.

13. Article 1, Section 8 of the Constitution of the United States.

14. Michael Hodges, at http://mwhodges.home.att.net, provides information and backup data for this Government versus Private-Sector Spending Chart. Permission was granted from Hodges to use his charts and data for this presentation.

15. Constitutions, of course, can and should be changed as the needs of those governed change.

16. Thomas Carlyle, rightly, said that the *wants* of an individual or population can never be satisfied. You give the lowest bootblack 100£s and soon he will want 200£s. This is human nature. So the best bet, for a government to maintain a reasonably contented and stabilized population, is to focus on keeping the population's expectations minimized instead of trying to satisfy people's wants. See Note 8.

17. David S. Landes, *The Wealth and Poverty of Nations,* (New York, NY: W. W. Norton & Company, Inc., 1998). Dr. Landes is professor emeritus of history and economics at Harvard University and also author of *Revolution in Time* and *Prometheus Unbound.*

18. Michael Hodges, concerned about the financial problems facing his grandchildren, provides valuable information about financial aspects of our federal government and national spending trends. His website at http://mwhodges. home.att.net is packed with factual and useful data, charts and analysis. See Note 13.

19. Named after Charles Ponzi, who in 1920 collected more than $9 billion from investors by selling promissory notes paying "fifty percent profit in forty-five days." Ponzi paid the matured notes held by early investors by money collected from later investors. Word of enormous profits spread, causing greedy investors to buy into the scam. For more information, visit http://www.mark-knutson.com.

20. Debt statistics obtained from the Federal Reserve, http://www.federalreserve.gov.

21. Bankruptcy statistics obtained from http://www.abiworld.org/stats; college degree statistics obtained from http://www.pueblo.gsa.gov.

22. Federal Department of Debt reported federal debt as of September 30, 2001 was $5,807,463,412,200.06. As of 20 June 2002, the national debt was $6,101,371,914,990.35. It blew by the $6 trillion mark by a paltry $101 billion, http://www.brillig.com/debt_clock.

23. Three largest intra-governmental debts are: (1) Federal Old-age and Survivors Insurance Trust Fund, $893.5 billion; (2) Civil Service Retirement and Disability Fund, $497 billion; and (3) Federal Hospital Insurance Trust Fund, $168.9 billion.

24. 1990 U.S. Federal Census age distribution follows: under 5 years—7.6 %; 5 to 19 years—21.3%; 20 to 44 years—40.1%; 45 to 64 years—18.6%; over 65 years—12.5%. http://www.infoplease.com/ipa/A0110384.html.

25. Twenty-six percent of elders (65-years old or older) are still working. Thus, 26 percent times 13 percent shows that about 3.25 percent of America's total workforce are senior citizens, adding this to 54%, plus adding about 3 percent for young people in the work force, provides an approximate figure of 60%. Data obtained from the *World Almanac and Book of Facts, 2000*.

26. Total government debt of $7.1 trillion divided by the working population of 165 million (275 million times 60%).

27. As of 27 Sept 2002, the national debt is $6,222,554,066,955.09. Thus, during the past year it has increased more than $415,000,000,000.00 with very little public attention from the press or politicians.

28. Ross Perot, *United We Stand*, (New York, NY: Hyperion, 1992).

29. Green Party, P.O. Box 1134; Lawrence, MA 01842. Website at http://www.greens.org.

30. Libertarian Party, 2600 Virginia Avenue, NW, Suite 100; Washington, DC 20037. Website at http://www.lp.org.

31. William E. Simon, see Note 2.

32. http://www.rutgers-newark.rutgers.edu/pubadmin/resource /direc-body.

33. Walter A. Burien, Jr., CAFR1@aol.com; http://www.rense.com.

34. Rick Boettger, *The Deficit Lie: Exposing the Myth of the National Debt,* (Arlington, TX: The Summit Group, 1994).

35. David S. Landes, *The Wealth and Poverty of Nations: Why Some Are So Rich and Some So Poor,* (New York, NY: W. W. Norton & Company, Inc., 1998).

36. Steven Conover's insight on debt and growth is available at http://web2.iadfw.net/scsr. Here, the ideas he uses are paraphrased and abbreviated.

37. Ibid.

38. Paul Treanor. For a comprehensive discussion of the ills of democracy, refer to the following website: http://web.inter.nl.net/users/Paul.Treanor/dem.wrong.html. Views presented here on the problems with a democracy were strengthened by Treanor's thoughtful discussion.

♭♭ Six ♭♭

Nobody Ever Told Me[1]

(A Status Report)

Nobody ever told me there'd be days like these
Strange days indeed—strange days indeed

Everybody's runnin' and no one makes a move
Everyone's a winner and nothing left to lose

Everybody's flying and never touch the sky
There's a UFO over New York and I ain't too surprised

John Lennon's UFO experience was far from unique. Since mankind first viewed the heavens, many people have witnessed strange lights, unexplained mysteries and unidentified flying objects (UFOs). As we increased in numbers and invented our own flying machines, more-and-more eyes have been drawn to the sky, thus unexplained sightings multiplied. These sightings haven't been isolated to one culture, but have been made by countless credible witnesses in every age and every region of planet Earth.

On July 2, 1947, a strange day indeed, witnesses in and near
Roswell, New Mexico, observed a disc-shaped object moving swiftly
in a northwesterly direction through the sky. During the night an
explosion was heard at Corona, New Mexico. The following
morning, Mac Brazel, foreman of a nearby ranch discovered a great
deal of strange debris, including chunks of extremely light and tough
metallic material scattered about the area. Some of the material was
stamped with hieroglyphics and the metallic material had unusual
properties. The material could not be dented by the impact of a
hammer, yet it could be rolled by hand into a ball and would snap
back into its original shape with no wrinkles.

A U.S. Air Force investigation team soon searched the site and,
two-and-a-half miles southeast of the debris field, they discovered a
crashed UFO. Nearby, several dead extraterrestrials were allegedly
found. The Air Force quickly announced that the wreckage was the
remains of a weather balloon and commenced an elaborate cover-up.
There were too many witnesses to too many of the details, and over
the years the Air Force cover-up unraveled as eye-witness participants
broke their ranks of silence; thereby, allowing investigators to piece
together closer-to-the-truth versions of the event.[2, 3]

Within two months of the Roswell incident (and it is doubtful the
timing was a coincidence), Lt. Gen. Nathan Twining said UFOs
"were something real and not visionary," and recommended an
official UFO investigation. By the end of 1947, the Air Force
established Project Sign, under Lt. Gen. Twining's command, to
investigate UFOs. Remarkably, during the summer of 1948, Project
Sign investigators determined that some UFO sightings could only be
otherworldly vehicles. Air Force Chief of Staff Gen. Hoyt S.
Vandenberg promptly rejected their report on the grounds the case
was unproven. Then, in short order, Project Sign's advocates of an
extraterrestrial visitation were reassigned or left the service.[4] Project
Sign was succeeded by Project Grudge (1949-1952) and Project Blue
Book (1952-1969).

The United States Air Force had the task of identifying UFOs well in hand. Or did they? Project Blue Book was a low-priority operation headed by a low ranking officer—a captain. The final "Blue Book" report was subcontracted to the University of Colorado. A committee, led by University of Colorado's Edward Condon, was assembled to perform an independent study of the Blue Book data on thousands of sightings. The Condon report concluded: no alien craft or alien had been found; there was no evidence that UFOs were a threat to national security; and the majority of sightings were explainable by known activities (e.g., airplanes, meteorology experiments, missiles, weather, balloons, reflected lights, astronomical events, pranks, etc.). Therefore, there was no need for further investigations. This was what the Air Force needed to get out of the UFO business; so they promptly closed down the project.

The Condon report failed to emphasize that fully one-third of the cases examined by the Project Blue Book team remained unexplained. Dr. Alan Hyneck, head of Northwestern University's astronomy department and one of America's most respected astronomers, was Project Blue Book's chief scientific advisor.[5] Initially a complete flying-saucer skeptic, Professor Hyneck disagreed with Condon's conclusions, because he believed there were too many unexplained sightings by multiple and independent reliable individuals to sweep under the rug. So, he grouped the thousands of unexplained sightings into categories and, in 1972, wrote a book entitled *The UFO Experience*. This is a classic study by *the* UFO expert, a scientist, who believed it was unscientific to ignore the vast amount of empirical data obtained from thousands of concerned, rational, reliable and independent witnesses. One of Hyneck's UFO categories was *Close Encounters of the Third Kind*, which became the model for a very popular movie with the same name.[6]

Since the closure of the Blue Book Project many unidentified objects have continued to be sighted internationally,[7] but the U.S. military has, at least publicly, washed their hands of UFO investigations. UFO sightings have been sporadic and no unidentified flying object or alien capture has been reported publically by the U.S. military. Thus, the mainstream of the world's population believes that UFOs can be explained by real, this-planet or outer-space objects and events or they are the creation of pranksters or hallucinations. These folks will never believe in the existence of flying machines from an alien culture until the aliens and their hardware become regulars on the television talk shows. Yet, thousands of rational people believe they have seen alien spacecraft and/or aliens, so they believe that intelligent other-world entities exist; no one can convince them otherwise.

The UFO phenomenon is considered by most to be an occult subject, such as ESP, mind travel, reincarnation, astrology, fortune telling, etc. This is a nonrational comparison and assessment. We know that the human mind has definite limits for acceptance and accountability. In history this has been proven repeatedly. Often a revolutionary idea is at first scoffed at and shunned, only to be adopted later as a universal fact. The time may not be right for understanding aliens, because maybe the aliens want it that way or we are not willing to treat the idea of UFOs and aliens with the amount of resources and scientific investigation the subject deserves.

Andy Wright, who has been quiet for awhile, is certain in his belief of angels, but considers those who believe in UFOs and aliens as strange indeed and probably under the devil's influence. Me? After reading and analyzing a significant amount of UFO literature, watching and hearing a number of eyewitness accounts on television and having a faint grasp of space's immensity, I suspect that some form of UFOs are real. But I don't trust eyewitness accounts, because of the tricks our senses and minds play. Therefore, the bottom line is I don't have a clue. UFOs remain another one of our sweet mysteries.

♬♬ UFO Has Landed ♬♬

No matter what I believe, late on a lazy, hazy summer afternoon, on July 2, 1997, another strange day indeed, in central Iowa, along

U.S. Interstate 35, the police and radio stations began receiving call after call about a single craft UFO. The shape, size, headings, speed and altitude of the sightings varied, but generally it was a silver-shaped disk, headed south southwest. Similar sightings occurred within a three-hour time frame in Kansas, Oklahoma, Texas, and Mexico.

This was an exciting time for our survey team. We had been traveling for what seemed an eternity, had made a low-altitude pass over North and Central America, and now we were ready to complete the surface examination and make our status report. There were six of us and my dual duties were navigation officer and status reporter. My Lord our spirits were high, especially mine since I nailed the navigation and parked us right on target on the valley floor nestled in the Sierra Madre Occidental Mountains of 0723-3 (called planet Earth by its inhabitants). This was no mean feat for one in their second renewal.[8]

The crew members called me "Navigator," and I could detect a friendlier tone in their rationality after we landed. I won't say I was strutting around, but I was more than a little proud of my navigation. True we had precision astro instruments, and fellow galanauts had been here more than two-thousand times in the past. Nevertheless, it took some doing to sling shot our space craft past 10^{14} stars and black masses, find the optimum intergalactic entryways, and accelerate at the proper angle through the universe bubble, to land on this beautiful, blue, insignificant rock. I say insignificant, but it had several outstanding features that were extremely important to us, including an intense electromagnetic field that would allow us to replenish our craft's power system. Also it had been populated by our ancient ancestors, using archaic but successful random cellular casting.

As we moved from our craft, we felt no sense of motion. Light was fading and the photons diffused and refracted over the western range of mountains in a multitude of hues—mostly oranges, purples and shades of silver. The mountaintop purples deepened and blackened, and the whites and reds of the mountain flowers became tinged with a twilight color of lavender. The scars etched on the mountainsides dimmed, and the million shades of green mutated together in a shadowy dance.

Suddenly, like a hidden magician crowning his spell, the terrain was cloaked in darkness. It was a soft, peaceful darkness that hid the jagged mountains surrounding us on three sides and heightened our senses of sound, smell, feel and life perception. There seemed to be cellular life in every crevice of the landscape. We had to adjust our optical sensors due to the lack of surface light. The mountainous jungle landscape had been pushed and shoved and smoothed out in places by four-plus billion years of solar winds, meteor bombardment, core and subsurface upheavals and overgrowth from the evolution of cellular life. The visual effects, the sounds, the aromas washed over us in a harmonic cadence of immense, soothing pleasure. Our crew's rationality merged, and our common thought was "Blessed, Blessed! Our kind populated this oasis."

From these surroundings we took strength that would be needed for our difficult tasks and return journey. It was a tender time—the time of awakening for earth creatures of the night. The cry of a whippoorwill jarred us back to reality, but I recalled the words of one of our authors, who said "Nature teaches us the poorness and ugliness of our inventions." In the grip of the moment and for some unknown reason, I mocked a human sound, "Yo Ho!" And, out of the darkness the mountain walls caught the sound of my yell and flung it back, clear and lilting as a special welcome—"YO HO, Yo Ho, yo ho." Silently my captain chastised me and sternly ordered me to tend my tasks. There would be no more "yo hos."

We were located 25 degrees latitude and 105 degrees longitude on the 3^d distant mass from star 0723's epicenter, which we long ago had labeled 0723-3. This precise location had been used by us in the past as it was distant from the major population centers of capricious humanoids, thereby giving us a base of operations with a measure of privacy and safety.

Our first task was to stretch our weary bodies, make repairs to our craft and replenish it for the long journey back home. We had mastered the use of harmonic photon accelerators, bidirectional gravity shields and bidirectional mass convertors which enables us, within limits, to convert mass to energy and energy back to mass. This ability permits us to remove the cloak of illusion from the dimension called time and the parameter called motion and allows us to travel at speeds beyond light speed. The fuels we use for our craft are electromagnetic energy and photons (the most plentiful material in the universe). Our bidirectional gravity shields allow us to accelerate and deaccelerate, using the great masses located throughout the universe. Our photon nets and gravity shields are in great need of repair. This will be done by our engineering officer. Our crew consists of the captain, engineering officer, astro physics officer, statistician and me, the navigator. I've listed us in decreasing order of rank, so you see as the lowest ranking member of the crew I can't strut too much.

After we completed our repairs and rested, we made thirty-six high-speed circumplanet passes and: analyzed the mass makeup and core temperature patterns; calculated the orbit trajectory with other cosmos masses; and determined that 0723-3 had an eighty percent probability of surviving cosmic or internal core destruction for another five-billion years. In other words, cosmically 0723-3 was positioned at about half life. This successfully met the first goal of our mission. Next, we proceeded with our second mission goal—a two-part, fact-finding survey. The two parts of the fact-finding survey are (1) Fate of our probe X-E047 that disappeared on this planet fifty years earlier, and (2) Planet Status Summary.

♪♪ Part One: Status of X-E047 ♪♪

X-E047 was not a complicated survey-mission flight like our own. Rather, it was a routine training flight of a four-being craft. The captain of X-E047 was an experienced officer in his fifth renewal, but all other crew members were first-renewal trainees. Their mission to 0723-3 was their final training mission and test before receiving their full commissions as fleet officers. The craft was a fleet-standard, but had been retrofitted with newly designed electromagnetic sensors. Our task was to determine the cause of the craft's disappearance.

We found it amusing how often humanoids changed the nomenclature they used to describe their landscape, but at fifty-year intervals, we recorded their major divisions. At the last position report, X-E047 was in the southwestern United States.

Once made, sound waves don't disappear, although they slowly dissipate and it quickly becomes difficult to differentiate between later and earlier sound waves. Gravity and electromagnetic fields trap sound signatures at their origins. Our scientists developed a sensitive sound differentiator, but we had to be within five miles of the original sound imprint for accurate analysis, and the sound differentiator accuracy improved almost linearly as the distance to original sound origination point decreased. Fortunately for us, humanoids had developed a computer Internet, which we used to fix X-E047's crash point near Corona, New Mexico.

There it was a simple matter for our instrumentation to analyze the explosion signature and determine that an immense lightening strike had reversed the polarity on the ship's photon power plant, blowing it apart. We knew our ships were susceptible to this type of catastrophic malfunction, especially when blocked from direct star light and had designed a lightening shunt which required crew resetting when tripped. We concluded the inexperienced crew had failed to maintain or reset the shunt, resulting in the loss of X-E047. The crews' physical bodies had long ago dissolved, their energy being converted to boost the nearest electromagnetic field. Body dissolving and energy conversion takes place within one year for those in their first renewal. One year extensions are acquired for each renewal. If our medical technicians can service injuries before energy conversion occurs, we may continue to exist. If not, our physical bodies and life forces are melded to the universe's mass and energy field.

We found X-E047's wreckage material had been moved to an area near Groom Lake, Nevada called Area 51. Where, to our amazement, humanoids still were trying unsuccessfully to analyze and reproduce our craft materials. They don't understand that they already have the material in abundance. They call it sand. They just need to build a foundry, housed at absolute zero temperature, that is capable of simultaneously flashing (raising the temperature of the material to 10,000° F in 100 microseconds), while subjecting the material to a magnetic field intense enough to realign the atomic structure.

Enough! Enough!! What kind of science fiction malarkey is this? It is another example of mixing facts with a runaway imagination to set the stage for what would be an interesting perspective—the perspective of an unbiased outsider[9] reviewing the condition and status of our planet. But, so far, no aliens, if they did help populate or help control the evolution of our planet, have felt obliged to honor us with such a status report. So, we will complete the aliens' task, using the biased offerings (facts) of our own scientists, researchers and demographers.

♫♫ Planet Earth Status Report ♫♫

The increasing human population (now more than six-billion inhabitants) and their activities are exerting a mounting negative pressure on planet Earth's resources. This has led to severe pollution of air, water and land; a rapid rate of deforestation; and the extinction of many subhuman species.

Humans are creatures of habit and repetitious behavior. After learning to mix lime and clay with sand, gravel, binding agents and water to create concrete mixtures, bricks and asphalt, they have used their mixtures to paste ribbons and structures over the planet's surface. Wherever they go, they soon congregate and denude the landscape and start covering it with their concrete and asphalt.

Humans are restless, selfish, sexually obsessed, energetic, short sighted and often downright stupid. It seems they are driven: to reproduce; invent new things; build things, then tear down, ruin, and abandon them; consume what they touch; accumulate possessions and then try to hold onto and protect these possessions; fight and kill; and scurry about from one place to another. The affluent among them often make everyone's lives more difficult by their hoarding and over consumption. Humans don't know how to govern themselves; practice an amazing array of religions; make poor energy choices; consistently show lack of consideration for others of their own kind and other species; have accelerated their unhealthy use of drugs; don't give the proper time and instruction in rearing their young; and seem bent on instant gratification at the expense of planning and conservative action, through which they could pass on a better world to their progeny.

♬ Planet Earth's Environment ♬

Before the twentieth century the interactions between humans and their environment were relatively simple and localized. The complexity and scale of these interactions have increased and will continue to increase, especially as resources become scarcer and competition for them increases. What was once local pollution incidents, now may involve many nations. Questions of ecological preservation versus economic growth now involve complex interrelationships, as in the case of the interaction between energy use and crop production, deforestation and climate change. Despite their inventive progress and improved global social interchange, during the twentieth century, through their collective excesses humans have abused their home planet to such an extent that the comforts, beauty, and the ability of Earth to rejuvenate itself have all been seriously compromised.

According to 2,500 climatologists assembled by the United Nations, our twentieth century legacy looks like a global exercise in environmental genocide. The following list of broad facts demonstrates the scope of this dismal report; each of these facts brings with them associated and negative side effects.

❏ Unchecked population growth is stressing our planet resources beyond repair.

❏ Our greatest resources (air, water and land) are all being polluted or depleted at alarming rates.

❏ Expanding urbanization, agriculture and forestry has altered Earth's environment and ecology.

❏ Increased exploitation of water systems for agriculture, industry and for waste disposal is depleting water tables and contaminating significant amounts of the remaining water.

❏ Fossil fuel (coal, gas and oil) burning is on pace to double the atmospheric carbon dioxide concentration by the middle of this century, as well as significantly increasing the emissions of sulphur and nitrogen.

❏ The average planet surface temperature is increasing and bringing about profound changes on our planet.

❏ Human activities are eliminating other species at alarming rates.

❏ Our collective energy choices are unwise and are dictated by special interest groups that control the political process.

❏ The concentration of ozone in the stratosphere has decreased, due to the release of nitric oxides and chlorine compounds.

❏ The disparity of the "good life" between the richest and poorest continues to be an enormous disgrace.

Human population growth is the underlying cause of most of the world's environmental problems. As our numbers increase, more pollution is generated, more habitats and species are destroyed, and more natural resources are used up. Even if new technological advances and conservation measures were able to cut in half the environmental impact that each person has, as soon as the world's population size doubled, environmentally the earth would be no better off than before.

♦♦ Population Growth and Its Consequences ♦♦

In 1994, the Population Division of the United Nations predicted that the 5.63-billion humans alive in 1994 would increase to 10.02 billion by 2050. Andy Wright reminds me again-and-again to beware of my facts and how these facts are used! Here is another example of why Andy's advice is wise: When the United Nation's demographers did their biennial update of world population numbers and projections in October of 1998, they reduced the 1994 projected global population total for 2050 to 8.9 billion. Two-thirds of their reduction from earlier predictions was because of falling fertility, and one-third of the fall was the result of rising mortality from AIDS.[10]

Within the space of four years, their estimates had decreased a whopping 1.1-billion souls. This demonstrates that humans are proficient at extrapolating past trends to the future, assuming the variables that established those past trends remain consistent, but we "suck" at predicting the future behavior of old variables and the introduction of new variables. Why? Because, they are mysteries beyond our knowledge. None of us know the future. The United Nation's demographers currently estimate that Earth's population will peak and stabilize at approximately 10 billion in 2200. Other estimates predict that our numbers will continue to rise above 19 billion in the foreseeable future, but the United Nation estimates are the best we have, and although their estimates have scaled down, the almost certain impact of future population growth on our collective environment is, at best, appalling.

Although the rates of population increase are slower in the developed nations than in the developing areas of the world, larger amounts of resources per person are used in the developed nations.

So, each citizen from the developed world has a greater environmental impact than does one from a developing country. Conservation strategies that would lessen environmental impact on Earth are essential in both developed and developing nations.

While undeveloped countries are jeopardizing our future with unchecked population growth, the developed countries are jeopardizing our future (and theirs) with their unwise use of resources. The following statistics gathered by the United Nations and presented by Paul Erhlich[11] and Worldwatch Institute are eye-opening testimony to environmental stresses.

❑ Americans eat 815-billion calories of food each day; that's roughly 200 billion more than needed and is enough to feed 80-million starving people. We also throw out 200,000 tons of edible food daily; and the average American generates 52 tons of garbage by age 75.

❑ The average American's daily consumption of water is 159 gallons, while more than half the world's population lives on 25 gallons.

❑ More than 1-in-5 people in the world do not get enough to eat and approximately 2-billion people lack access to clean drinking water. Throughout the developing world, 95 percent of urban sewage is discharged untreated into surface waters.

❑ Approximately 30,000 species of animals, plants, fungi, and microorganisms become extinct annually.

❑ Eighty percent of the corn grown and 95 percent of the oats are fed to livestock. Fifty-six percent of available farmland is used for beef production.

❑ One-third of the world's fish catch and more than one-third of the world's total grain output are fed to livestock. It takes an average of twenty-five gallons of water to produce a pound of wheat in modern Western farming systems. It takes 5,214 gallons of water to produce a pound of beef.

❏ Americans constitute 5 percent of the world's population, but consume 24 percent of the world's energy. On average, one American consumes as much energy as two Japanese, six Mexicans, thirteen Chinese, thirty-one Indians, 128 Bangladeshis, 307 Tanzanians, or 370 Ethiopians.

❏ On average, only 0.1 percent of pesticides applied to crops reaches the pest, the rest poisons the ecosystem. Each year, 25-million people are poisoned by pesticides in less developed countries, and more than 20,000 die.

For now (and for many of us, especially Americans), the broad and detailed facts, listed above, don't directly influence our daily lives on a level that stirs us into action. So, like insidious cancers, they continue on without appropriate action by people and their governments. There are many "voices" trying to make us understand the depth and potential consequences of these facts. Some of their dialogue with supporting factual details follows.

♬ Environmental Degradation and Its Consequences ♬

Similar to glass panes in a greenhouse, gases in the earth's atmosphere allow the sun's radiation to heat the earth but are barriers to infrared energy radiating back out from the earth and escaping into space. These gases, primarily carbon dioxide, methane, nitrous oxide, and water vapor maintain a global temperature acceptable to life. This process is referred to as the "greenhouse effect." As the gases increase, more heat is trapped within the atmosphere, and the worldwide temperature edges upward. Within the last century, the amount of carbon dioxide in the atmosphere has increased dramatically, largely because of the practice of burning fossil fuels—coal, petroleum and its derivatives.

Evidence continues to indicate that increases in atmospheric carbon dioxide and other "greenhouse" gases are raising Earth's surface temperature. The United Nations Intergovernmental Panel on Climate Change (IPCC) has concluded there is a "discernible human influence" on the global climate. However, there is disagreement among scientists on how much of the warming is due to human activity and how much to natural causes, such as sunspots. There also is uncertainty whether the increased temperatures of the twentieth century are a trend or a natural cyclical variation. While future global temperatures may be a mystery, there is no myth and no question about the temperature increases of the twentieth century.

Global surface temperature has increased about 1.8° F within the past century.[12] Scientists have predicted that unless dramatic action is taken, temperature will continue to rise between 1.8°-and-6.3° F over the next century. This may not seem like much, but global temperature was only about 4° F cooler during the last ice age. So, the consequences of a modest increase in temperature will be significant. Sea levels will rise, many plant and animal species will become extinct, agriculture will be disrupted, and the frequency of severe weather and droughts is likely to increase.

In the early 1980s, Dr. Norman Meyer, a leading authority on greenhouse gases, in his book *The Sinking Ark*, estimated that about 200 species were going extinct on planet Earth each year.[13] Only twenty years later, zoologists and botanists estimate that we have increased the rate of extinction to approximately 30-thousand species per year. Only about 1.4-million species, out of an estimated total that range from five-million to a hundred-million, have been identified and catlogued.[14]

Dr. Jane Lubchenco believes that, unless substantial and immediate human efforts are directed toward environmental stewardship, biological life forms on planet Earth have entered their "End Game."[15] She bases her conclusions on facts. Some are listed below:

❏ Close to 50 percent of the land surface of the planet has been transformed by humans, through activities such as filling in wetlands, converting tall grass prairies into cornfields, or converting forests into urban areas.

❏ Humans have more than doubled the amount of available nitrogen in the environment because of excess fertilizer use and burning of fossil fuel.

❏ Rates of species extinction are 100 to 1000 times what they would be without human-induced changes in the planet. On land, this is largely caused by habitat loss and species invasions that are crowding out native species. In water, this is caused by over-fishing, as well.

❏ At current rates, by 2150, man-made events and phenomena will have engineered the single-largest mass extinction of species in measurable geologic time. Processes currently in motion have put one-in-eight plant species at risk.

❏ While human domination of land masses is clear, the current data also indicates a dramatic alteration of Earth's oceans. Infra-red satellite imagery has identified some 50 "dead zones" in the world's coastal areas. These "dead" ocean zones have little or no oxygen. The largest in the Western Hemisphere is in the Gulf of Mexico, caused by excess nitrogen and phosphorus flowing down the Mississippi River. Many signals of degraded water include toxic algal blooms, coral bleaching and sudden disappearance of fish from key fisheries.

❏ The Earth's ice cover is melting in more places and at higher rates than at any time since record keeping began. Many scientists suspect that the enhanced melting is a sign of human-assisted global warming, caused by the unprecedented release of carbon dioxide and other greenhouse gases over the past century.[16]

Some of the most dramatic reports come from the polar regions, which are warming faster than the planet as a whole and have lost large amounts of ice in recent decades. The Arctic-sea ice, covering an area roughly the size of the United States, shrank by an estimated 6 percent between 1978 and 1996, losing an average of 34,300 square kilometers—an area larger than the Netherlands—each year. The Arctic sea ice has also thinned dramatically since the 1960s, the average thickness dropping from 3.1 meters to 1.8 meters—a decline of nearly 40 percent in less than thirty years.

The massive Antarctic ice cover, which represents some 91 percent of Earth's ice, is also melting. Within the past decade, three ice shelves have fully disintegrated and two more are expected to break up soon. Icebergs as large as the state of Delaware have broken off Antarctica in recent years, posing threats to open-water shipping.

Outside the poles, most ice melts have occurred in mountain and subpolar glaciers, which have responded much more rapidly to temperature changes. The World Glacier Monitoring Service scientists predict that, if the warming trend continues, up to a quarter of global mountain glacier mass could disappear by 2050.

The Earth's ice cover acts as a protective mirror, reflecting a large share of the sun's heat back into space and keeping the planet cool. Loss of the ice not only affects the global climate, but also raises sea levels and sparks regional flooding, which damages property and endangers lives. Although, the disappearance of Earth's ice cover would significantly alter the global climate, the net effects remain unknown. Excessive ice melts in the Arctic could also have a cooling effect in parts of Europe and the eastern United States, as the influx of fresh water into the North Atlantic may disrupt ocean circulation patterns that enable the warm Gulf Stream to flow north.

As mountain glaciers shrink, regions that rely on glacial runoff for water supply will experience shortages. The Quelccaya Ice Cap, the traditional water source for Lima, Peru, is now retreating by some 30 meters a year—up from only 3 meters a year before 1990—posing a threat to the city's 10-million residents. And in northern India, a region already facing severe water scarcity, an estimated 500-million people depend on the tributaries of the glacier-fed Indus and Ganges rivers for irrigation and drinking water. But as the Himalayas melt, these rivers are expected to swell initially and then fall to dangerously low levels, particularly in summer. In 1999, the Indus reached record high levels because of glacial melt. The glacial area of the Alps in Western Europe has shrunk by 35-to-40 percent and volume has declined by more than 50 percent since 1850. Closer to home, in the Glacier National Park, located in America's Rocky Mountains, since 1850, the number of glaciers has dropped from 150 to fewer than 50. Overall, if the present warming trend continues, glaciers could be reduced to only a small fraction of their present mass within decades.

Large-scale ice melts would also raise sea levels and flood coastal areas, currently home to about half the world's people. Over the past century, melting in ice caps and mountain glaciers has contributed on average about one-fifth of the estimated 4-to-10 inch global sea level rise, with the rest caused by thermal expansion of the ocean as the Earth warmed.

Wildlife is already suffering as a result of global ice melt—particularly at the poles, where marine mammals, seabirds, and other creatures depend on food found at the ice's edge. In northern Canada, reports of hunger and weight loss among polar bears have been correlated with changes in the ice cover. And in Antarctica, loss of the sea ice, together with rising air temperatures and increased precipitation, is altering the habitats as well as feeding and breeding patterns of penguins and seals.

Scientists at the National Center for Ecological analysis in Santa Barbara, California, analyzed distribution patterns of thirty-five species of European Butterfly. They found that for two-thirds of the species, their range of habitat had shifted northward by 22-to-150 miles. In the United Kingdom the British Trust for Ornithology and the Institute of Terrestrial ecology analyzed the nesting habits of twenty species of birds. They found these birds were laying their eggs earlier in the spring; meteorological spring was coming earlier in the northern hemisphere; and autumn was coming later. Alpine plants that thrive on cold weather are being found only at higher and higher elevations. In the Antarctic, warming temperatures have affected the supply of tiny, shrimp-like krill, subsequently causing a 40 percent population drop among the Adelie penguins that feed on them. In Fairbanks, Alaska, the number of days 40-below F° in the late 1990s was half what it was in the 1950s. The permafrost is warming by an estimated two-to-four degrees centigrade.

What is clear is that fundamental shifts are underway in the operation of the planet. Changes in the highlands are most dramatic. The earth appears to be "breathing deeper." The earth is breathing earlier, too. Spring was starting about a week earlier in the 1990s than it was in the 1970s. Migrating red-winged blackbirds arrived three weeks earlier in Michigan in 1997 than they did in 1960.

As world population hit six billion, water tables fell on every continent, major rivers are drained dry before they reach the sea and millions of people lack enough water to satisfy basic needs.[17]

Water tables are now falling in China, India, and the United States, which together produce half the world's food.

In China, water tables are falling almost everywhere that the land is flat. Under the North China Plain, the country's breadbasket, water tables are falling by 1.5 meters, or roughly 5 feet per year. Where wells have gone dry, farmers have been forced either to drill deeper or to abandon irrigated agriculture, converting back to lower-yield rain-fed farming.

In India, a country whose population now exceeds one billion, the pumping of underground water is now estimated to be double the rate of recharge from rainfall. The International Water Management

Institute, the world's premier water research group, estimates that India's grain harvest could be reduced by up to one-fourth as a result of water depletion.

Rivers running dry provide another manifestation of water shortages as growing populations require more water. The Yellow River, the cradle of Chinese civilization, first ran dry in 1972. Since 1985, it has run dry for part of each year. In 1997, it failed to reach the sea during 226 days, or roughly seven months of the year.

During the dry season, the Ganges River has little water left when it reaches the Bay of Bengal. India, with more than a billion people taking the lion's share of the water, is leaving too little for the farmers of Bangladesh during the dry season.

In central Asia, the Amu Darya, one of two rivers that once fed the Aral Sea, is now drained dry by farmers in Turkmenistan and Uzbekistan. As this Sea has shrunk to scarcely half its original size, the rising salt concentration has destroyed the fish, eliminating a rich fishery that once landed 100-million pounds of fish per year.

Similarly, the Colorado, the major river in the southwestern United States, rarely ever makes it to the Gulf of California. The fishery at its mouth that once supported several thousand Cocopa Indians has now disappeared. Today the Nile, like many other major rivers, has little water left when it reaches the sea. Even though virtually all the water in the river is now claimed, the population of the three principal basin countries—Egypt, the Sudan, and Ethiopia, where most of the water originates—is projected to increase from 153 million today to 343 million in 2050, generating intense competition for water.

Water that seeps through porous rocks and is stored beneath the ground is called groundwater. In the United States, approximately half the drinking water comes from groundwater. Presently, groundwater in the United States is being withdrawn approximately four times faster than it is being naturally replaced. The Ogallala Aquifer, a huge underground reservoir stretching under eight states of the Great Plains, is being drawn down at rates exceeding 100 times the replacement rate, suggesting that agricultural practices depending on this source of water may have to soon be curtailed.

In *Pillar of Sand: Can the Irrigation Miracle Last*, Sandra Postel, the author, reports that the number of people living in countries experiencing water stress will increase from 467 million in 1995 to more than three billion by 2025. As water becomes scarce, the competition for water between cities and countryside intensifies. In this competition, farmers almost always lose. In North Africa and the Middle East, the region ranging from Morocco in the west to Iran in the east, virtually every country is experiencing water shortages. As cities grow, countries take water from agriculture to satisfy expanding urban water needs. The countries then import grain to offset the water losses. If the world stays on the current population trajectory, a growing share of humanity may simply lack the water needed for a decent life and water will become a bigger source of conflict than oil.[18]

The ozone layer, a thin layer in the upper part of earth's atmosphere, helps shield us from the sun's ultraviolet rays. In the 1970s, scientists discovered that the ozone layer was being destroyed by chlorofluorocarbons (CFCs)—chemicals used in refrigeration, air-conditioning systems, cleaning solvents, and aerosol sprays. CFCs release chlorine into the atmosphere. In turn, the chlorine breaks ozone down into oxygen. Because chlorine is not affected by this interaction, each chlorine molecule can destroy ozone for an extended period. Even if we ceased using CFCs tomorrow, the existing chlorine molecules in the atmosphere would continue to erode the ozone layer.

Increased ultraviolet radiation leads to accelerated growth of skin cancers and cataracts and reduces the ability of people's immune systems to fight off infection. Additionally, the growth rates of the world's oceanic plankton, the base of all marine food chains, is negatively affected.

United Nations' initiatives led to international agreements for phasing out the use of ozone-depleting chemicals in Montréal in 1987 (Montréal Protocol on Substances that Deplete the Ozone Layer). The Montreal Protocol is working.[19] Global observations have shown that the combined abundance of chlorine and bromine containing ozone-depleting substances in the lower atmosphere peaked in 1994 and has now started to decline. Assuming continued compliance to the Montreal Protocol, including amendments, the ozone levels are projected to return to their pre-1980 levels by about 2050. Without the international corrective actions initiated by the Montreal Protocol, the ozone depletion would be about ten times larger than it is today. However, springtime depletion of ozone in Antarctica continues unabated at the same levels as observed in the early 1990s. Large depletions of ozone have been observed in the Arctic in most years since 1990, which, in spite of general global warming, has been characterized by unusually cold and protracted winters.

Some good news has arrived. For the first time since 1993, global emissions of carbon from the combustion of fossil fuels declined last year, falling 0.5 percent to 6.32 billion tons. This decrease marks the first pause in the carbon emissions escalation since economic collapse cut emissions in central Europe dramatically in the early 1990s. But unlike that reduction, or the previous decline connected with the oil crisis of the 1970s, the latest downturn did not result from a major economic disruption. Still, it is not yet clear how long-lasting the new trend will be.[20]

Carbon dioxide is a by-product of burning coal, oil, and natural gas, and is believed by many scientists to be a chief contributor to global climate increases. The decline in emissions in 1998 is a sign that it may be less difficult to slow global warming under the Kyoto Protocol than predicted. The recent decline in emissions stems in part from improved energy efficiency and from falling coal use, spurred by new efficiency standards and the removal of energy subsidies. Also, much of the economic growth of the last two years has come from information technologies and services, sectors that are not major energy users. Operating the entire global Internet requires less electricity than New York City uses. Meanwhile, industries such as steel production and other resource-intensive sectors are growing more slowly.

The unlinking of carbon emissions from economic growth is seen in China, the world's second largest emitter. Its economy grew 7.2 percent in 1998, while emissions dropped 3.7 percent, following a smaller decline the previous year. This compares with a steady 4-percent annual increase in China's emissions in the previous two decades. The reasons for the sharp cut in China's emissions are not fully known, but one factor is a recent $14 billion cut in its coal subsidies.

Carbon emissions and economic growth unlinking was also evident in the United States in 1998, where emissions increased 0.4 percent while the economy grew 3.9 percent. Still, U.S. emissions in 1998 were 10.3 percent above 1990 levels. Under the Kyoto Protocol, the United States was supposed to reduce total greenhouse gas emissions to 7 percent below the 1990 level by 2010.

Slower growth in carbon emissions will make it slightly easier to achieve the ambitious goals of the Kyoto Protocol. However, to reach those targets, and to reduce emissions in developing countries, accelerated adoption of new energy technologies will be needed. Recent double-digit growth rates for solar and wind technologies, and the imminent commercialization of hydrogen fuel cells, herald a new, less-carbon-intensive energy system in the early twenty-first century. However, the pace of development will be heavily influenced by government decisions on fossil fuel subsidies and taxes, and on the rate of adoption of market incentives for new energy technologies.

After cutting petroleum dependence during the 1970s and 1980s, the world has been on an "oil binge" during the last decade, raising consumption by nine million barrels per day. The shift to gas-guzzling sports utility vehicles in the United States, the boom in truck transport in Europe, and the doubling of global air travel in the last twelve years have all played a role in driving oil consumption up. The United States, with 4 percent of the world's population, is consuming nearly 25 percent of the world's oil, and is now importing over half its supply.[21]

Because of rising demand, oil consumption is once again challenging global production limits. Meanwhile, the economies of Asia and Latin America are working hard to replicate the kind of oil-based economies they see in the north. If China alone were to use as much oil per person as the United States does, world oil production would have to double in order to supply it. But no credible geologist believes that the world will ever come close to doubling production.[22]

While oil is abundant enough to meet the energy needs of a billion people in industrial countries today, it cannot meet the needs of more than six-billion affluent consumers several decades from now. If continuing oil dependence is unrealistic from a resource perspective, from an ecological perspective it's preposterous. Burning vast quantities of oil also contributes to the buildup of carbon dioxide in the atmosphere, a trajectory that must end soon or we may disrupt virtually every ecosystem on the planet. The real price of oil is not the $34 per barrel that consumers are now paying, but the losses entailed in global warming-related melting of the Arctic ice cap and the ongoing destruction of many tropical coral reefs—damage that future generations will not be able to reverse no matter how hard they try.[23]

The economies of the twentieth century were fueled by coal and oil, but this century must be powered by a new generation of energy sources. The same technological revolution that created the Internet and so many other wonders can be used to efficiently harness the world's vast supplies of wind, biomass, and solar energy—thousands of times more abundant on an annual basis than the fuels we now use.

Already, the market for these technologies is growing at double digit rates, and automakers that once seemed wedded to the internal combustion engine are developing a new generation of hydrogen fuel cell cars. Daimer Chrysler has committed $1.5 billion to getting 100,000 of these vehicles on the market by 2004. There is hope that the world's transport fleets can be freed of dependence on oil fired internal combustion engines.[24]

It's time for energy companies, one of which recently announced that its BP logo stands for 'Beyond Petroleum,' to put their investment dollars where their corporate rhetoric is, and for consumers to stop complaining about oil prices, and start purchasing more fuel-efficient cars. And it's well past time for politicians to provide targeted tax incentives that will spur the market for a new generation of fuels and engines.[25]

A significant portion of industry and transportation is based on the burning of fossil fuels, such as gasoline. As these fuels are burned, chemicals and particulate matter are released into the atmosphere. These chemicals interact with one another and with ultraviolet radiation in sunlight in various and dangerous ways. Smog, usually found in urban areas with large numbers of automobiles, is formed when nitrogen dioxide is broken down by sunlight. When sulfur dioxide and nitrous oxide are transformed into sulfuric acid and nitric acid in the atmosphere and return to earth in precipitation, they form acid rain. Acid rain is a serious global problem, because few species are capable of surviving such acidic conditions. Acid rain has made numerous lakes so acidic that they no longer support fish populations. Acid rain is also thought to be responsible for the decline of many forest ecosystems worldwide. Germany's Black Forest has suffered dramatic losses, and recent surveys suggest that similar declines are occurring throughout the eastern United States.[26]

Air pollution, both indoors and outdoors, is a major environmental health problem affecting developed and developing countries alike. It comes from sources of dust, gases and smoke, and is generated mainly by human activities—traffic, industry, etc.[27] Air pollutants are suspended particulate matter, gases and vapors that are present in the atmosphere in abnormally high concentrations. The main components of suspended particulate matter are coarse particles such as soil and mineral ash or fine particles found in wood smoke or coming from engine exhausts. Gaseous air pollutants are principally oxides of nitrogen, ozone, carbon monoxide, sulphur dioxide, ammonia and volatile organic compounds.

Every year millions of people die or suffer serious health effects from air pollution: mainly respiratory diseases, asthma, chronic obstructive pulmonary disease, cardiovascular disease and lung cancer. Studies consistently show that life expectancy is significantly reduced in communities with high levels of particulate matter. Indoor air exposure to suspended particulate matter increases the risk of acute respiratory infections. In Asia, such exposure accounts for between one-half to one-million deaths every year. Approximately 35 percent of asthma cases and 25 percent of respiratory diseases are linked to air pollution in some populations.

Indoor air pollutants are an even greater threat to the health of millions. Pollutants released indoors are about one thousand times more likely to reach people's lungs than pollutants released outdoors. Two billion people, mostly in developing countries, use wood, coal or other biomass fuels (cow dung, crop residues and grass) for their cooking and heating, thus they constantly breathe pollutants.

Pesticide residues on crops and mercury in fish are examples of toxic substances that are encountered daily. Many industrially produced chemicals may cause cancer, birth defects, genetic mutations, or death. Although a growing list of chemicals has been found to pose serious health risks to humans, the vast majority of substances have never been fully tested. Preliminary results indicate that these chemicals, in trace amounts, may disrupt development and lead to a host of serious problems in both males and females, including infertility, increased mortality of offspring, and behavioral changes such as increased aggression.[28]

Fortunately, not everyone has been oblivious to the dangers inherent in our deteriorating environment and dwindling resources. On April 22, 1970, the first Earth Day, approximately 20-million Americans gathered at various sites to protest individual, corporate and governmental abuse of the environment. Earth Day, the events leading up to it, and its aftermath led to increased environmental awareness. Several grassroots environmental organizations were established to work for political change, including the Environmental Defense Fund in 1967, Friends of the Earth in 1968, Greenpeace in 1970, the Natural Resources Defense Council in 1970, and the Sierra Club Legal Defense Fund in 1971. The Environmental Protection Agency (EPA), an independent agency of the United States government, responsible for protecting the environment and maintaining it for future generations, was established in 1970.

Slowly, as the insidious negative effects of environmental degradation have become obvious to more people, political parties have "crept up" around the world that emphasize environmental protection. One of the more successful has been the Green Party of West Germany. In 1993, twenty-three Green Parties from eastern and western Europe formed the European Federation of Green Parties, hoping that together they would have a greater voice in polices impacting environmental issues.

The first major international conference on environmental issues was held in 1972 and was sponsored by the United Nations. The United Nations Environmental Program (UNEP) was created from this conference. A major focus for UNEP has been the study of ways to encourage sustainable development—increasing standards of living without destroying the environment. The United Nations Conference on Environment and Development, called the Earth Summit, was held in 1992. The conference produced treaties to reduce emission of gases leading to global warming and to require countries to develop plans to support biodiversity or protect endangered species and habitats. Notwithstanding a lot of supportive rhetoric, the United States fought for scaling back the global warming treaty requirement and President George Herbert Walker Bush refused to sign the biodiversity treaty.

In November 1992 a warning-to-humanity document was signed by 1,500 scientists from around the world, including 99 Nobel laureates.[29] This document reported that human beings and the natural world are on a collision course, which may alter the living world so that it will be unable to sustain life in the manner that we know.

Negotiations on the Kyoto Protocol to the United Nations Framework Convention on Climate Change (UNFCCC) were completed in 1997, committing the industrialized nations to legally binding reductions in emissions of six greenhouse gases. The United States signed the Protocol in 1998, but failed to obtain congressional ratification. This treaty would have committed the United States to a target of reducing greenhouse gases by 7 percent below 1990 levels during a "commitment period" between 2008-2012.[30]

President George Walker Bush, bowing to the will and opinions of big business, ambushed the environmental Protocol in 2001, just as his father had done to international environmental initiatives in 1992. President Bush said that the agreement on global warming was fatally flawed and was not well balanced, as it didn't include developing nations in binding agreements. Bush said, "The goals are not realistic, however, that doesn't mean we cannot continue to work together—and will work together—on reducing greenhouse gases." The Protocol calls on all parties—developed and developing nations—to take steps to formulate programs to improve greenhouse gas emission factors, activity data, models, and national inventories of emissions. All parties are committed to formulate, publish, and update climate change mitigation and adaptation measures, and to cooperate in promotion and transfer of environmentally sound technologies and in scientific and technical research on the earth's climate system.

Are you in the market for junk? Peter N. Spotts reports that near Earth space may have just what you're after. Roughly 10,000 objects of space-age litter large enough to track from the ground—from old satellites and spent fuel tank stages, lens caps, tie-down straps, and bits of explosive bolts—encircle the planet. And that doesn't include the millions of smaller bits of orbital debris ringing Earth. Approximately 45 percent of that junk has been discarded by the United States, approximately 45 percent by the former Soviet Union, and the remaining 10 percent by other nations of the world.[31]

Only four collisions between a spacecraft and debris have occurred since space flight began. But concern is growing that as the number of satellites multiplies, along with human reliance on them for cell phones to digital directions to grandmother's house, so are the chances that orbiting junk could knock out satellites and threaten human presence in space. Now that we've done a number on Earth's environment, we've started messing up outer space, where our growing junk yard, increasingly, imperils satellites and astronauts.

♪♪ Poverty and Its Consequences ♪♪

The final agenda in our status report is a discussion of the poor. As communications improve and the poorer segments of our population become more aware of the magnitude of their disparities with the rich, there is going to be continued and violent repercussions. As reported in the previous chapter, this gap in wealth that separates the rich and poor, according to Dr. David S. Landes, is the single greatest danger facing the world of the Third Millennium; superceding the threat of nuclear war, overpopulation and environmental deterioration. Of course, all of these problem areas are interlaced. Landes' research shows the gap between income per head in the richest industrial nation, say Switzerland, and the poorest country, Mozambique, is about 400-to-1.[32]

United Nations statistics show that now about two billion of our world's population of six billion are poor. What is poverty? Who are the world's poor women and men? What are their aspirations? Why do the poor remain poor? To help answer these questions, as the new millennium began, the World Bank sponsored a study of the poor called the "Voices of the Poor Project." The study collected the voices of more than 60,000 poor women and men from sixty countries, in an effort to understand poverty from the perspective of the poor themselves. The researchers visited poor urban and rural communities around the world, discussing with the poor such issues as: What is a good life and bad life?; What is the quality of poor people's interactions with government and institutions?; and How have gender and social relations changed over time?[33]

This research chronicled the struggles and aspirations of poor people for a life of dignity. The voices of the poor reveal that poverty is multidimensional and complex, it's: voiceless, powerless, and filled with insecurity and humiliation. The study showed, in spite of diversity and location specificity, there is a striking commonality of experience across countries, cultures, rural and urban areas, and age and gender divides.

Not surprisingly, lack of food, shelter, clothing, poor housing and uncertain livelihood sources were critical and mentioned everywhere. Having enough to eat the whole year round was mentioned again and again in many countries.

In the urban areas of countries that have undergone severe crises of economic restructuring, study teams were shocked to learn about quiet and hidden starvation. Those who starve are often too proud to beg and too decent to steal. The research team in Russia wrote, "A woman told us that sometimes she did not have food for several days and was only drinking hot water and lying in bed not to spend energy."

Poverty is much more than lack of income alone. For the poor, the good life or well being involves both material and psychological dimensions. Well being is: peace of mind; good health; belonging to a community; safety; freedom of choice and action; a steady source of income; and food.

The poor describe ill-being as lack of material things—food especially, but also lack of work, money, shelter and clothing—and living and working in unhealthy, polluted and risky environments. They also defined ill-being as bad experiences and bad feelings about the self. Perceptions of powerlessness over one's life and of voicelessness was common; so was anxiety and fear for the future. Insecurity has increased. Violence is on the rise, both domestically and in the society. And the poor feel they have been bypassed by new economic opportunitics.

Following are some of their voices:[34]

Poor woman in Moldova — Poverty is pain; it fecls like a disease. It attacks a person not only materially but also morally. It eats away one's dignity and drives one into total despair.

Young woman in Jamaica—Poverty is like living in jail, living under bondage, waiting to be free.

Poor person in Georgia—Poverty is lack of freedom, enslaved by crushing daily burden, by depression and fear of what the future will bring.

Poor person in Nigeria—If you want to do something and have no power to do it, it is talauchi (poverty).

Poor older woman in Ethiopia—A better life for me is to be healthy, peaceful and live in love without hunger. Love is more than anything. Money has no value in the absence of love.

Blind woman from Tiraspol, Moldova—For a poor person everything is terrible—illness, humiliation, shame. We are cripples; we are afraid of everything; we depend on everyone. No one needs us. We are like garbage that everyone wants to get rid of.

Older man, Egypt—My children were hungry and I told them the rice is cooking, until they fell asleep from hunger.

Tra Vinh, poor person in Vietnam—Poor people cannot improve their status because they live day by day, and if they get sick then they are in trouble because they have to borrow money and pay interest.

Physical health, strength and appearance are of great importance to the poor. The body is poor people's main asset, but one with no insurance. If it deteriorates, hunger and destitution hover at the doorstep. Bad living and working conditions, together with material poverty, make the poor highly vulnerable to becoming weak through sickness, or to permanent disability or death through illness and accident. Shortage of food and sickness not only cause pain, they weaken and devalue the asset. Poor people are more often sick, and sick for longer periods of time, and less able to afford treatment than the better off. So, "they just sleep and groan (Malawi)." Anguish and grief over watching loved ones die, because of lack of money for health care is a silent crisis of poverty.

Many people described security as peace of mind or confidence in survival. Survival referred not just to livelihood, but also to sheer physical survival in the face of rising corruption, crime, violence, lack of protection from the police and absence of recourse to justice, wars between ethnic groups, tribes and clans; frequent natural disasters, and the uncertainties of season and climate. Lawfulness and access to justice were widely seen as crucial aspects of well being. In the Kyrgyz Republic people said, "Among all the well being criteria, peace is the most important." In Russia, it was "the absence of constant fear." In Ethiopia, women said "we live hour to hour worrying if it will rain." The bad life is deeply embedded in insecurity and feeling vulnerable. A discussion group in rural Ethiopia concluded that "Life in the area is so precarious that the youth and every able person has to migrate to the towns or join the army at the war front in order to escape the hazards of hunger escalating over here." In Chittagong, Bangladesh, vulnerability was defined by slum-dwellers as "The failure to protect their young daughters from hooligans as well as protect themselves both from the harassment of outsider hoodlums and the police."[35]

With increased economic hardship and a decline in poor men's income earning opportunities, poor women across the world report "swallowing their pride" and going out to do demeaning jobs to bring food to the family. In their struggles to adapt to changing economic roles in the household, women widely report greatly increased work burdens; and men in many communities express frustration and humiliation with the lack of livelihood opportunities. This loss of traditional male "breadwinner role" and female "caretaker role" is traumatic for both genders, and family breakdown, domestic violence and increased alcoholism among men are often mentioned. Two poverty-stricken women voice their opinions:[36]

> Woman from El Gawaber, Egypt—Problems have affected our relationship. The day my husband brings in money we are all right together. The day he stays at home (out of work) we are fighting constantly.

> Elderly woman, Uchkun Village, The Kyrgyz Republic—The unemployed men are frustrated because they no longer can play the part of family providers and protectors. They live on the money made by their wives, and feel humiliated because of this.

Government corruption emerges as a core poverty issue. Poor people engaged in the study reported hundreds of incidents of corruption as they attempt to seek health care, educate their children, claim social assistance, get paid, attempt to access justice or police protection, and seek to enter the marketplace. In their dealings with officials, poor men and women are subject to insults, rudeness, harassment, and sometimes assault by officials. Poor people's evaluations of institutions that are important in their lives show that while politicians, state officials and public servants are sometimes viewed as important they rarely show up as effective, trustworthy, or participatory. There are exceptions. The poor want governments and state institutions to be more accountable to them. The poor must rely on informal networks and local institutions to survive, including the local holy men and their own kind. Following are additional comments that illustrate the poor's relationship to their governments:[37]

> Poor person in Brazil—The municipal Congressmen are all thieves … they do not solve anything, there are no schools, no health care. They do not vote issues that interest the people.

> Discussion group in Foua, Egypt—Nobody is able to communicate our problems. Who represents us? Nobody.

> Poor person in South Africa—We keep hearing about monies that the government allocates for projects, and nothing happens on the ground.

> Poor person in Armenia — People place their hopes in God, since the government is no longer involved in such matters.

> Poor person in Benin—Church affiliated entities represent probably the most visible and far reaching safety net presently operating in Benin.

> Poor person Vares, Bosnia and Herzegovina—No one helps, not anyone. I would gladly help someone, but how when I am in need of help myself. This is misery (jad). Our souls, our psyches are dead.

Poverty in America? You bet and in some poverty-stricken areas it's just as bad as any situation in developing countries! For instance, the following is the tape-recorded statement of an eleven-year-old girl as she was approached by a social worker at an emergency shelter in

Seattle, Washington: *"So don't tell me you knows 'bout homeless kids. And don't ask me if I understand what happenin' to my family bein' we got no home. They invisible and so is me. I not here anymore. I died three years ago. Hey, you wastin' your time talkin' to a dead person."*[38]

The "Voices of the Poor Project" study showed that extreme poverty declined only slowly in developing countries during the 1990s: the share of the population living on less than $1 a day fell from 28 percent in 1987 to 23 percent in 1998, and the number of poor people remained roughly constant, as the population increased. The share and number of people living on less than $2 per day—a more relevant threshold for middle-income economies such as those of East Asia and Latin America—showed roughly similar trends.

In general, poverty declined in countries that achieved rapid growth, and increased in countries that experienced stagnation or contraction. But on average, income inequality within countries has neither substantially decreased not increased over the last thirty years. However, in line with Dr. David Landes's conclusions, since within-country inequality has increased in some populous countries, overall more people have been affected by increases in inequality than by decreases.[39]

What drives this inequality? The Voices-of-the-Poor-Project study found no simple and clear answers. It's a mystery, but cross-country analyses and case studies have generated some insights into the link between inequality and several policy and institutional factors. For example, policies fostering stable economic conditions, openness to trade, and moderate size of government tend to stimulate growth, but haven't been found to systematically affect the distribution of income. Policies that reduce inflation from very high levels appear to benefit the poor more than the average. If growth is strong in areas where the poor live and sectors where they are employed (for example, smallholder agriculture), they benefit more; if growth takes place in areas or sectors that are not accessible to the poor, inequality can increase. Domestic policy distortions that hinder agriculture (along with international trade barriers) have restrained growth in rural incomes in many countries. This has also been reflected in rising regional inequality, as in poor regions farming is often the dominant sector of activity.

By and large poor people feel they have not been able to take advantage of new economic opportunities due to lack of connections and lack of information, skills and credit. Unemployment and lack of food and money are problems in many communities. The poor report experiencing life as more insecure and unpredictable than a decade or so ago. This is linked to: jobs that are unreliable and with low returns; loss of traditional livelihoods; breakdown of the state; breakdown of traditional social solidarity; social isolation; increased crime and violence; lack of access to justice; extortion; and brutality from the police rather than protection. Illness is dreaded, and lack of affordable health care pushes many families into indebtedness and destitution.

In presenting the study findings during their 1999 Annual Meeting, World Bank President, James Wolfensohn said: *"These are strong voices, voices of dignity. There needs to be a passionate rededication to each other as we enter the next century. All of us have to assume a responsibility for global equity which is the only assurance of peace."*[40]

Isn't it interesting that the World Bank (the world of high finance) financed this study of the poverty-bound dregs of society. Listen closely to Wolfensohn's words—*"All of us have to assume a responsibility for global equity which is the only assurance of peace."* This is precisely what Dr. Landes is telling us.[41] While Wolfensohn surely is sincere about the plight of the poor, a major concern of the "haves" is to keep giving the "have-nots" enough crumbs to keep the peace and protect the haves' assets (and the "t" can be deleted from assets).

♪♪ Status Report Postscript ♪♪

In 1975, an organization called the Club of Rome published a book-length article entitled "The Limits to Growth," in which they predicted mass famines, due to increased population, environmental collapse and a worldwide lack of raw materials. These mass famines were to occur by 1990 at the latest.[42] It seems in every era, there are those who examine facts and fit them to "worst-case" scenarios that fail to materialize. Their predictions have failed because of the diversity, resourcefulness, ingenuity and will-to-live of mankind.

Like the title of John Lennon and Yoko Ono's album "Milk and Honey," many of us have been privileged to live in lands of "milk and honey" where natural resources and opportunities are plentiful and seemingly endless. But, make no mistake about it, that is becoming an ever narrowing and dangerous point of view!

Science and common sense (our closest allies) tell us that no population having a fixed amount of space, human or otherwise, can grow indefinitely. Eventually some controlling variable, such as food, water, air, predators or catastrophic events, will limit population growth.

The facts gathered from reliable sources and presented in this chapter clearly show humans have changed and stressed planet Earth's environment. Bluntly put, *"We have messed our nests*!" Some of these changes—such as the destruction of the world's tropical rain forests to create grazing land for cattle or the drying up of almost three-quarters of the Aral Sea (once the world's fourth-largest freshwater lake) for irrigation purposes or the generation of greenhouse gases—have helped alter climate patterns that, in turn, have changed the distribution of species and now threaten mankind's well being.

Species in an ecosystem interact with one another, either directly or indirectly. The interreaction may be subtle, but it is present. For example, American ecologist Robert Paine, in a rocky intertidal region of the Pacific coast, found a stable invertebrate community dominated by fifteen species, including starfish, mussels, limpets, barnacles, and chitons. Paine removed the starfish from the area. Although it hadn't been obvious, the starfish were preying on one of the mussel species. With the starfish removed, the population of this mussel increased, and the mussel out competed the other species of invertebrates. Thus, the loss of one species, the starfish, indirectly led to the loss of an additional six species and a transformation of the community. Typically, because the species that coexist in natural communities have evolved together for many generations, they have established a balance, and without human intervention their populations remain relatively stable.[43]

Many of the facts catalogued in this short status report have been collected by the United Nations. Most of us consider peace-keeping is the main purpose of the United Nations, and only the most ardent supporters would claim the organization has been successful at keeping the peace. But, the United Nations' leadership and importance in establishing and maintaining world demographics, documenting and publicizing the plights of the underprivileged around the world, and tracking and leading the corrective action on world problems such as population growth and environmental destruction cannot be overstated. Two prime environmental examples of the United Nations value are (1) the 1987 Montreal Protocol on ozone-depleting substances, and its subsequent Amendments and Adjustments, and (2) the 1997 Kyoto Protocol on substances that alter the radiative forcing of the climate system. Both of these protocols defined substantial world problems and provided remedies. Perhaps, just perhaps, there is more to "keeping the peace" than placing troops and trying to negotiate "peace settlements" between warring factions.

With all the bad environmental and economical-equity news, the good news is that much of our planet Earth is still an oasis and global environmental or economical collapse is not inevitable. Surely an alien survey team, even one capable of destroying us, would recognize enough good on Earth to want us alive, if for no other reason than to laugh at the way we go about solving our problems. Folly and positive sentiments aside, population growth, conservation and equity strategies need to become more widely accepted and implemented. It is in our individual and collective interests to be more fully engaged in improving our environment and assisting the poor, thereby ensuring our own and our descendants' health, prosperity and well being. The resolutions to our problems will be varied and fitful, and delays in corrective action will increase our collective pain. Certainly, the answers are mysteries, but let's resolve to not use the dodge, *"Nobody ever told me"* about the problems.

Chapter Notes

1. "Nobody Ever Told Me" is a song written by John Lennon and released by Yoko Ono on the *Milk and Honey* album. Unfortunately, Lennon was assassinated before *Milk and Honey* was finished. The lyrics were the result of Lennon's startling UFO encounter, August 23, 1974, at his New York City penthouse apartment on 53^d Street. He and his friend May Pang, who also witnessed the UFO, called the police and newspaper; they were informed by both sources that multiple calls had been received about the same strange sighting. A number of reputable celebrities, such as President Jimmy Carter, Jackie Gleason and Walter Chronkite have seen UFOs. Jim Hickman at http://jhickman@itlnet.net. "Nobody Ever Told Me" sheet music, Ono Music Limited, BMG Music Publishing Limited, London, England, 1980.

2. Stanton Friedman and William Moore, *The Roswell Incident*, (New York, NY: MJF Bks; Fine Communications, 1980).

3. Kevin Randle and Donald Schmitt, *UFO Crash at Roswell,*(New York, NY: Avon, 1991).

4. Jerome Clark and Marcello Truzzi, *UFO Encounters*, (New York, NY: Signet, 1993).

5. Dr. Alan Hyneck was also a scientific advisor on the Air Force's Sign and Grudge UFO Projects.

6. Alan Hyneck, *The UFO Experience*, (Chicago, IL: Henry Regnery Co., 1972).

7. Concerned civilian UFO trackers logged 2781 sightings for North America in the 1990s.

8. Our culture now has the option of twelve renewals for each individual. A renewal is equivalent to the time it takes for 100 revolutions of 0723-3's orbit about star 0723.

9. There isn't an unbiased human on planet Earth, so to find an unbiased entity, if such exists, it would have to be an alien.

10. Information from Worldwatch Institute's Lester R. Brown and Brian Halweil report, October, 1999: "The HIV epidemic itself is a severe international problem. Nowhere is this more evident than in sub-Saharan Africa, a region of 800 million people, where the epidemic is spiraling out of control. If a low-cost cure is not found soon, countries with adult HIV infection rates over 20 percent, such as Botswana, South Africa, and Zimbabwe, will lose one fifth or more of their adult population to AIDS within the next decade." http://www.worldwatch.org.

11. Paul Erhlich's website at http://www.pbs.org/kqed/population-bomb.

12. In January 1999 NASA announced that 1998 was the warmest recorded year in history. "There should no longer be an issue about whether global warming is occurring, but what is the rate of warming, what is its practical significance and what should be done about it," said Dr. James Hansen, a scientist with the NASA Goddard Institute for Space Studies. The NASA report concluded that the average worldwide temperature in 1998 was 58.496 degrees, topping the record of 58.154 degrees set in 1995. NASA researchers collected data from thousands of meteorological stations around the world. The warmest years of the twentieth century all occurred after 1979. The six hottest years in the last one-thousand years were 1990, 1995, 1997, 1998, 1999, and 2000.

13. Norman Meyer, *The Sinking Ark*, (New York, NY: Pergamon PR, Franklin, 1979).

14. Species information obtained from the World Resources Institute at http://www.wri.org.

15. Dr. Jane Lubchenco is the Distinguished Professor of Zoology at Oregon State University and chairperson of the National Science Board's Task Force on the Environment. In August, 1999, she presented the National Science Board's findings at the XVI International Botanical Congress where more than 4,000 scientists from 100 countries met to discuss the latest research on plants for human survival and improved quality of life. The International Botanical Congress is held only once every six years. Visit Ellen Wilson at ewilson@burnessc.com.

16. Facts about Earth's diminishing ice cover were extracted from "Melting of Earth's Ice Cover Reaches New High" by Lisa Mastny. Ms Mastny is a WorldWatch Institute staff researcher. For more information visit http://www.worldwatch.org.

17. Lester R. Brown and Brian Halweil, *World Watch Magazine,* (September, 1999). Information about world water shortages was extracted and abbreviated from the article, "Populations Outrunning Water Supply." Visit http://www.worldwatch.org.

18. Sandra Postel, *Pillar of Sand: Can the Irrigation Miracle Last*, (New York, NY: W. W. Norton, 1999).

19. Ozone level status information was extracted from World Meteorological Organization/UNEP, "Scientific Assessment of Ozone Depletion: 1998," WMO Global Ozone Research and Monitoring Project, Report 44, (Geneva, 1998).

20. Christopher Flavin, *World Watch Magazine,* (July 1999). Information about reduction in carbon emissions rates was extracted from Flavin's article "World Carbon Emissions Fall." Flavin, at the time, was Senior Vice President and Energy Analyst, later acting President, at the Worldwatch Institute located in Washington, D.C., for more details visit http://www.worldwatch.org.

21. Christopher Flavin tells what the real price of oil is in his 28 September 2000 article published in *The International Herald Tribune.*

22. Ibid.

23. Ibid.

24. Ibid.

25. Ibid.

26. Michael Zimmerman, "Environment," *Microsoft Encarta Encyclopedia* (CD-ROM, 1998). Dr. Zimmerman is dean of the College of Letters and Science and professor of biology at the University of Wisconsin, Oshkosh.

27. Air pollution information derived from World Health Organization (WHO), Fact Sheet 187, September 2000. For more than 20 years the WHO with the UN Environmental Program (UNEP) assessed trends in ambient air pollution. This program was replaced by the Air Management Information System (AMIS).

28. Zimmerman, see Note 26.

29. This warning was coordinated by Dr. Henry Kendall, Nobel Laureate and chairman of the Union of Concerned Scientists.

30. Facts obtained from the Congressional Research Service Report for Congress 98-2 entitled *Global Climate Change Treaty: The Kyoto Protocol*, by Susan R. Fletcher, Senior Analyst in International Environmental Policy Resources, Science, and Industry Division, March 6, 2000.

31. Peter N. Spotts, staff writer for *The Christian Science Monitor*, researched and wrote an article about space debris in 1999. The data was obtained from that article. For additional information, visit http://www.csmonitor.com.

32. David S. Landes, *The Wealth and Poverty of Nations,* (New York, NY: W. W. Norton & Co., 1998).

33. "Voices of the Poor Project," the study was managed by the Poverty Group in the Poverty Reduction and Economic Management Network, World Bank. Team leader was Deepa Narayan. http://www.worldbank.org /poverty/data/trends/what.htm.

34. Ibid.

35. Ibid.

36. Ibid.

37. Ibid.

38. Sharon Quint, *Schooling Homeless Children: A Working Model for America's School,* (New York, NY: Teachers College, 1994). This isn't part of the "Voices of Poor Project," but sadly illustrates poverty exists

side-by-side with affluence in America. In 1999, the Dow Jones average hit 11,000, while homelessness hit 3,000,000.

39. Landes, see Note 32.

40. See Note 33. James Wolfensohn was referring to the study results of the "Voices of the Poor Project."

41. Landes, see Note 32. According to Dr. Landes, the gap in wealth that separates the rich and poor, is the single greatest danger facing the world of the Third Millennium; superceding the threat of nuclear war, overpopulation and environmental deterioration.

42. Donella Meadows, et al, *The Limits of Growth: A Report for the Club of Rome's Project on the Predicament of Mankind,* (New York, NY: New American Library, 1972).

43. Yvonne Baskin, *The Work of Nature, Natural History*, 1997. Ms Baskin reported on Dr. Robert Paine's research; http://www.anapsid.org. Professor Paine was professor of zoology, University of Washington.

𝄞𝄞 Seven 𝄞𝄞

Seasons in the Sun[1]

(Genealogy)

We had joy we had fun
We had seasons in the sun
But the wine and the song like the seasons
Have all gone.

Goodbye Papa it's hard to die
When all the birds are singing in the sky

We had joy we had fun
We had seasons in the sun
But the stars we could reach
Were just starfish on the beach.

We don't know where or when we originated, what our fundamental purpose is, or our final destination. For that matter, we don't know with certainty, even though we may think we do, where we will be and what we will be doing next week. But, in spite of these mysteries and our limited "starfish" reach, we, each in turn, fulfill our destiny and have our "seasons in the sun."

Millions are fascinated with the question of how our own seasons in the sun started, and we have spent countless hours tracing our genealogical roots as far back as we can find ancestral links. Family members devour information about their ancestors and elapsed time seems to enhance the value of the information. The fact that the stories are about ordinary people and everyday life (not about the exploits of the famous) doesn't detract from their interest. A simple bill of sale signed by one's ancestor and dated back to the Revolutionary War era or perhaps to the seventeenth century is considered a priceless family treasure. Family historians who undertake the task of tracking down their ancestors soon find that the number of ancestors quickly becomes unmanageable, so they focus their search on one or two family surnames. The simple arithmetic of cataloging your direct ancestors back to the early 1600s, when many family ancestors first found their way to America, adds up to about thirteen generations and the potential number of ancestors that it took to create you in this relatively short time span exceeds 8,000.[2] If you back up seventy generations the collective number of your forebearers could exceed billions, and this only takes you back to about the time of Christ.[3]

Richard Dawkins suggests that people should revere their ancestors, because their ancestors enabled their own existence, and only the smallest minority of organisms born will have a descendant alive a thousand generations later. All organisms that ever lived can lay proud claim to the fact that not a single one of their ancestors died in infancy. They all lived long enough to propagate their species. We all inherit our genes from an unbroken line of successful ancestors, and that is evolution at work.[4]

Science has found that our bodies are vessels for maintaining this unbroken genetic chain. In each of our body cells, 50 percent of our genes are inherited from our mother and 50 percent from our fathers. Each gene, in turn, came from only one of our four grandparents, and so on back to our own Adam and Eve. These genes do not blend; they recombine and function side-by-side to make each of us unique. The body, then, is a vehicle for the gene. Genes perpetuate themselves by controlling our bodies to survive and have sex.

Dawkins likens this process to a continuously living river of genes. Each species of life has their own, but different, river. A new species comes into existence when an existing species divides in two. At that point, the river forks into two rivers each going their separate ways. Why does a species divide? All of the answers to this question are unknown, but one answer is geographical separation. For example, the river of grey squirrel genes has separated from the river of red squirrel genes and while these squirrels may now share the same territory, they don't mate. Their river of genes, sexually and in other ways are different rivers. This same story underlies the much earlier separation between humans and apes. As our separate rivers flow longer in time, we tend to become more-and-more different.[5]

There are now between five million and one-hundred million separate genetic rivers as this is the current range of estimates of species on earth. It is also estimated that the current number of species represent about one percent of the species that have lived but whose river of genes have dried up or become extinct.[6]

Edward O. Wilson, imminent Harvard naturalist and reductionist colleague of Dawkins, used decades of research and study of social insects (primarily ants) and animals as the basis for his controversial book, *Sociobiology: The New Synthesis.* At least, his scientifically supported arguments for genetic determinism were controversial in the nurture-over-nature dominated academic climate of the 1970s. Wilson expanded his synthesis to include social vertebrates (apes and primates) and man and tells us that human beings inherit a propensity to acquire behavior and social structures, a propensity that is shared by enough people to be called human nature.[7] The defining traits include division of labor between the sexes, bonding between parents and children, heightened altruism toward closest kin, incest avoidance, suspicion of strangers, tribalism, dominance orders within groups, male dominance overall, and territorial aggression over limiting resources. The channels of human psychological development, however much we might wish otherwise, cut more deeply by the genes in certain directions than in others. So while human cultures vary greatly, they inevitably converge toward these traits we call human nature. Wilson collaborated with Charles Lumsden in a search for the basic process that directed the evolution of the human mind. They concluded this process is a form of interaction between genes and culture, where this "gene-culture coevolution" is an eternal circle of change in both heredity and culture.[8,9] Research to date seems to bear out the accuracy of their conclusion.

♭♭ Evolution and Our Earliest Ancestors ♭♭

The idea that populations (both genetically and environmentally) can be transformed over time into different descendant populations has been considered since early history, but before the eighteenth century the idea was unsupported by scientific evidence. The growth and study of natural history led to an increasing knowledge of living organisms and fossils, and the concept of evolution began to attract more proponents. In 1809 Jean-Baptiste Lamarck argued that the patterns of resemblance found in various creatures arose through thousands of years of evolutionary modifications—for example, lions, panthers and other catlike animals had all descended from a common ancestor.[10] Charles Lyell, an English geologist, in the early 1800s, found tools under layers of sediment and concluded they had to be at least 100,000 years old, and, if there were tools that old there had to be people that ancient too. To a society accustomed to believing that Earth had been created only about 6,000 years earlier, this was an unbelievable revelation.[11] So, the notion of man evolving from an ancient species didn't have many disciples until after Charles Darwin's 1859 book, *On the Origin of Species by Means of Natural Selection*.[12]

Darwin observed that while offspring inherit a resemblance to their parents, they are not identical to them. Animal breeders, he noted, were able to change the characteristics of domestic animals by breeding those having the most desirable qualities such as speed in racehorses. Darwin reasoned that, in nature, individuals with qualities that made them better adjusted to their environments would have higher fitness, leading to a population that is well adapted to the environment it inhabits. When environmental conditions change, populations require new properties to maintain their fitness. Either the survival of a sufficient number of individuals with suitable traits leads to an eventual adaptation of the population as a whole, or the population becomes extinct. Thus, according to Darwin, evolution proceeds by the natural selection of well-adapted individuals over a span of many generations.[13]

The inheritable part of Darwin's theory was verified by Gregor Mendel who discovered that characteristics are transmitted across generations in discrete units, now known as genes.[14] Because different individuals have different assortments of genes—no two humans (except identical twins) are precisely alike genetically—the total number of genes available for inheritance by the next generation can be large and will have great genetic variability. Sexual reproduction ensures that the genes are rearranged.

Natural selection is not the only source of genetic change in the evolution of species. Gene frequencies may also change by the chance failure of progeny to reproduce the exact gene proportions of their parents. This is termed genetic drift. Also, failure to carry the full range of genes in the parent population occurs when a few individuals migrate and found a new, isolated population. Mutations can change gene frequencies, but such changes occur at low rates relative to the changes brought about by the recombination of genes in offspring.

The science of heredity underwent a Promethean leap forward in 1953, when James Watson and Francis Crick demonstrated that genetic material is composed of two nucleic acids, deoxyribonucleic acid (DNA) and ribonucleic acid (RNA).[15] Nucleic acid molecules contain genetic codes that dictate the manufacture of proteins, and the latter direct the biochemical pathways of development and metabolism in an organism. Mutations are now known to be changes in the position of a gene, or in the information coded in the gene, that can affect the function of the protein for which the gene is responsible. Natural selection can then operate to favor or suppress a particular gene according to how strongly its protein product contributes to the reproductive success of the organism. These findings have made it possible to study evolution at the molecular level, tracing the history of changes in particular genes and in gene organization.

Today, evolutionary studies extend into all branches of geology and biology. These studies show that the present state of all forms of life, from bacteria to humans, have been achieved by evolution. Evolution is scientifically accepted as underlying modern biology, but our understanding of evolution depends on interpretations of incomplete rock, fossil and genealogical records, so the details and theories continue to be debated and updated and differences in interpretations are plentiful.[16,17] Many questions still need to be answered and many problems need to be resolved before the facts of evolution are securely knitted together in a complete history.

The mysteries of evolution deepen as we regress in time, but the scientific consensus is that life originated about 3½-billion years ago, when Earth's environment was much different from that of today. Experiments have shown that complicated organic molecules, including amino acids, can arise spontaneously under conditions that are believed to simulate the earth's primitive environment. Concentration of these molecules evidently led to the synthesis of active chemical groupings of molecules, such as proteins, and eventually to interactions among chemical compounds. A genetic system arose through natural selection into the complicated mechanisms of inheritance known today. The earliest organisms must have fed on nonliving organic compounds, but chemical and solar energy sources were soon tapped. Photosynthesis freed organisms from their dependence on organic compounds and also released oxygen so the atmosphere and oceans gradually became more hospitable to advanced life forms.

The earliest organisms were already cells, resembling modern bacteria. These simple single-cell forms lived without oxygen, but they diversified into an array of adaptive types from which blue-green algae descended and evolved into cell bodies that photosynthesize, and some tiny bacteria evolved into cell bodies that release energy during respiration. These cells led to the appearance of multicellular plants and animals, which from fossil evidence are known to have first appeared about 670-million years ago.[18] Between about 670-and-570-million years ago, there was a remarkable burst of evolutionary diversification. The earliest body fossils consist chiefly of impressions belonging to jellyfish and their allies. At about the same time, burrowing worms appeared with more advanced body structures. At least one wormlike lineage that pursued a swimming mode of life evolved a stiff dorsal cord and eventually an articulated internal skeleton that supported the body to improve swimming efficiency; thus, fish arose from the early invertebrates.

In order for complex animal communities to develop, plants needed to first become established to support herbivore populations, which in turn probably supported predators and scavengers. Land plants appeared about 400-million years ago, and finally land vertebrates (amphibians at first) rose from freshwater fish nearly 360-million years ago. The subsequent spread of land vertebrates made them increasingly independent of water. Dinosaurs and mammals shared the terrestrial environment for about 135-million years.[19] The mammals, however, survived a wave of extinction that eliminated dinosaurs about 65 million years ago, and subsequently diversified into the species, habitats and modes of life that we know today. Fossil records display a wide variety of evolutionary trends and patterns. Lineages may evolve slowly at one time and rapidly at another time; they may follow one pathway of change for some time only to switch to another pathway. And, they may diversify rapidly at one time, then shrink under widespread extinctions. The key to many of these patterns is the rate and nature of environmental change. Species become adapted to the environmental conditions that exist at a given time, and when change leads to new conditions, these species must evolve new adaptations or become extinct.[20]

What a story! Yes, this tale of our deep history and early evolution on planet Earth is quite a story. The idea that our Adam and Eve were nonliving organic compounds, converted into living cells by chemical and solar energy, is difficult to comprehend—let alone believe. If the essence of it hadn't been demonstrated again and again by the research, analysis and synthesis of hard evidence by thousands of dedicated scientists, it would be unbelievable. *It is unbelievable* to millions, like Andy Wright, who still stake their belief on an omnipotent creator, who in one fell swoop created the universe and our fully-developed Adam and Eve. But, to those who believe the evidence of science, this story is the only one that makes sense.[21] This story, then, while debatable and filled with mysteries, best describes the genesis of our genealogical seeds.

> *The heritage of the past is the seed*
> *that brings forth*
> *the harvest of the future.*[22]

Perhaps a more amazing chapter in the saga of our genealogy begins as the cellular seeds evolved into our human roots. Humans belong to an order of mammals, the primates, which existed before the dinosaurs became extinct. Early primates were tree dwellers. Many of the primate attributes—short faces, overlapping visual fields, grasping hands, large brains, and perhaps even alertness and curiosity—must have been acquired as tree dwelling adaptations. Descent from trees to forest floors and eventually to open country is associated with the development of unique features of the human primate, especially erect posture and bipedal movement.

In November 1994, an upper jaw of early *Homo*, the genus to which modern humans belong, was recovered along with primitive stone tools at Hadar, Ethiopia. Dated to 2.33-million years ago, they represent the oldest firmly dated association of stone tools with a fossil human ancestor.[23] Hadar is also the famous home of "Lucy," the most complete example of the small-brained, big-jawed, upright-walking ancestor of man. However, no tools were found with Lucy. The jaw and tools were discovered in a geological layer laid down approximately 700,000 years after Lucy lived at Hadar.[24]

Lucy's age was estimated to be 3.18 million years; she was found by Donald Johanson and Tom Gray on November 30, 1974. They had taken a Land Rover out to map an area near their campsite. After a long, hot morning of mapping and surveying for fossils, they were walking back to the vehicle, through a gully, when Johanson spotted the forearm bone of Lucy. That night there was much celebration and excitement over the discovery of what looked like a fairly complete female hominid skeleton. There was drinking, dancing, and singing; the Beatles' song "Lucy in the Sky with Diamonds" was played over and over. (This is evidence that, when we can, we take our music wherever we go.) At some point during that night—no one remembers when or by whom—the skeleton was given the name "Lucy." The name has stuck. After two weeks of extensive excavation, screening, and sorting, several hundred fragments of Lucy's bones were recovered.[25]

Who better to guide us through the dawn of mankind's genealogy on Earth than one of the discoverers of Lucy—Donald Johanson? Dr. Johanson, an outstanding paleoanthropologist, used his field and laboratory work, plus the work of other evolutionary detectives, e.g.: archeologists, biologists, geologists and other paleoanthropologists to document our earliest ancestors. In his book, *Ancestors*, Professor Johanson narrates the epic of human evolution, and tells us the major lineage links are classified in chronological order: *Australopithecus afarensis, Australopithecus boisei, Homo habilis, Homo erectus, Homo neanderthalensis,* and finally us, *Homo sapiens*.[26]

With each step forward in the evolutionary process our ancestors developed bigger bodies and bigger brains. Lucy was an *Australopithecus afarensis*—an ape that stood up. In 1959, Mary Leakey found a 1.75-million-year old skull at Olduvai Gorge in northern Tanzania that was first thought to be human, but the brain case was too small, the teeth too large, and the facial features too strange for it to belong to Homo. They nicknamed it Zinj and it was classified as *Australopithecus boisei*. In 1964, also at the same Olduvai site, Louis Leakey discovered our earliest ancestor to be classified in the genus, *Homo*. They called it *Homo habilis* because the tools discovered with the skeleton indicated it was an able, handy, tool maker and a mentally skillful hunter or scavenger.

Professor Johanson reports that the *Australopithecus robustus* were a group of humanlike creatures about four-feet tall, having tiny crested heads and wide, thickly enameled, nickel-sized teeth, which led to them being called "The Nutcracker People." This species is extinct and cannot be our direct ancestor. But, if Lucy and the *afarensis* First Family at Hadar were our species' great-grandparents, if the *Homo habilis* crowd at Olduvai were our grandparents, and *Homo erectus* our parents, then *Australopithecus robustus* were our great-great-uncles and aunts. The *robustus* were living at the same time—and sometimes in the same places—as their cousins, *Homo habilis*. More than three-hundred *robustus* fossils have been found at six different African sites. The ages of this extinct species range from two million to 900,000 years old. The Swartkrans Cave in South Africa produced more *Australopithecus robustus* fossils than any other site.[27]

The fossil evidence supports that *Homo erectus* also lived in the Swartkrans Cave about one-million years ago, but we must jump 200,000 years forward and move to Java in Southeast Asia for the earliest find of *Homo erectus*. In 1891, a Dutch military surgeon on duty in Java, discovered a skull which is the earliest *Homo erectus* skull discovered and became known as the "Java Man." *Homo erectus* was the first big hominid. Tall, thin and barrel-chested, it was about 14 percent bigger than *Homo habilis* and well adapted to long-distance ranging. *Homo erectus* were our first world travelers and their fossils have been found in Europe, India, Africa, Java, and China. The "Peking Man" fossil was discovered in China and is dated about 500,000 years ago.[28]

Homo Neanderthals first appeared around 130,000 years ago and disappeared from the fossil record around 35,000 years ago. Johanson believes they evolved in Europe, and that remained the center of their range. As far as scientists now know the *Neanderthals* were never in Africa, and, like the *Australopithecus robustus*, may not be in our direct ancestry.[29] The fossil evidence shows that *Neanderthals* coexisted with *Homo sapiens* for about 60,000 years. After about 35,000 years ago, no other form of early manlike creatures (other than our *Homo sapiens* ancestors) have been found.[30]

Somewhere, between 100,000 and 500,000 years ago, the origins of *Homo sapiens* evolved. A major debate that has not been conclusively answered is (1) Did *Homo sapiens* originate in one place, Africa, and radiate out to the rest of the world? or (2) Was our species born in geographically separate places that slowly overlapped as *Homo sapiens* evolved? According to DNA analyses, we can trace our genetic ancestry to a female who lived in Africa perhaps 150,000 years ago, but Richard Leakey reminds us that this one female was part of a population of as many as 10,000 individuals. The DNA analysis (with more than 4,000 living people from diverse nationalities now tested) has revealed there is no evidence of interbreeding with pre-modern populations. The implication is that modern newcomers completely replaced ancient populations—the process having begun in Africa about 150,000 years ago and then having spread through Eurasia over the next 100,000 years.[31]

A number of *Homo sapiens* fossils have been excavated from caves situated at the mouth of the Klasies River in South Africa. These archaic *Homo sapiens* have been dated between 115,000 and 75,000 years old—the oldest known modern *Homo sapiens* remains found anywhere in the world. In a symposium, held in October 1997 at the Cold Spring Harbor Laboratory, New York, geneticists, who had before them an immense amount of data regarding human populations, declared that *Homo sapiens* originated in Africa and radiated out to the rest of the world. Both Donald Johanson and Richard Leakey believe the evidence supports that *Homo sapiens* originated in one area—Africa. Studies suggest separation between Africans and Asians about 100,000 years ago, between Asians and Australians nearly 50,000 years back, and between Asians and Europeans about 35,000 years ago.[32]

As we come forward in time, between 75,000 and 35,000 years ago, more and more *Homo sapiens* appear. They have been found in abundance in Africa, Europe, Asia and Australia. Then, about 35,000 years ago a robust, tall and intelligent *Homo sapiens*, called Cro-Magnon appeared on the scene. To this point in the history of our ancestors, scientists have only fossils, rocks, earth, bones, and stone tools and implements to use as a basis for reconstructing the past.

From the period 35,000 to 10,000 years ago, countless *Homo sapiens* records begin to appear and show that our ancestors spread to North and South America. There are more than seventy sites of Cro-Magnon cave art in France alone, dating from about 28,000 to 10,000 B.C. This art suggests that man became more adept at using language and communicating. The famous cave at Lascaux, France was discovered in 1940 when a dog fell into a crack in the ground. The boys with the dog widened the crack and slipped down into a cavern hundreds of feet long. There they found the rock walls adorned with spectacular, ancient paintings of horses, deer and bison.[33] Our ancestors were multiplying and spreading out in every geographical direction, and their activities and creativity left us thousand upon thousands of treasures and *mysteries* to explore.

♭♭ Ancient Wonders ♭♭

About 6,000 years ago in ancient Babylonia, the Sumerians were the first to leave written records. During that time great civilizations began to rise all across the world. As these civilizations arose they began to build cities and edifices. But, the march of time is relentless in its agenda to cover over each of us, after our seasons in the sun, and this includes our deeds and structures. Only bits and pieces of structures built before Christ now survive, except the pyramids.

> *All things dread Time,*
> *but Time dreads the Pyramids*
> Arabic Proverb

The Egyptian pyramids were built long before Caesar, before Moses and the Exodus, or before Mesopotamia's ancient city. The pyramids have stood like silent sentries for almost 5,000 years—time enough for the Roman Empire to rise and fall a dozen times. More than eighty of these man-made mountains stand on the west bank of the Nile River, stretching 400 miles between Abu Roash and El Kula. The majority of them were built within fifty miles of Cairo. And, they were all built within the space of 160 years, from about 2650 to 2490 B.C. Early Greek historians named the Great Pyramid of Khufu (Cheops) as the most marvelous of the ancient world's Seven Wonders. It was also the oldest of the Seven ancient Wonders. Today, Cheops is the only one of these seven ancient wonders to survive intact. Cheops is the largest and most complex pyramid, sprawling across thirteen acres of desert and standing 450 feet high.[34]

Unfortunately those inconsiderate Egyptians didn't leave a record of how they built the pyramids or why they built them. This has led to almost five millenniums of speculation, but the answers remain a mystery. The "how" is a significant puzzle, because some of the limestone blocks weigh between twenty and thirty tons and they have been cut, polished and placed with such precision that their yards-long joints rarely exceed a hundredth of an inch. Think of the remarkable engineering skill that it took to position these huge blocks on a thirteen-acre plot so they fit almost perfectly at the top. This building feat would be a monstrous undertaking with today's equipment, tools and technology. If the pyramids didn't exist, the current universal consensus of our scientist and engineers would be: "four-thousand years ago, they couldn't have done it." The "why" is just as puzzling and may have its basis in religion or, as some have conjectured, the pyramids were giant make-work projects, like President Franklin D. Roosevelt's WPA in the 1930s. But, in the year 2002 A.D., the answers remain educated guesses.

Notwithstanding countless mysteries, we can be certain that our ancestors were propagating on every continent and, using Dawkins' analogy, the river of human genes was becoming a torrent. All of the world's six billion human beings are descended from one or more of the five basic racial types of mankind—Australoid, Capoid, Mongoloid, Negroid and Caucasoid. One reason our genetic river has swollen is all of these racial types can and have interbred, and the interbreeding diversity seems to help fight off predators (germs and parasites) to the human body. Dr. K. K. Verna tells us,[35] "In Mexico 60 percent of its population are a result of hybridization between Europeans and Red Indians. In the Urals most people are hybrids between Caucasoids and Mongoloids. In fact it is estimated that half of humankind today is made up of people, who represent racial intermixing not far back in the past. There is ample evidence that the most different looking individuals from the most remotely separated parts of the world can interbreed if given the opportunity. Norwegians, Australian aborigines, Bushmen, Malays and South American Indians are all perfectly capable of interbreeding and producing healthy and completely fertile offspring." So billions of us hardy souls have a mixture of these five racial types in our genealogy, and the rate of mixing is increasing with each generation.[36]

♬ Early North American Inhabitants ♬

Thousands of archaeological sites in North America provide evidence of prehistoric cultures and societies. One site is special—Russell Cave in Alabama. No other site in North America has revealed so detailed a record of occupation for so long a period of time—9000 B.C. to 1650 A.D. The cultural remains lie where the occupants left them, layer-upon-layer in a record that reads like the pages of a book. An archaeologist, trying to determine when man first came to America and how man lived during the hundreds of centuries before the Europeans arrived, is like a child trying to solve a picture puzzle when he has only one-tenth of one percent of the pieces in his possession.[37]

In Russell Cave, archaeologists uncovered stone implements, tools of bone and wood, and jewelry fashioned from shells and bone. They also uncovered fragments of baskets, pottery, seeds, human skeletons and charcoal remains. Many of the tools and weapons uncovered resembled objects associated with cultures found to the east, west, south and north of the Alabama site.[38] Just how and why they came to be in this cave in Alabama is open to speculation. One theory put forth deals with the migration routes of early man. During the last ice age, there was a slow but steady movement of Paleo-Indians across North America, presumedly from west to east and north to south.[39] Later there was movement of archaic people, both north and south along the Appalachian Ridge. These people traveling in either direction, for whatever reason, carried their material culture with them. Can this be why the jointed fish hook associated with northern cultures was found in Russell Cave or why a primitive spear associated with the Aztec culture and peoples of Minnesota was also found in the lower levels of the cave? It has been suggested that the area around Russell Cave was an ancient meeting ground.

While Russell Cave is special, it is not unique, because early archaeological sites have been discovered all across America. At the

Brown's Valley Site located in Traverse County, Minnesota, bone fragments and tools were discovered in 1933. This was a burial ground for Paleo-Indians who lived here about 8,000 to 10,000 years ago. Flaked stone blades were found among the burial remains that were made from a dark brown translucent flint which comes from the area of Dodge, North Dakota.[40]

The Koster farm in Greene County, Illinois, is one of the most important archaeological sites in North America. In 1969, Dr. Stuart Struever of Northwestern University was shown artifacts dating to 1000 A.D. in a field on the Koster farm. Archeological excavations have revealed an archaeological treasure—at least twelve cultures (horizons) separated from one another by sterile soil. Horizon 12, the oldest yet excavated, revealed habitation of the site by man from 8,000 to 10,000 B.C.[41]

Summer digs at the Koster farm is an interdisciplinary effort involving 225 students and professionals. Northwestern University and the National Science Foundation provide significant funding for this project. A total picture of the plants, animals, shells, diets, health, economy, and social organization of each horizon is beginning to take shape. At least 250 archaeological sites have been identified in the area, including the Titus site now under investigation two miles from Koster. The sites have been preserved both by natural forces and by the relative isolation of the area.[42]

The Itasca Bison Kill site is located in north central Minnesota. The site dates from 7,000 to 8,000 years ago. Artifacts found in lake marl below peat deposits and on an adjacent slope suggest that the site was used in the fall for bison hunting, as the animals migrated to their wintering grounds, and in the spring to hunt turtles and fish. Activities evident in the camp were meat processing, bone-and-stone-tool manufacturing, hide preparation, and woodworking.[43]

Early American remains, known as Kennewick Man, were the subject of anthropological, cultural and legal controversies since their discovery in 1996. These remains were found scattered over an approximately 300-square-foot area in the Columbia River, near the bank of a dammed lake-like section under the management of the U.S. Army Crops of Engineers in Kennewick, Washington. The government transferred the bones to the joint custody of five tribes for disposition. Radiocarbon dating established the age of the Kennewick Man as more than 9,000 years old.[44]

In the summer of 1940, Georgia and S. M. Wheeler explored rock shelters in Nevada's sunbaked Carson Sink area. Their work for the Nevada State Parks Commission ultimately documented twenty-six caves and shelters, most containing archaeological materials. In a small cave, dubbed the Spirit Cave, the Wheelers found and removed some well preserved human burial bones. Not long afterward, they learned disappointing news about the apparent age of their find when a reigning expert placed the age of the burial at approximately 1,500-to-2,000 years. Because their discovery was made in 1940, the archaeologists had to accept an expert opinion—the advent of radiocarbon dating was still more than a decade away. The mummy was placed in a well-crafted wooden box. Cataloged and curated in the Nevada State Museum, it remained there until the University of California Riverside Radiocarbon Laboratory began experiments to determine if it was feasible to date hairs recovered from archaeological sites. Dr. Taylor of the California Riverside laboratory contacted the Nevada State Museum to determine if the museum had any ancients with hair on their heads. Assured that such samples were available and could be used, Taylor went to Carson City and one of the mummies he took samples from was the Wheeler's mummy. Taylor's laboratory results indicated Wheeler's mummy dated back more than 9,000 years ago. Further tests confirmed that, indeed, the Spirit Cave mummy, one of the most complete and well-preserved set of human remains found in North America, was more than 9,000 years old.[45]

The surprising date for the Spirit Cave man was discovered about the same time the Nevada State Museum learned that another skeleton in its collection dated to more than 9,200 years ago. This skeleton, known as the Wizard's Beach man, was found in 1978 when a prolonged drought lowered the level of Pyramid Lake northeast of Reno. The discovery site is only about 100 miles from Spirit Cave.[46]

The Templeton site on the Shepaug River in Washington, Connecticut, was first excavated in 1977. A wide variety of artifacts for woodworking, bone working, hide working, tool manufacturing, food processing, and hunting were found. These artifacts included a fluted point, drill, gravers, graving spurs, knives, etc. A carbon-14 date of 10,200 years old was obtained.[47]

Archaeologist Roger W. Moeller, who led excavations of the Templeton site, reports that Paleo-Indian sites are found in all forty-nine continental states and across Canada, but no given region can boast large numbers or closely spaced camps. The Paleo-Indians camped in an area to exploit a particular resource and then moved to the next seasonally available resource. The implications of Indians intentionally destroying their environment to obtain basic necessities for life and then moving on should sound the death knell for the Noble Savage concept and should make contemporary people feel less guilty about being a source of environmental degradation.[48]

The Meadowcroft Rockshelter site located near Avella, Pennsylvania is one of the few sites in North America that has produced artifacts in levels dated older than 12,500 years ago. Meadowcroft Rockshelter was excavated from 1973 until 1978 with additional excavations to make repairs and check data in the 1990s. Radiocarbon dating showed some of the Meadowcroft Rockshelter material to be more than 19,000 year's old, but controversy concerning contamination of samples has not been resolved, and many scientists believe that the more accurate dating is approximately 12,500 years ago.[49]

If scientists are bothered with radiocarbon dating of more than 19,000 years ago, they have major problems with radiocarbon dates exceeding 200,000 years old that have been recorded from artifacts found at the Calico Early Man Archaeological Site located near Barstow, California. More than 12,000 stone tools dating back perhaps 200,000 years have been located in an excavation begun in 1964 by Dr. Louis Leakey. It is one of the oldest sites of prehistoric tools in the Western Hemisphere. After Leakey's death in 1972, Ruth D. Simpson took over directorship; she died in 2000. Work at the site continues to this date. The Calico site is a center of major controversy in American archaeology. Its antiquity is beyond the acceptance of most American archaeologists, who believe that the human occupation of North America only occurred through an ice-free corridor during the last glacial period from 10,000 to 13,000 years ago.[50] It is only recently that some North American archaeologist have begun to accept that the ancient migration to the Americas was both through an ice-free corridor from the north and along a coastal route.[51] In spite of the multitude of mysteries, there can be no doubt that beginning many thousands of years ago mankind was spread across America, from north to south and from sea to shining sea. The genes from these people (often referred to as savages or aborigines) are now intertwined in millions of Americans, including the Cherokee Indian genes residing in the body of this chronicler.

Influence of Geography

No matter which age we lived in, geography (the lay of the land, temperature, and availability of water) has been a significant factor in determining where we live and our levels of prosperity and health. The economist, John Kenneth Galbraith tells us that if one marks off a belt a couple of thousand miles in width encircling the earth at the equator one finds within it no developed countries and everywhere within this belt the standard of living is low and the span of human life is short. Most underdeveloped countries lie in the tropical and semitropical zones.[52] Geography isn't the only factor causing their impoverishment and poor health, but it undeniably is a major factor, and it illustrates that nature like life is not always fair. Further it illustrates that the limited capabilities and actions of man cannot easily find remedies to the realities of nature and life.

For man, excess heat poses more problems than excess cold. Hot, damp climates sap man's energy and productivity. Worse, insects swarm as temperature rises and parasites within them mature and breed. The result is faster transmission of disease and development of immunities.

Returning to America, thankfully we find a land that has the good fortune of being far enough from the equator and the extremes of the North and South Poles to afford us a better opportunity for a good life. And, by the sixteenth century more-and-more people were learning about this land of opportunity.

♭♭ Our Modern Ancestors ♭♭

During the sixteenth century, when the influx of Europeans commenced in North America, there were more than 500 Indian tribes scattered across every region of the land. Many of these tribes were affiliated with other tribes, some organizing themselves into great Indian Nations.[53] Five of the great Indian Nations known as the Civilized Tribes were the Chickasaw, Cherokee, Choctaw, Creek and Seminole. Some of the other major tribes included: Algonkin, Apache, Catawba, Chippewa, Comanche, Delaware, Erie, Huron, Illinois, Iroquois, Kickapoo, Miami, Mohegan, Navajo, Ottawa, Pequot, Pueblo, and Winnebago.[54] But the Indians' technology, or the lack of it, and their number of warriors, proved to be no match for the onslaught of Europeans, from the sixteenth through the nineteenth century. Sadly, 1500 A.D. marked the beginning of the end for many Indian cultures.

How many Indians were in America before 1500 A.D.? The estimates range between 500 thousand and 16 million. William Denevan's scholarly attempt to reconcile the many conflicting estimates, concluded that about 4-million Indians lived above the Rio

Grande in 1500. While the answer is a mystery, there is a certainty: The Indian populations of North and South America suffered a catastrophic collapse after Columbus' discovery of the Americas in 1492.[55] Recent U.S. Census data shows the total Indian population in America is now about two million.[56] Think about that for a moment. Since America's current population exceeds 265 million, that means most of our ancestors were transplants, less than thirteen generations ago, from other parts of the world. The U.S. emigration statistics show that approximately 50-million legal emigrants have entered the U.S. during its entire history. Almost 7 million came from Germany, about 5.1 million from England; about 5 million from Austro-Hungarian, almost 5 million from Italy, almost 5 million from Mexico, about 4.5 million from Ireland, almost 4 million from Canada, about 3.3 million from Russia, about 1.4 million from the Phillippines, and about 1.1 million from Sweden. In substantial numbers (less than a million), emigrants came from Africa, Scotland, China, Caribbean/West Indies, Korea, Dominican Republic, Cuba and Vietnam. And, in smaller numbers emigrants came from almost every country in the world to the United States of America.[57]

What caused so many of our ancestors to uproot from their homelands and come to America? Well you can be sure that most of them weren't the contented, affluent, highly educated, or leading citizens of their respective countries. Circumstances have to be terrible for most humans to leave their land of birth. The emigrants were escaping jail, poverty, and persecution of all types. Not all, but most were the dregs of their homeland's society. If white, they were mostly poor, uneducated whites; if they were yellow, they were mostly poor, uneducated yellows; and if they were black, they were mostly poor, uneducated blacks. To this mix, we add the red men who were characterized as savages and already present in America. These, then, were our ancestors and represent a fair description of our collective heritage.

As our genealogy unfolded, our population expanded. And, it's interesting to see this population growth juxtaposed against a time line and a few world events. It's next to impossible to pinpoint exact population numbers, so there is an unknown error factor in the following numbers, especially those estimated prior to the nineteenth century, and even more so for the numbers prior to the fall of Rome. But, the population totals are sufficiently accurate to portray significant trends.

Year		Event	World Population
10,000	B.C.	End of last Ice Age	4,000,000
8000	B.C.	Domestication of plants and animals	5,000,000
3000	B.C.	Bronze Age; use of wagons	
1500	B.C.	Iron Age begins	
550	A.D.	Fall of Rome	250,000,000
1347	A.D.	Black Death/Plague; 75-million people die	
1492	A.D.	Europeans discover the Americas	
1567	A.D.	Two-million S. Am. Indians die of typhoid	450,000,000
1800	A.D.	Smallpox vaccination introduced	
1803	A.D.	U.S. Industrial Revolution begins	One billion
1903	A.D.	First airplane flight	
1916	A.D.	World War I	Two billion
1941	A.D.	World War II	
1945	A.D.	Atomic bomb detonated	
1954	A.D.	Vaccine for polio	Three billion
1966	A.D.	Moon landing	
1973	A.D.	U.S. Supreme Court legalizes abortion	Four billion
1978	A.D.	Test-tube baby born	
1987	A.D.	New world population milestone	Five billion
1998	A.D.	First cloning of sheep and monkeys	
1999	A.D.	New world population milestone	Six billion

One interesting comparison of the above population time line is that it took almost 12,000 years (until about 1950) after the Ice Age ended for earth's population to reach three billion; then in approximately fifty years the population doubled, adding another three billion. Another interesting fact about population growth is that it is becoming increasingly urbanized. For example, in 1800 London was the world's most populated city with one million; today more than 326 metropolitan areas in the world exceed that population. It doesn't require genius to understand that in the twenty-first century the human river of genes is approaching the fully-flooded stage. There are so many people on Earth that soon we may not even be able to reach the starfish.[58]

But here in America's melting pot, with our ragtag ancestry, it's not immodest to say *we've done well*. In spite of our problems, we have built a country that, by almost any comparative measure of excellence, has no peer on our planet. And we've done it with those who answered the beckoning call of our first lady—the Statue of Liberty. This call symbolizes our genealogy:

> *Give me your tired, your poor,*
> *Your huddled masses yearning to breathe free.*
> *The wretched refuse of your teeming shore.*
> *Send these, the homeless, tempest-tost to me,*
> *I lift my lamp beside the golden door!*
> Emma Lazarus

The Statue of Liberty, a gift from France in 1884, has been the portal to the American dream for millions of our ancestors. Life was not easy for our ancestors, but like us they derived comfort from their family, friends and the satisfaction of working and helping others. As Terry Jacks tells us it may be *hard to die when all the birds are singing in the sky. But most of us have joy and fun during our seasons in the sun, even though the stars we reach are just starfish on the beach.* And, we can be thankful that our ancestors conspired so our own seasons in the sun were in the United States of America.

♪♪♪♪

Chapter Notes

1. "Seasons in the Sun" was written by Canadian singer and songwriter Terry Jacks. Jacks's recording of the song was a big hit in 1973 and 1974. Ten million copies of the award winning song were sold worldwide.

2. This calculation uses thirty years as a generation span and assumes that your ancestry relationships were all direct parent-to-child; i.e., no marriages of cousins, aunts or uncles. But while there are few relationships where we end up being our own grandpas, like the novelty tune "I'm My Own Grandpa" outlines, we all have multiple marriages of cousins in our distant and not-so-distant genealogies that dramatically reduce the actual number of our ancestors.

3. This calculation also uses thirty years as a generation span, and assumes no marriages of cousins, aunts or uncles. But the best estimate of world population at the time of Christ was about 250 million; so, obviously, multiple marriages of cousins dramatically reduce the actual number of our ancestors. One in the same ethnic group probably would need to back up no more than ten centuries to find a common cousin with all those presently living in his group.

4. Richard Dawkins, *River Out of Eden*, (New York, NY: BasicBooks, 1995).

5. Ibid.

6. Species estimates by World Resources Institute, http://www.wri.org.

7. The terms "man" and "mankind" are used throughout this book as synonyms for human beings. The terms aren't meant to be sexist and apply equally both to male and female human beings.

8. Charles J. Lumsden and Edward O. Wilson, *Genes, Mind, and Culture*, (Cambridge, MA: Harvard University Press, 1981).

9. Charles J. Lumsden and Edward O. Wilson, *Promethean Fire*, (Cambridge, MA: Harvard University Press, 1983).

10. Jean-Baptiste Lamarck, *Philosophie Zoologique*. Lamarch, a French professor of worms and insects, coined the word invertebrates to describe his worms and insects.

11. Charles Lyell, "Biography of Charles Lyell," (England: Encyclopaedia Brittanica, 11th Edition, 1910-1911). http://www.gennet.org/facts/lyell.html.

12. Charles Darwin, *On the Origin of Species by Means of Natural Selection, A facsimile of the First Edition*, (HUP, 1964).

13. Ibid.

14. W. Bateson, ed., *Mendel's Principles of Heredity*, (England: Cambridge University Press, 1902). Mendel was a Czechoslovakian monk who tested the genetic history of peas. The results of his meticulous observations became known as Mendel's Laws of Heredity. When published in 1866, his work had little impact. It wasn't until the twentieth century that the enormity of his work was appreciated.

15. James Watson and Francis Crick are the Harvard microbiologists who co-discovered the fundamental properties of DNA. A discovery that ranks in importance with any in our world's history.

16. James W. Valentine, "Evolution," *Microsoft® Encarta® 98 Encyclopedia*. Segments of this early discussion of evolution were abridged from Valentine's presentation on evolution.

17. Preston Cloud, *Oasis In Space*, (New York, NY: W.W. Norton & Company, 1988). Portions of this discussion on evolution were abridged from Preston Cloud's incredible book–*Oasis In Space*.

18. Scientists call the period from about 670-million years ago to about 250-million years ago the Paleozoic Era.

19. The period from 250-million years ago to about 65-million years ago is referred to as the Mesozoic Era and is known as the age of reptiles and flowering plants. The Cenozoic Era extends from about 65-million years ago to the present, and it is referred to as the age of mammals.

20. Valentine, see Note 16.

21. Andy Wright is quick to remind us that what makes sense isn't always the truth. For example less than 600 years ago, most everyone believed the Earth was flat, because that is what made most sense to their senses. Of course, we now are certain they were all wrong.

22. Inscription on the National Archives Building, Washington, D.C.

23. William H. Kimbel of the Berkeley-based Institute of Human Origins (IHO) and an international team of scientists reported the finds in the December 1996 issue of *Journal of Human Evolution*.

24. Hadar is a remote site in northern Ethiopia, which is located in Africa's Great Rift Valley. The Great Rift Valley, is a scar on Earth's surface that extends approximately one eighth of its circumference, from Israel to South Africa's Mozambique. The Great Rift Valley is formed at the boundary and from the clashing of two giant tectonic plates that form Earth's crust. Along this rift, the earliest fossils of our species, Homo, have been found. This has led to Africa being called the "Cradle of Civilization."

25. Dr. Donald Johanson is an Honorary Board Member of the Explorers Club, a Fellow of the Royal Geographical Society and recipient of several international prizes and awards. http://www.asu.edu/clas/l*ho/science.htm, 3/14/99.

26. Donald Johanson, Lenora Johanson with Blake Edgar, *Ancestors, In Search of Human Origins*, (New York, NY: Villard Books, 1994).

27. Ibid.

28. Ibid.

29. F. Clark Howell, *Early Man*, (New York, NY: Time-Life Books, 1970). Howell's book clearly shows *Neanderthals* as having been found not only in Europe but also in Africa. Two decades later, in 1994 updated information and better dating techniques have altered that conclusion, which serves to illustrate that the tapestry of our earliest genealogy is not fixed and will change with future discoveries.

30. Johanson, see Note 26

31. Richard Leakey, *The Origin of Humankind*, (New York, NY: Harper Collins Publishers, Inc., 1994).

32. Ibid.

33. Ibid.

34. "The Great Pyramid of Giza;" http://ce.eng.usf.edu/pharos/wonders/pyramid.html. Cheops was the tallest manmade structure on Earth for more than forty-three centuries.

35. K. K. Verma and Rashmi Saxena, "Essays on Man," 1998. Both Dr. Verman and his daughter Dr. Saxena are zoology professors; http://www.biol.tsvkuba.ac.jp/.

36. Ibid.

37. Russell Cave National Monument, The Southeast's Most Complete Record Through Time; http://www.pride-net.com.

38. Ibid.

39. The Paleo-Indian period was the earliest firmly established era of human activity in the New World and extended from about 8,000 B.C. to 10,000 B.C.

40. Minnesota Prehistory; http://www.emuseum.mnsu.edu.

41. Stuart Struever and Felica Holton, *The Koster Site: Secret in a Cornfield,* (Prospect Heights, IL: Waveland Press, Inc., 1999).

42. Ibid.

43. "The Itasca Bison Kill Site," The Institute for Minnesota Archaeology; http://fromsitetostory.org.

44. "Kennewick Man," The Burke Museum of History and Culture at the University of Washington; http://washington.edu/burkemuseum. The five tribes were: Colville Confederated Tribes, Nez Perce Tribe, Confederated Tribes of the Umatilla, Wanapum Band, and Yakama Confederated Tribes.

45. D. R. Tuohy and Amy Dansie, *An Ancient Mummy from Nevada*, Nevada Department of Cultural Affairs; http://dmla.clan.lb.nv.us.

46. Ibid.

47. Roger W. Moeller, "A View of Paleo-Indian Studies in Connecticut,"Archaeological Services. www.siftings.com/paleo.html.

48. Ibid.

49. An interesting discussion of this controversy by Dr. Mark McConaughy, who helped excavate Meadowcroft Rockshelter, can be found at http://members.delphi.com/MCCONAUGHY/web/Meadowcroft.

50. "Calico Early Man Site," Bureau of California Land Management, Barstow Field Office; http://www.ca.blm.gov/barstow.

51. Don Alan Hall, "Mammoth Trumpet" pp. 5-10. Papers presented by scientist at the 63rd Annual Meeting of the Society for American Archaeology at Seattle were reflective of this acceptance.

52. David S. Landes, *The Wealth and Poverty of Nations: Why Some Are So Rich and Some So Poor,* (New York, NY: W. W. Norton & Company, Inc., 1998).

53. http://www.indiancircle.com.

54. http://www.tolatsga.org.

55. *U.S. News* cover story by Lewis Ford, "Mysteries of Science, How Many People Were Here Before Columbus," August, 1997.

56. Only the Apache, Cherokee, Chippewa, Choctaw, Navajo, Pueblo and Sioux tribes have populations of more than 50,000: 1990 U.S. Census.

57. These statistics came from Ellis Island's presentation: "The Peopling of America," http://www.ellisisland.org.

58. Terry Jacks, see Note 1.

Eight

Ah, Sweet Mysteries!

(What the Facts Reveal)

*A*h! *Sweet mystery of Life, at last I've found thee, Ah, I know at last the secret of it all.* Rida Johnson Young's lyrics continue on to give us an answer: *All the longing, seeking, striving, waiting, yearning; the burning hopes, the joy and idle tears that fall! For 'tis love and love alone, the world is seeking . . . 'Tis the answer, 'tis the end and all of living . . .* The love that the heroine sings of in this operetta is romantic love.[1]

Our choice of music mirrors us; and, for this reason, it was used to introduce each chapter in this book. In attempting to match chapter subject matter with appropriate music, the lyrics of thousands of songs were visited. Not surprising, more than 90 percent of the songs were found to be about love or the mating game. The lyrics and harmony of love cross all musical boundaries: popular, country and western, blue grass, classical, operas, ballads, blues, rock, show tunes, hymns, etc. Since our music is a reflection of our culture, there can be no doubt that human beings have a "love affair" with the concept of love. *LOVE* is in all our minds, regardless of our cultural diversities. So who can deny its importance, especially if we broaden the concept to include other types of love; e.g.: love of God, love of work, brotherly love, and love of good works.

Love is the universal emotion implying a deep fondness or devotion. Like our fingerprints and DNA, it is both universal and uniquely personal. Unlike our fingerprints or DNA, it's undefinable by a digital presentation. Ask a thousand people to define love and, while there will be some common ground in their answers, you will get thousands of different answers and examples. Ask these same thousand the identical question one year later and, most likely, not all of their answers will remain constant—because love has a fleeting quality. There is no single definition of an individual's love, because love, too, is a sweet mystery.

Since we evolved into thinking beings, mankind has wrestled with the important mysteries, questions and issues addressed in this book (fantasy, religion, mysteries of the mind, what makes us killers, do we have free will, where did we come from, what's our purpose, how do we govern ourselves to reduce the disparities between the haves and have-nots while maintaining freedom and safety, and where are we going). And, as before, the questions and issues survive without final answers. While we "wrestlers" are left with our opinions, the answers remain cloaked in mystery.

On the difficult questions, there remain clouds of confusion and disagreement. Based on religious choice alone, at least two-thirds of the world's population disagree with our conclusions. But, that shouldn't bother us, because less than 600-hundred years ago 99 percent of the people knew Earth was flat, and they were wrong. Did this error impoverish their lives or doom them to some purgatory? Were the few souls who had the right answer rewarded in some substantial way? I doubt it made any more difference at that time than most of our disagreements do today.

Ideas, issues and truths evolve just as species evolve. As human beings whose common ancestries appear to have originated in Africa more than 100,000 years ago, our disagreements and behavior differences may seem endless. However, in fact, they are quite small compared to our agreements and common responses to most of life's challenges.

A predominate theme of this book[2] is that each of us is controlled by three principal factors that play out against the background music of random chance: (1) our genetic makeup (nature); (2) our environment (culture or nurture); and (3) our free will that is influenced by the first two factors much more than most of us would choose to believe. All of these factors are products of evolution. The first factor, genetic makeup, is totally beyond our direct personal control. Each of us is stuck at birth, for good or bad, with our own unique genetic code.[3] The second factor, our environment, we have almost no control over during the first decade of our life; and, in the total scheme of life's circumstances, little control after that. Only the third factor, our will, has a measure of freedom that we may personally control. And, the nineteenth century German philosopher, Arthur Schopenhauer probably was close to the truth when he postulated that *we can do as we will but not will as we will*. None of these factors are mutually exclusive. Rather, they are mixed together in this "pot" we call life that is: sometimes peaceful, serene and homogeneous; sometimes glorious; sometimes fraught with upheaval and horrific experiences; and most of the time, for most of us, bubbling somewhere in between these extremes.

Our collective actions show we have a propensity for survival and self-gain at the expense of others and may lie, cheat and even kill if it serves our purpose. Fortunately, we have just as great a propensity for cooperation and good. Instilled within the majority of us from our genetic makeup and nurture is the ability to consider the many sides of an issue and determine right, wrong and points of confusion in between. Killers usually know that killing is wrong. And most of us have our own internal Andy (Always) Wright, who helps us recognize before we act whether our actions are right, wrong or some shade of grey in between these extremes. We should strive with all our will to listen to that mysterious, noble voice within us and do right as we see it. Any person who does so consistently *is good*—the highest achievement for any human. Being a good person is within our reach and has little to do with circumstances, race, sex, age, social or financial status, intelligence, physical ability or beauty.

All of us can listen to ourselves and exercise our will to be good. The highest achievement in life is that simple. And good has as many forms, hues and shapes as there are human beings, which means, to be good, we don't need to be Mother Theresa, Mahatma Gandhi or Albert Einstein clones. Love, while a sweet mystery, is the most important manifestation of goodness. This is not psycho babble, a faith-based platitude or a warm fuzzy feeling. The facts, reason and experience have demonstrated it's the truth.

To the question, "What is the purpose of life?" Preston Cloud proposes a worthy goal for each of us: "To live with as much grace and integrity as possible, to enjoy and improve it while you have it, and to leave the world no worse for your having been there."[4] This language is more sophisticated, but it's synonymous with "Being Good."

A reality that may seem depressing, although it shouldn't, is that within ten million years—a blink of the eye on eternities' scale—and probably much less time, everything we (the greatest and the least of us) are or do, including our bones and vestiges of our cities and handiwork, will be gone and forgotten. Except, perhaps, some microscopic measure of our genetic and/or nurturing links will survive. The nature that spawned us will see to it, covering over our bodies and deeds.[5]

So, we should not bow easily to another's wisdom on the important questions and mysteries of life, unless it agrees with our own reasoning and common sense. In the first place, the wisest among us aren't that much wiser than the average person.[6] In the second place, depending on the question and our emphasis, we may be more correct for the time rather than one far wiser. And, thirdly in the long-term scheme it will make little difference whether you or one who disagrees with you is (was) right or wrong. This third fact doesn't diminish the importance of our decisions and actions. Why? Because our decisions and actions are important to us and the ones we care about for now and for the near-term.

Fortunately, on planet Earth; music, rhythm, symmetry and love abound. These extensions of our nature and nurture bring great comfort and joy. Love, good works, family, music and the bounty of Earth is experienced even by those caught up in poverty and war. Still, there is too much needless discord, caused by heeding the bad advice and demands of others. Advice and demands that conflict with our own reasoning and feelings. Each of us is unique and our uniqueness has as much right for expression and action as that of others, as long as those actions don't encroach on the rights and safety of others.

> *Believe nothing, no matter where you read it,*
> *or who said it—even if I have said it—unless*
> *it agrees with your own reason*
> *and your own common sense.*
>   Buddha

At some point, many of us come to realize that those seeking ease and happiness have made poor choices, because ease is a short-lived comfort, and the truest happiness arrives only as a by-product of service to others. Sometimes life seems so complex, but a successful formula is quite simple—Be good and do all that you can do for others, because this is the essence of happiness. This process involves hearing others; yet, in the deepest sense it means we correlate the ideas of others with our own ideas and experience and **listen to ourselves**,[7] just as Buddha, the enlightened one, advised in the above quote.

Understanding the importance of our own views and decisions, relative to other human beings, we should smile more, lift our chins higher and renew the vigor and spring in our step.

> *I see trees of green, red roses too*
> *I see them bloom for me and you*
> *And I think to myself what a wonderful world.*
>
> *I see skies of blue and clouds of white*
> *The bright blessed day, the dark sacred night*
> *And I think to myself what a wonderful world.*

Louie Armstrong (Satchmo) summed up the human condition (and a fitting view) with six short lines from his hit song, "What a Wonderful World."[8]

Although each of us are born with the sexually transmitted and terminal disease called *life*, when the positive sides of living are balanced against the tribulations and problems (most due to our own ignorance and muck ups), mankind throughout our history has found planet Earth to be a hospitable oasis and we have experienced many more good moments than bad.[9] Satchmo is right: we've been blessed with a wonderful world—a world of boundless wonders that is filled with much more love than hate.

A world where our mysteries are sweet because they supply us meaningful challenges, furnish us joy for each inkling of a solution, fuel our hopes and, last but not least, provide us constant refuge from burdens too awesome to bear.

Ah, sweet mysteries!

♪♪♪♪

Chapter Notes

1. "Ah, Sweet Mystery of Life" is Victor Herbert's theme score for the operetta *Naughty Marietta*; words by Rida Johnson Young and music by Victor Herbert.

2. This isn't meant to imply that this is an original theme. Thinkers have scrutinized and massaged aspects of this theme for centuries.

3. DNA associated discoveries and cloning promise to challenge the universal stability of this fact. But, to date this is a possibility; not a fact.

4. Preston Cloud, *Oasis in Space*, (New York, NY: W. W. Norton & Company, 1988). Cloud, professor emeritus of geology at the University of California, Santa Barbara is also author of *Resources and Man, Adventures in Earth History, Cosmos, and Earth and Man*.

5. The facts show this statement to be reality, but thankfully these facts don't prevent us hoping (many even believing) that somehow we are destined to have everlasting life in some distant paradise.

6. Marvin Minsky, *The Society of Mind*, (New York, NY: Simon & Schuster Inc., 1988). Minsky, cofounder of MIT's Artificial Intelligence Laboratory, has studied the IQ and ability variances among us and found that the brightest have only marginally greater ability than the least of us. A genius develops creative expertise in areas and thinks in novel ways, but Minsky found ordinary people also think in novel ways and any person who can walk and speak coherently has the better part of the intelligence of those we call a genius.

7. "Listen" means to make a conscious effort to hear; attend closely; give heed; and take advice. Obviously, there are those who have limited capability of listening to themselves, because of disease, accidents or age.

8. "What a Wonderful World," words and music by George David Weiss and Bob Thiele; artist: Louie Armstrong, 1967; http://www.geocities.com.

9. If, throughout our lives, we each balanced the things that give us pleasure or contentment (such as eating; drinking; cultivating personal relationships;

fantasizing; gaining sense of accomplishment as we increase our mastery of things and ideas; sleeping; awakening; making love; participating in an array of entertainment activities; communing with nature; etc.; etc.) versus the things that cause us grief and pain (such as hunger, hurt, depression, sense of futility or failure, rejection, fear, sickness, and death), most of us will find the balance heavily favoring pleasure and contentment.